National Parks
OF NORTH AMERICA

CANADA · UNITED STATES · MEXICO

OVERLEAF: Pacific Rim National Park Reserve, Canada

Yosemite National Park, United States

Tulum National Park, Mexico

Arches National Park, United States

National Parks

OF NORTH AMERICA

CANADA · UNITED STATES · MEXICO

Prepared by the Book Division
National Geographic Society
Washington, D.C.

National Parks
OF NORTH AMERICA

CANADA · UNITED STATES · MEXICO

Published by
The National Geographic Society

Gilbert M. Grosvenor,
President and Chairman of the Board

Michela A. English, *Senior Vice President*

Prepared by the Book Division

William R. Gray,
Vice President and Director

Charles Kogod, *Assistant Director*

Barbara A. Payne, *Editorial Director*

Staff for this book

Leah Bendavid-Val, *Managing Editor*

Mary B. Dickinson, *Editor*

Lyle Rosbotham, *Art Director*

Carolinda E. Hill, Margaret Sedeen,
Text Editors

Susan C. Eckert, Victoria Garrett Jones,
Senior Editorial Researchers

Jennifer C. Urquhart, *Staff Writer*

Leslie Allen, David Dunbar, Seymour
L. Fishbein, Catherine Herbert Howell,
Alison Kahn, Richard Olsenius, Melanie
Patt-Corner, Cynthia Russ Ramsay, John
F. Ross, Thomas Schmidt, *Writers*

Michael A. Gross, Christy M. Nadalin,
Researchers

Suez B. Kehl, *Assistant Art Director*

Carl Mehler, *Map Editor and Designer*

Karen Dufort Sligh, *Illustrations Assistant*

Lewis R. Bassford,
Production Project Manager

Sandra F. Lotterman, *Editorial Assistant*

Karen F. Edwards, Elizabeth G. Jevons,
Peggy J. Oxford, *Staff Assistants*

Sven M. Dolling, Thomas L. Gray, Dean A.
Nadalin, Tracey M. Wood, *Map Researchers*

Tibor G. Tóth, Martin S. Walz,
Map Relief and Production

NGS Cartographic Division, *Country Maps*

Barbara Brownell, *Concept Development*

Arturo Gómez-Pompa, University of
California, Riverside; Rodolfo Dirzo, National
Autonomous University of Mexico,
Consultants for Mexico

Manufacturing and Quality Management

George V. White, *Director*

John T. Dunn, *Associate Director*

Vincent P. Ryan, *Manager*

R. Gary Colbert

Diane L. Coleman, *Indexer*

Contents

Library of Congress CIP Data: page 336

Yoho National Park, Canada

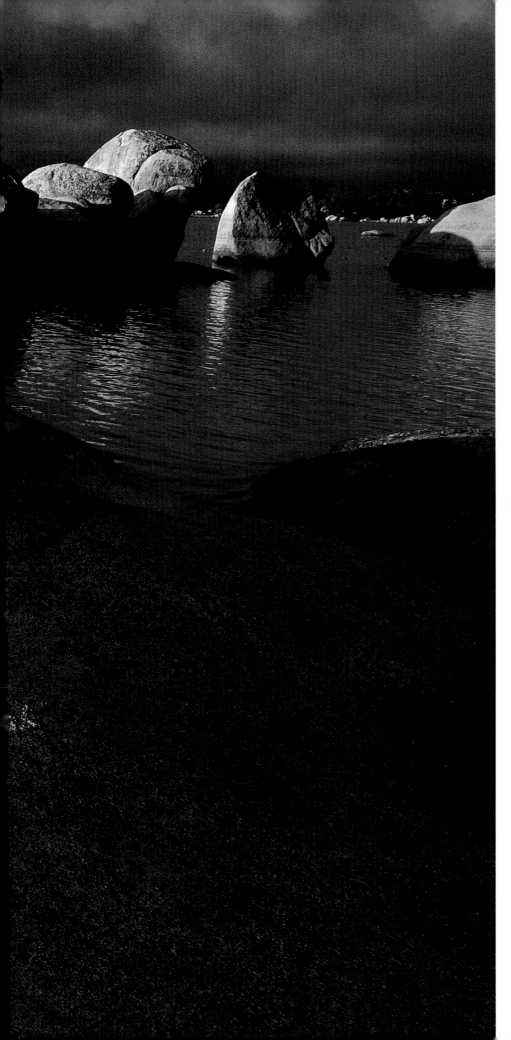

Introduction

BY WILLIAM R. GRAY

The first true mountain I ever climbed—at six years of age—is in a national park: Old Rag Mountain in Shenandoah; and the tallest mountain I ever climbed is in another national park: Mauna Loa in Hawaii Volcanoes.

I've always sought the exuberance and commanding presence that flow from soaring heights. The national parks of North America literally burst with majestic peaks; but they also enfold much more—a seemingly endless, inspiring array of canyons and deserts, of rivers and lakes, of coastlines and islands, of forests and caverns.

In the pages of this book, you will be refreshed by visiting familiar sanctuaries in Canada and the United States—Banff, Yellowstone, the Great Smokies; you will be surprised by remote and wonderful realms there—Auyuittuq, Guadalupe, Katmai; and you will be astonished as you discover a nation full of remarkable, lesser known parks—the lakes, mountains, valleys, and archaeological wonders of Mexico. The national parks of all three countries of North America are presented here in a comprehensive volume that captures the breathtaking grandeur and sublime beauty of the continent.

The April 1916 issue of NATIONAL GEOGRAPHIC magazine was largely devoted to national parks and was credited with helping to influence the creation of the U.S. National Park Service—the first in the world. Since then, the protection of parklands for the good of all has spread around the globe, and the earth's wild heritage is being preserved.

To continue the family cycle, I plan to take my six-year-old daughter to climb Old Rag Mountain this year.

Constitución de 1857 National Park, Mexico

ARCTIC OCEAN

ELLESMERE
ISLAND
NATIONAL
PARK RESERVE

*Baffin
Bay*

NORTH BAFFIN
NATIONAL PARK
(Proposed)

AUYUITTUQ
NATIONAL
PARK RESERVE

AULAVIK
NATIONAL PARK
(Proposed)

Beaufort Sea

*Banks
Island*

Baffin Island

*Foxe
Basin*

ARCTIC CIRCLE

IVVAVIK
NATIONAL PARK

*Victoria
Island*

ALASKA
(U.S.)

VUNTUT
NATIONAL PARK

YUKON

TERRITORY

NORTHWEST TERRITORIES

Hudson

*Great
Bear
Lake*

Mackenzie

Yukon

C A N A D A

KLUANE
NATIONAL
PARK RESERVE

Liard

★ Whitehorse

NAHANNI
NATIONAL
PARK RESERVE

★ Yellowknife

Thelon

*Great
Slave
Lake*

Back

*Hudson
Bay*

WOOD BUFFALO
NATIONAL PARK

Peace

L. Athabasca

BRITISH

COLUMBIA

ALBERTA

SASKATCHEWAN

MANITOBA

Churchill

Nelson

*James
Bay*

ONTARIO

*Queen
Charlotte
Islands*

GWAII HAANAS
NATIONAL
PARK RESERVE
(Proposed)

R O C K Y

Fraser

Athabasca

Edmonton ★

JASPER
NAT. PARK

ELK ISLAND
NATIONAL
PARK

PRINCE
ALBERT
NATIONAL
PARK

*Saskatchewan
River*

*Lake
Winnipeg*

PUKASKWA
NATIONAL
PARK
(Proposed)

*Vancouver
Island*

GLACIER
NATIONAL PARK

MOUNT
REVELSTOKE
NATIONAL PARK

YOHO NATIONAL PARK

BANFF
NAT. PARK

Vancouver

KOOTENAY
NATIONAL PARK

● Calgary

WATERTON
LAKES
NATIONAL
PARK

Regina ★

GRASSLANDS
NATIONAL PARK
(Proposed)

RIDING
MOUNTAIN
NAT. PARK

★ Winnipeg

PACIFIC

PACIFIC RIM
NATIONAL
PARK RESERVE
(Proposed)

★ Victoria

M

T

S.

Columbia

Missouri

OCEAN

Snake

UNITED STATES

Lake Superior

Albany

L. Michigan

Mississippi

M O U N T A I N S

ICELAND

GREENLAND
(DENMARK)

ARCTIC CIRCLE

*Davis
Strait*

ATLANTIC

OCEAN

*Labrador

Sea*

Strait

Caniapiscau

N E W F O U N D L A N D

Churchill

TERRA NOVA
NATIONAL
PARK

GROS MORNE
NATIONAL PARK
(Proposed)

★St. John's

*Island of
Newfoundland*

MINGAN ARCHIPELAGO
NATIONAL PARK RESERVE

*La Grande
Rivière*

FORILLON
NATIONAL
PARK

CAPE BRETON
HIGHLANDS
NAT. PARK

QUEBEC

St. Lawrence River

PRINCE EDWARD
ISLAND

PRINCE EDWARD ISLAND NAT. PARK

R. de Rupert

★Charlottetown

NEW
BRUNSWICK

KOUCHIBOUGUAC NATIONAL PARK

FUNDY NATIONAL PARK

Québec
★

Fredericton★

★Halifax
NOVA SCOTIA

LA MAURICIE
NATIONAL
PARK

KEJIMKUJIK
NATIONAL
PARK

Montréal

Ottawa Ottawa

GEORGIAN
BAY
ISLANDS
NATIONAL
PARK

ST. LAWRENCE
ISLANDS
NATIONAL
PARK

L. Huron

Toronto
★ *L. Ontario*

BRUCE PENINSULA
NAT. PARK (Proposed)

L. Erie

POINT PELEE
NATIONAL PARK

0   400 mi
0   400 km

NATIONAL PARKS OF
Canada

Icy realms of polar bears and white wolves, mountain strongholds of bighorn sheep, rain forest homes of rare owls, golden grasslands ranged by bison—Canada encompasses all of them. The country treasures its rich wilderness heritage and protects 85,000 square miles of it in a network of 37 national parks and reserves (parklands where native peoples retain hunting and fishing rights). By the year 2000, as many as 16 parks and 40,000 square miles may be added to the system.

Canada began setting aside land for parks in 1885, when it established a health and pleasure resort at what is now known as Banff, in the Rocky Mountains. The first parks were viewed primarily as recreational resources, but over the years parks have also become conservation areas, where the flora, fauna, land, and water are kept free from exploitation and development.

In 1930, parliament passed the National Parks Act, which promised that all such lands "shall be maintained and made use of so as to leave them unimpaired for the enjoyment of future generations." This policy of "use and protect" ensures not only that people will continue to find opportunities here for recreation and inspiration, but also that parks will remain protected places for future generations of all living things.

Aulavik

*I*n some years the shores of Aulavik National Park, on the northeastern end of Banks Island, remain icebound all through summer. Sections of the Thomsen River—considered the northernmost navigable waterway in the world—may stay frozen until late June, but then the river's lazy flow makes for easy canoeing. The Thomsen and its tributaries twist through tundra meadows, shallow canyons, and desertlike badlands. Here the ground thaws only for a short time, providing a very brief growing season for the grasses, sedges, heathers, and dwarf willows that mantle the hummocky terrain.

This frigid outpost in the far reaches of the Northwest Territories is home to one of the largest concentrations of musk oxen. Some 70,000 roam the island—25 percent within the boundaries of the park. They paw through the snow for willows and grasses, using sharp hooves that also serve as weapons against arctic wolves. As a first line of defense, musk oxen bunch together around their young, confronting predators with a buffer of horns.

Aulavik is home to polar bears in the summer months, when melting sea ice forces them ashore. By October they depart and roam across the frozen M'Clure Strait, on the park's northern boundary, to stalk bearded and ringed seals at their breathing holes.

Hundreds of archaeological sites, some dating back 3,500 years, offer glimpses of the island's earliest cultures. Today, only about 140 people live at Sachs Harbour, 155 miles southwest of the park.

There are no facilities in Aulavik, but air charters from Inuvik, 450 miles away, provide access to this remote Arctic park.

PARK DATA

TERRITORY: Northwest Territories

ESTABLISHED: 1992 (agreement to establish)

AREA: 4,710 sq mi (12,199 sq km)

CLIMATE: Precipitation slight, with most rainfall occurring in July and August; winter temperatures dropping as low as −50°F (−46°C)

NATURAL FEATURES: Canyons, tundra, badlands; meandering rivers

CULTURAL FEATURES: Archaeological sites representing thousands of years of human history

FLORA: Dwarf willows, heathers, sedges, grasses

FAUNA: Polar bears, musk oxen, arctic wolves and foxes, Peary caribou (an endangered species); snowy owls, gyrfalcons, and sandhill cranes

UNIQUE FEATURE: Thomsen River—considered the world's northernmost navigable waterway

From a meadow high above the Thomsen River, a park patrolman surveys Aulavik, one of Canada's newest national parks. Though empty in appearance, the tundra is inhabited by arctic hares, lemmings, ground-nesting birds, and the arctic foxes that prey on them.

17

Auyuittuq

Although Auyuittuq means "the land that never melts" in Inuit, Aksayook Pass provides an ice-free corridor in summer that leads backpackers through the magnificent, glacier-hewn terrain of Auyuittuq National Park Reserve on central Baffin Island. Pinnacles, fanged peaks, and the dizzying, vertical face of 5,485-foot Mount Thor stand out amid the rubble of boulders and gravel ridges deposited by moving ice. Hanging glaciers spill down from the Penny Ice Cap, decorating somber granite with glossy white.

Steep terrain, icy streams that swell with rain or meltwater, and unpredictable weather make the 60-mile hike between North and South Pangnirtung Fiords a challenging trek. Trailheads at both ends of the park are accessible from the Inuit communities of Pangnirtung and Broughton Island by boat or snowmobile, depending on the season.

Willow herb blossoms emblazon low terrain in Auyuittuq's Weasel River Valley during the fleeting summer. Short of wildlife except for birds, foxes, ermines, and arctic hares, Auyuittuq lures visitors with imposing ice-carved landscapes.

Stones arranged in human shape mark trails, caches, and hunting and fishing sites. Called *inukshuk*s after the Inuit term meaning "looks like a person," the cairns have become symbols and logos for Inuit organizations.

Banff

*F*irst and most famous of the national parks of Canada, Banff is filled with glittering snow-capped peaks, valleys draped in ever-green forests, turquoise lakes, flowered alpine meadows, glaciers, hot springs, waterfalls, and abundant wildlife. Four mountain parks—Banff and its neighbors Jasper, Yoho, and Kootenay—contain such a large and representative segment of the Canadian Rockies that they have been collectively designated a UNESCO world heritage site.

Banff topography is characterized by sweeping, U-shaped valleys that separate the parallel Front and Main Ranges of the Rockies, mountains made of sedimentary rocks that were uplifted and folded, then shaped by glaciers. Banff's highest peaks are in the Main Range, which forms the Continental Divide. At Valley of the Ten Peaks, this soaring watershed forms a rampart about 8 miles long and more than 3,000 feet high from base to ridgeline.

Variations in topography, soil, moisture, and temperature create three complex vegetation communities in Banff. In the montane zone, alders, willows, birches, and cottonwoods grow in sheltered valley bottoms and along watercourses. Douglas firs and lodgepole pines form the predominant forest cover on the lower slopes. Subalpine forest, the park's most widespread habitat, extends from the montane up to about 6,500 feet. Above that is the alpine zone, where even hardy spruces become stunted by wind and cold. With a ground cover of shrub willows,

Glaciers and countless conifers cling to slopes high above Marvel Lake in Banff National Park.

grasses, sedges, and heathers, this zone resembles Arctic tundra. Flowers here put on dazzling displays throughout the brief growing season, with saxifrages, mountain avens, and alpine forget-me-nots blooming in quick succession.

Mountain goats and small mammals such as marmots, weasels, and pikas survive on storm-swept heights. Pipits, larks, and rosy finches breed on the alpine tundra, but only white-tailed ptarmigans live here year-round.

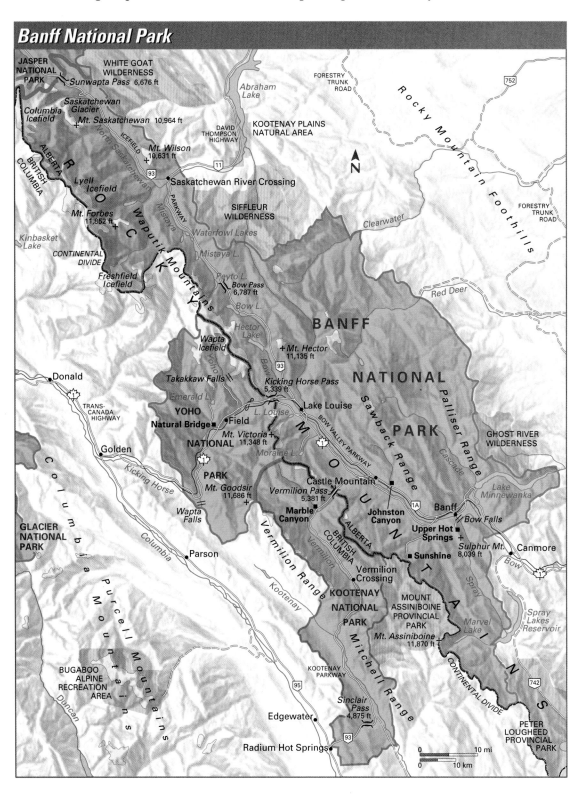

Banff National Park

MANY LANDFORMS in Banff stand as monuments to the power of ice. During the Pleistocene epoch, which ended some 10,000 years ago, vast ice fields sprawled along the Continental Divide. Huge rivers of glacial ice flowed down from the frozen fields, gouging V-shaped valleys into broad, U-shaped ones. The Bow and Athabasca Valleys are textbook examples.

On the sides of some mountains, the valleys of small tributary glaciers were often left "hanging" high above the deepened floor of the main valley when the ice retreated. The hanging valley on Mount Wilson (upper right) is hundreds of feet above the valley of the North Saskatchewan River.

As a glacier advances, it picks up and grinds down rocks in its path. When the ice retreats from a valley, this burden is deposited as till: unsorted boulders, gravel, sand, and rock flour (powdered rock milled by the grinding passage of ice). In places, the till eventually hardens into rock studded with cobbles and boulders. On the southern slope of Tunnel Mountain, near Banff townsite, wind and water eroded a relatively soft cliffside into freestanding pillars known as hoodoos (lower right).

BY THE AUTUMN of 1883, crews laying track for the Canadian Pacific Railway (CPR) had reached the Bow River Valley. On November 8, Frank McCabe, a section foreman, and William and Thomas McCardell, construction workers, spent their day off prospecting. They came across wisps of steam rising from the ground on the north side of Terrace (now Sulphur) Mountain, near the present townsite of Banff. Lowering a lantern into a hole, they discovered they were standing on the roof of a cavern. Several feet below steamed a pool of sulphurous water.

A short time later, William McCardell built a crude cabin at the site. Word of the mineral-rich waters spread quickly, and soon other shacks sprouted around what are now known as the Cave

and Basin Hot Springs and the Upper Hot Springs, all on Sulphur Mountain.

Competing claims came to the attention of the Department of the Interior in Ottawa. On November 25, 1885, the federal government set aside ten square miles on the northern slope of the mountain for public use rather than private enterprise. This tiny reserve was the third national park in the world (after Yellowstone in the United States and Royal National Park in Australia).

Regular service on the CPR began in 1886, and soon tourists were flocking to the "Mountain Playground of the World." To house them, the railroad built elaborate wilderness resorts. The Banff Springs Hotel attracted European aristocrats and American magnates. Chateau Lake Louise (below) appealed to climbers, hikers, and riders. Outfitters guided guests on excursions from Lake Louise to Columbia Icefield (opposite, lower). Other diversions included cruises and rowing on Lake Louise and Moraine Lake (right). In 1887, Banff constructed a bathhouse and a soaking pool to heighten enjoyment of the park's raison d'être—Cave and Basin Hot Springs (opposite, upper).

Bruce Peninsula

The 60-mile-long Bruce Peninsula separates Lake Huron from Georgian Bay. At its rugged tip are twin parks administered jointly: Bruce Peninsula National Park and its offshore neighbor, Fathom Five National Marine Park.

The peninsula park is dominated by the Niagara Escarpment, a wall of dolomitic limestone that arcs between New York and Manitoulin Island, in Lake Huron. Cliffs, cobbled beaches, and limestone slabs define the eastern edge of the park overlooking Georgian Bay. Gnarled eastern white cedars, junipers, and stunted spruces cling to sheer cliffs feathered with purple cliff brakes, wall rues, and other ferns.

Caves, sinkholes, and other karst features riddle the escarpment's easily dissolved limestone. Indian paintbrushes and bunchberries brighten woodlands dominated by maples and beeches. The forest around Cyprus Lake, one of dozens of ponds and lakes on the escarpment, is prime habitat for orchids. Beavers, minks, and weasels flourish in the patchwork of streams and cedar swamps at the headwaters of Crane River and Willow Creek.

Dolomite bedrock dips gently into Lake Huron along the park's western edge, where rocky shoreline alternates with sandy beaches. Yellow lady's-slipper is the most common of 25 orchid species growing near Dorcas Bay. This boggy area is also home to pitcher plants, tiny sundews, and butterworts.

Fathom Five's 20 islands duplicate the topography of "The Bruce," with sharp, east-facing dolomite cliffs gently sloping to the west. Waves have excavated caves on Bears Rump Island and whittled rocky stacks called "flowerpots" on Flowerpot Island. More than 20 ships are known to litter the bottom, sunk by treacherous reefs and shoals.

PARK DATA

PROVINCE: Ontario
ESTABLISHED: 1987 (agreement to establish)
AREA: 104 sq mi (270 sq km) authorized
NATURAL FEATURES: Niagara Escarpment, karst formations, flowerpots
FLORA: Cedars, spruces, maples, beeches, birches, aspens; 31 orchid species; 20 fern species; 5 species of insectivorous plants
FAUNA: Black bears, deer, foxes, beavers, fishers; 9 snake species, including the Massasauga rattlesnake; more than 300 bird species, including the pileated woodpecker

Crumbling spine of southern Ontario, the Niagara Escarpment (opposite) formed some 400 million years ago. Wildflowers (below) add touches of color to the park's woodlands. Few other sites in North America have as many wild orchid species.

27

Cape Breton Highlands

Alexander Graham Bell once said, "I have seen the Canadian and American Rockies, the Andes and the Alps and the Highlands of Scotland; but for simple beauty, Cape Breton outrivals them all."

Cape Breton Highlands National Park stretches across the northern part

of Nova Scotia's Cape Breton Island, embracing the best the island has to offer. Flanked on the east by the Atlantic Ocean and on the west by the Gulf of St. Lawrence, this magnificent preserve of highland plateau offers steep headlands, rich bogs and wind-blown barrens (home to rare arctic and alpine plants), crystalline lakes and swift-running streams, sandy beaches, Acadian forests, and deep canyons. Made of some of the oldest visible rock on the planet, this rugged land was shaped by uplift, erosion, and glaciers, beginning between one billion and 345 million years ago.

The most famous feature of the park—and the only means of vehicular

First light finds the cove at Presqu'île, where craggy head-lands and grassy slopes meet the surging sea— a recurrent theme at Cape Breton Highlands National Park.

access to it—is the 184-mile Cabot Trail. Named for John Cabot, who is said to have landed at Cape Breton while exploring for England in 1497, it is one of the most spectacular drives in North America. The trail begins and ends south of the park at Baddeck, Dr. Bell's summer home, but its most scenic section lies within park boundaries. Along the way, visitors can enjoy breathtaking views and go for walks to savor a diversity of habitats.

Isolated except in summer, the two-lane road hugs the Atlantic shore, following the natural curves of bays, coves, and headlands. At Lakie's Head, a lookout point begs a stop to scan the ocean for marine life. Veering west through lush forests and past cascading falls, the trail dips toward the Gulf of St. Lawrence. Here it skirts 1,000-foot cliffs, climbs forested ridges, descends into a valley, and exits the park near the Acadian village of Chéticamp.

Cape Breton's diverse habitats support a cornucopia of flora: Clusters of summer-ripened bunchberries (above) carpet the forest floor at Middle Head, which juts from the park's east coast. The primitive pitcher plant (right) prefers the boggy central and western highlands.

FOR THE THOUSANDS of Scots who immigrated to Nova Scotia during the late 18th and early 19th centuries, Cape Breton Island's misty peaks, lakes, and moorlike barrens and bogs must have salved many a homesick heart. Celtic culture lives on here and is celebrated each year with the Gaelic Mod at the Gaelic College of Celtic Arts and Crafts in St. Ann's, south of the park. Along with the Highland dance competition (left), the four-day festival, usually held in August, showcases traditional music, crafts, foods, and sports.

Cape Breton Highlands National Park

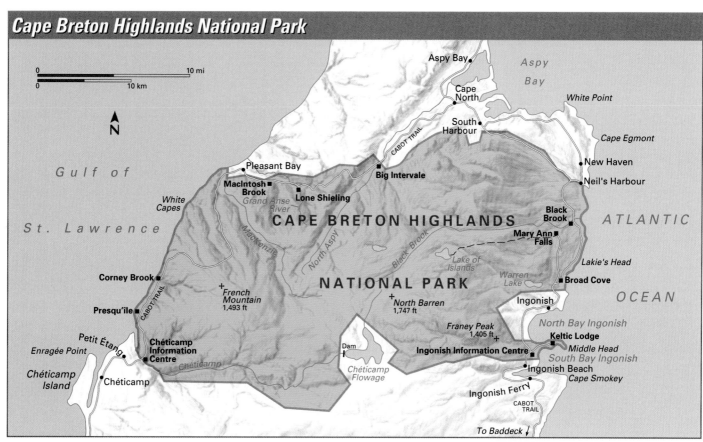

Elk Island

*C*anada's only fenced preserve protects an island of forested hills and rolling meadows surrounded by central Alberta's flat farmland. The 200-foot-high Beaver Hills are located in aspen parkland, which forms a transitional zone between open prairie and boreal forest. Woodlands, while mostly aspen, include a variety of conifers.

Established as a refuge for elk, the park also shelters 800 plains bison and 350 wood bison. Extensive ponds and wetlands lure migrating waterfowl to Elk Island, and trumpeter swans are being slowly reintroduced. From almost anywhere along the shores of Astotin Lake, birders can sight loons, grebes, and great blue herons.

PARK DATA

PROVINCE: Alberta
ESTABLISHED: 1913
AREA: 75 sq mi (194 sq km)
CLIMATE: Warm, dry summers; cold, dry winters
NATURAL FEATURES: Glacially formed "knob-and-kettle" terrain of small rounded hills and bowl-like depressions filled with some 200 ponds and lakes
CULTURAL FEATURE: Ukrainian Pioneer Home, a replica of dachas built by turn-of-the-century settlers
FLORA: Quaking aspens, balsam poplars, white and black spruces; open grass and sedge meadows; reed- and cattail-fringed wetlands; *Wolffia,* the world's smallest flowering plant
FAUNA: Plains bison, wood bison, moose, elk, deer, beavers; birds including loons, grebes, herons

Elk Island's Living Water Boardwalk curves 1,175 feet over the calm waters of Astotin Lake, gilded by a setting sun.

Ellesmere Island

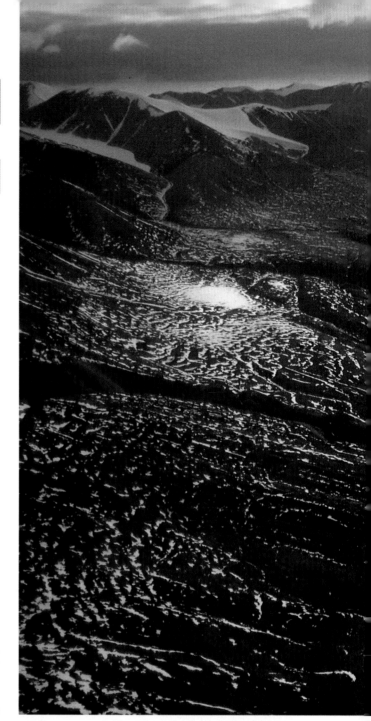

An ultimate wilderness about 500 miles from the North Pole, 360 miles from the nearest permanent settlement, and more than 1,200 miles north of the nearest tree, Ellesmere Island National Park Reserve encompasses little-known natural wonders and remarkably tough species of high Arctic plants and animals.

Stony peaks jut from a vast ice field 100,000 years old and more than half a mile thick. The ice buries most of the Grant Land Range, including 8,543-foot Mount Barbeau—the highest mountain in eastern North America. Icebergs trapped in Arctic Ocean pack ice stand along the shores like marooned sculptures, rough-hewn but incandescent in the sun. Thick ice shelves, trellised with meltwater during the summer, extend into the ocean for miles.

In summer, when the sun never sets, the lowlands near Lake Hazen and Tanquary Fiord are transformed. South-facing slopes reflect the sun's energy, helping to create thermal oases that burgeon with life. Heathers, willows, and other tundra plants attract shaggy musk oxen, arctic hares, collared lemmings, and Peary caribou, which are smaller than their mainland relatives. Polar bears, wolves, arctic foxes, and ermines prey on creatures that find sustenance in the harsh realm.

Park staff lead tours to Fort Conger, once used as a base by Arctic explorers, including Robert E. Peary on his 1909 journey to the Pole. Summer visitors who take the five-hour charter flight from Resolute Bay arrive in a brooding, near-barren landscape emerging only at the margins from its shroud of ice. Day hikes from Lake Hazen and Tanquary Fiord—sites of an airstrip and warden station—let visitors feel a special magic at the top of the world.

PARK DATA

TERRITORY: Northwest Territories
ESTABLISHED: 1988
AREA: 14,585 sq mi (37,775 sq km)
NATURAL FEATURES: Grant Land Mountains, plateaus, and polar desert; fjords, glaciers, ice fields, and the northernmost freshwater lake in Canada
CULTURAL FEATURES: Fort Conger, a scientific research base established in 1881; archaeological sites that date back some 4,000 years to early Inuit peoples
FLORA: Grasses, sedges, forbs, mosses, and lichens
FAUNA: Musk oxen, polar bears, arctic wolves, Peary caribou, arctic foxes and hares, ermines, collared lemmings; birds including ptarmigans, terns, eider ducks, snow geese, horned larks, hoary redpolls, snow buntings, and loons

Glacier-born Ruggles River (above) braids through a valley in Canada's northernmost park. Arctic hares (left) seek safety in numbers on a gravel plain. Skilled hunter, an arctic wolf (opposite) grasps a hare in its mouth. Other prey include musk oxen, ptarmigans, and Peary caribou.

Forillon

*J*utting into the Gulf of St. Lawrence like the beak of a great bird, Gaspé Peninsula marks both a beginning and an end. Here, in the early part of the 16th century, Jacques Cartier stepped ashore and began France's ventures in the New World. Here also the continental Appalachian Mountains end in a flourish of spectacular limestone cliffs.

Forillon National Park encompasses 93 square miles at Gaspé's eastern tip. Taking "Harmony between Man, Land, and Sea" for an interpretive theme, the park embraces a rich array of natural and cultural, marine and terrestrial features. Visitors can trek into remote wilderness areas or take gentle strolls along clearly marked paths. Plants typical of arctic-alpine zones meet upland firs and birches. Oaks, maples, and hemlocks usually found farther south flourish along river valleys.

Falling from cliffs along the shore, rocks large and small—loosened by the forces of ice, water, and wind—pepper the water and rocky beaches below. Several species of whales feed offshore. Harbor and gray seals frolic in the water and loll on the rocks. At the surf's edge, harlequin ducks bob, and waves of birds dive for fish or ride updrafts along the cliffs.

To introduce visitors at Grande-Grave to marine life, wet-suited naturalists dive and bring up lobsters, hermit crabs, sea stars, brittle stars, sea cucumbers, and other intriguing creatures; unharmed, the marine animals are later returned to the sea. Eager children line up to taste-test bits of kelp and sea lettuce retrieved by divers.

A trail leading to restored buildings that once were part of a fishing village lures visitors back in time and into the lives of Gaspé's cod fishermen.

PARK DATA

PROVINCE: Quebec
ESTABLISHED: 1974 official date; 1970 agreement to establish
AREA: 93 sq mi (240 sq km)
CLIMATE: Relatively mild winters and cool summers; average annual rainfall 44.3 in (112.5 cm)
NATURAL FEATURES: Limestone cliffs; mountainous coastal region
CULTURAL FEATURES: Restored buildings of fishing village, including Hyman & Sons store and cod-processing sheds; restored Xavier Blanchette farmstead
FLORA: Firs and birches in the highlands; maples in river valleys; wildflowers in abandoned farm fields
FAUNA: Moose, deer, black bears, foxes, lynx, snowshoe hares, groundhogs; marine mammals, including gray and harbor seals and several species of whales; numerous birds, including black-legged kittiwakes, black guillemots, ducks, and gulls

Sculptured by water, ice, and wind, limestone strata scallop Cap Bon Ami's shores. Thousands of seabirds colonize Forillon's cliffs. The park's name comes from a French word for "sea stack."

Fundy

*F*undy. For many people the name evokes one thing: the bay of giant tides. Sheltered between the southern coast of New Brunswick and the southwestern half of Nova Scotia, its mouth opening into the Atlantic-fed Gulf of Maine, the Bay of Fundy boasts the world's greatest range of tides. In the upper part of the deep, funnel-shaped bay the difference between high and low tide levels may be as much as 53 feet.

Fundy is also known for the land that adjoins the bay. An 80-square-mile

park preserves an 8-mile stretch of rocky, often fogbound bay shore, as well as an inland plateau of the geographically distinct Maritime Acadian Highlands Natural Region.

The park preserves the human story too, from Mi'kmaq Indians to European explorers and settlers—who were mostly farmers and lumbermen. The name "Fundy" may come from the Portuguese word *fundo*, which means "deep," or from the French *fendu*, which means "split."

Unquestionably, the tidal drama that plays out twice a day upstages all of the other attractions here. At high tide, water laps at steep cliffs of sandstone, shale, or hardened lava. Along the shoreline of the upper bay, thousands of years of erosion by wind and water have sculptured a gallery of fantastical grottoes and sea stacks known as "flowerpots."

Beachcombers delight in low tide, which transforms the shore into an expanse of mud-and-gravel flats and exposes a panoply of life—seaweeds, barnacles, periwinkles, sea anemones, sand hoppers, worms, mussels, whelks, crabs, clams, and an array of fish—all waiting under rocks or in tidal pools for the water's return.

Flanking the bay, the parkland plateau of rounded hills and deep valleys is a remnant of an ancient mountain range cut by streams and waterfalls, filled with small lakes, bogs, and beaver ponds, and covered by lush forests of spruce, fir, maple, and birch.

Wildlife is abundant in the park and includes snowshoe hares, beavers, porcupines, white-tailed deer, bobcats, moose, and black bears. Some 245 species of birds have been sighted here, especially during the spring and fall migrations. The park's many lakes and streams are rife with brook—or speckled—trout, and during the months of July and August, Atlantic salmon begin to make their run up the Upper Salmon River to spawn.

PARK DATA

PROVINCE: New Brunswick
ESTABLISHED: 1948
AREA: 80 sq mi (206 sq km)
ELEVATION: From sea level to 1,200 ft (365 m)
CLIMATE: Average annual rainfall more than 47 in (121 cm)
NATURAL FEATURES: Tidal flats, broad estuaries, coastal cliffs; interior plateau cut by deep valleys, rivers, and waterfalls
CULTURAL FEATURES: Remains of fields farmed by early settlers
FLORA: Spruces, firs, maples, and birches
FAUNA: Moose, black bears, deer, cougars, bobcats, porcupines, beavers, snowshoe hares; some 245 bird species; Atlantic salmon, brook trout

Faces of Fundy: On the high plateau beyond the bay shore, a white-tailed deer (opposite) feeds near an autumn-touched maple. Dickson Falls (left) tumbles past park visitors who watch from a walkway in the woods.

Georgian Bay Islands

Wind-sculptured pines, glacier-polished bedrock, and remote coves with cobbled beaches give a wild beauty to the park's 59 islands and shoals, a sampler of the 30,000 isles in Georgian Bay. Boreal and temperate species of plants and animals mingle here on the southern edge of the Canadian Shield, generating a surprising diversity. There are more species of reptiles and amphibians than in any other national park in Canada.

This rich mixture is most obvious on Beausoleil, the largest island in the park. Sparse soil in the cracks and crevasses of Beausoleil's northern half supports hardy shrubs, grasses, and gnarled white pines flagged by wind. American beeches, sugar maples, and red and white oaks thrive in the deep soils of the southern part of the island.

PARK DATA

PROVINCE: Ontario
ESTABLISHED: 1929
AREA: 4.6 sq mi (12 sq km)
NATURAL FEATURE:
Glaciated gneiss bedrock
CULTURAL FEATURES:
Prehistoric hunting and fishing camps
FLORA: Pines, firs, birches, maples, oaks, beeches, hemlocks; orchids
FAUNA: Variety of mammals; 18 reptile species, including the Massasauga rattlesnake and spotted turtle; 15 amphibian species; birds including red-shouldered hawks

Brébeuf Light (above) sweeps across the blue waters of Georgian Bay. The westering sun dips **into the bay off the isle of Beausoleil (right), which means "beautiful sun" in French.**

Glacier

The Selkirks of Glacier National Park have eroded slowly into angular mountains separated by deep, narrow valleys. Hundreds of glaciers and broad fields of granular snow drape the summits and alpine plateaus.

The combination of steep mountain walls, thick snowpacks, and often mild weather creates perfect avalanche conditions. Each winter, thousands of snowslides sweep down mountainsides at speeds of up to 200 miles an hour, clear-cutting paths that extend from the tree line to valley floors. Early green vegetation of the avalanche paths attracts birds and deer mice. Mountain goats, the park's most common large mammal species, descend from the heights to graze on shrubs. In the valleys, mild temperatures and abundant precipitation nourish lush forests.

PARK DATA

PROVINCE: British Columbia
ESTABLISHED: 1886
AREA: 521 sq mi (1,349 sq km)
CLIMATE: In winter, 30-55 ft (9-17 m) of snowfall
NATURAL FEATURES: Steep, craggy mountains and deep valleys; glaciers and ice fields; more than 20 percent of landscape scarred by avalanches
CULTURAL FEATURES: Rogers Pass designated a national historic site because of its importance in early rail travel; Glacier considered by many mountaineers to be their sport's North American birthplace
FLORA: Western red cedars and hemlocks in interior, or Columbia, forest; Engelmann spruces, subalpine firs, and mountain hemlocks at higher elevations; wildflowers
FAUNA: Grizzly and black bears, moose, mountain goats, marmots, pikas; 235 species of birds

Near Rogers Pass (left), trains that once brought mountaineers to Glacier from all over the world now haul freight to Pacific ports. Climbers on Illecillewaet Glacier in the 1930s (opposite) slowly chip their way to the top of an ice pinnacle called a serac.

43

Grasslands

The Great Plains were once
North America's counterpart
to East Africa's savanna—windswept,
nearly treeless grasslands supporting
huge populations of bison, pronghorn,
elk, deer, grizzlies, and prairie dogs.
One of the few remnants of this habitat
is protected in two disjunct blocks near
the Saskatchewan-Montana border.

The rolling terrain of Grasslands'
West Block is carpeted with mixed
grasses and widespread pincushion
and prickly pear cactuses. Black-tailed
prairie dogs inhabit densely populated
colonies, while golden eagles and
prairie falcons circle above, waiting to
pick off unwary rodents.

Pronghorn sprint across the flats,
kicking up rooster tails of dust. White-
tailed deer browse in wooded ravines
and willow thickets by the Frenchman
River, which plows a meandering
furrow the length of the West Block.

In the East Block, water and
wind ceaselessly sculpture the Killdeer
Badlands, creating deep gullies, flat-
topped buttes, hoodoos, and barren
clay hills known locally as "dobbies."

PARK DATA

PROVINCE: Saskatchewan
ESTABLISHED: 1975
(agreement to establish)
AREA: 350 sq mi (906 sq km)
NATURAL FEATURES:
Rolling prairie; Killdeer
Badlands; Frenchman River
CULTURAL FEATURES:
Tepee rings in the
Frenchman River Valley
FLORA: Saskatoons;
grasses; cactuses
FAUNA: Canada's only
black-tailed prairie dog
colonies; swift foxes (rein-
troduced); burrowing owls

Mixed grasses soften
the rumpled prairie
at 70-Mile Butte (right).
The purplish air sacs
of a male sharp-tailed
grouse (above) inflate
to attract mates during
courtship dances.

Gros Morne

Named for the great peak that looms over the rugged, mist-wreathed highlands of northwestern Newfoundland, Gros Morne evokes a sense of splendid isolation. It seems elemental and primordial—a vast landscape of grays, greens, and browns.

Along Bonne Bay and the Gulf of St. Lawrence are cliffs, grottoes, sandy beaches, sea stacks, and salt marshes. Lying between the sea and the Long Range escarpment is the coastal lowland, which consists of bogs and a series of forested ridges running parallel to the coast and the Long Range.

In 1987, UNESCO designated Gros Morne a world heritage site. Several rich fossil areas here preserve a record of the earth's past, and an unusual sequence of displaced ocean crust and mantle rocks is evidence for plate tectonics. About 450 million years ago, continents came together, crushing seafloor between them and creating the Appalachian range. A fragment of seafloor became the Tablelands plateau—a flat-topped, yellow-brown mountain where little vegetation will grow. Over several million years, the Appalachians wore down, and the crust readjusted along existing fault lines. Part of the crust rose along the Long Range Fault, creating the escarpment and high plateau. In the last two million years, glaciers cut deep valleys in the rock; as the ice melted, seawater flooded the valleys, producing fjords.

Gros Morne's human story dates back some 4,500 years, when Maritime Archaic Indians came here seeking seals, caribou, fish, small mammals, seabirds, and walruses. Paleo-Eskimos arrived about 2,700 years ago. There is also evidence for the arrival of a more recent Indian culture, which may have been Innu or Mi'kmaq.

PARK DATA

PROVINCE: Newfoundland
ESTABLISHED: 1973 (agreement to establish)
AREA: 697 sq mi (1,805 sq km)
HIGHEST POINT: Gros Morne, 2,644 ft (806 m), the second highest peak in Newfoundland
CLIMATE: Cool and breezy in summer; cool, clear, and snowy in winter
NATURAL FEATURES: Long Range Mountains, Tablelands plateau, steep cliffs, coastal lowland; fjords and fjordlike lakes
CULTURAL FEATURES: Archaeological sites dating back to Maritime Archaic Indians, 2 Paleo-Eskimo cultures, and an unidentified recent Indian culture; 19th-century villages and summer fishing premises
FLORA: Boreal forest and tuckamore; bog, fen, marsh, and seashore plants; wild orchids
FAUNA: Woodland caribou, moose, black bears, lynx; river otters, whales, seals; many bird species

Dwarfed by a wall of rock, a canoeist glides through mist. Cool air cascading off the park's plateau can cause high winds that make canoeing hazardous.

Gwaii Haanas

"Islands of wonder and beauty" is how some translate Gwaii Haanas, the Haida name for this park reserve in the remote Queen Charlotte Islands of British Columbia. Encompassing the southern end of Moresby Island and 137 other islands, the reserve is accessible only by boat or aircraft. The islands lie at the edge of the continental shelf, and from them rise the spectacular, rugged peaks of the Queen Charlotte Mountains. Fjords and bays penetrate rocky shorelines, and a temperate rain forest blankets steep slopes with huge spruces, hemlocks, and venerable cedars that may be more than a thousand years old.

Much of Gwaii Haanas seems pristine wilderness, but a closer look reveals traces of the sophisticated culture that developed on these islands. A Haida heritage site, Gwaii Haanas is part of the archipelago that has been home to the Haida for 10,000 years. Today, the reserve is largely uninhabited, and once thriving villages have been swallowed up by an ever encroaching forest.

Carved mortuary poles provide a haunting tribute to past splendors at Ninstints (opposite). Until the 1860s, when disease struck, some 300 Haida occupied the then flourishing village on Anthony Island, now a UNESCO world heritage site, in the southwestern part of the archipelago. In an 1878 photograph taken farther north at the still inhabited village of Skidegate (above), poles arrayed around waterfront dwellings reveal the richness of the Haida culture.

Gwaii Haanas National Park Reserve

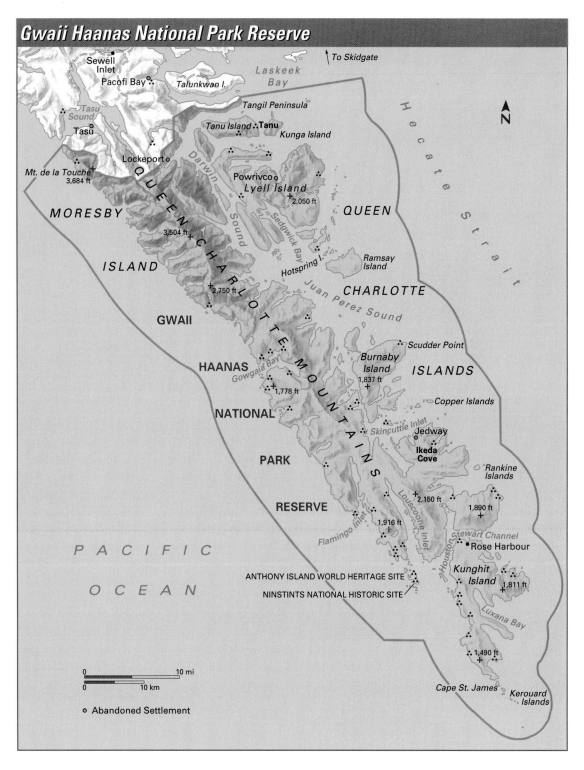

To Skidgate

Sewell Inlet
Pacofi Bay
Talunkwan I.
Laskeek Bay
Tangil Peninsula
Tasu Sound
Tasu
Tanu Island ∴Tanu
Kunga Island
Lockeport
Darwin Sound
Mt. de la Touche 3,684 ft
Powrivco
Lyell Island 2,050 ft
QUEEN
MORESBY
Sedgwick Bay
Hecate Strait
3,504 ft
ISLAND
2,750 ft
Hotspring I.
Ramsay Island
CHARLOTTE
GWAII
Juan Perez Sound
HAANAS
Gowgaia Bay
1,778 ft
Scudder Point
Burnaby Island 1,837 ft
ISLANDS
NATIONAL
Skincuttle Inlet
Jedway
Copper Islands
PARK
Ikeda Cove
Rankine Islands
RESERVE
Louscoone Inlet
2,150 ft
1,890 ft
1,916 ft
PACIFIC
Flamingo Inlet
Stewart Channel
Rose Harbour
OCEAN
ANTHONY ISLAND WORLD HERITAGE SITE
NINSTINTS NATIONAL HISTORIC SITE
Kunghit Island 1,811 ft
Houston Stewart Channel
Luxana Bay
1,490 ft
Cape St. James
Kerouard Islands

QUEEN CHARLOTTE MOUNTAINS

0 ——— 10 mi
0 ——— 10 km

○ Abandoned Settlement

PARK DATA

PROVINCE: British Columbia
ESTABLISHED: 1988 (agreement to establish)
AREA: 577 sq mi (1,470 sq km)
NATURAL FEATURES: Rugged mountains; fjord-cut coastlines
CULTURAL FEATURES: Remains of Haida villages (elaborate mortuary or commemorative poles still at Ninstints); Anthony Island designated UNESCO world heritage site
FLORA: Temperate rain forest, including spruces, hemlocks, and cedars that may be more than 1,000 years old
FAUNA: Black bears, pine martens, weasels, otters, deer mice, shrews, bats, and Sitka black-tailed deer (introduced); Pacific white-sided dolphins; seabirds (including 12 species that breed here) and many forest birds (including the northern saw-whet owl)

Low tide in Burnaby Strait (opposite) exposes a sea star and other marine creatures. Such abundance along the continent's northwestern coast provides food for wildlife and humans alike. "The tide is out, our table is set," say coastal Indians farther to the north.

Since the 1970s, the Haida have been working in concert with conservationists to protect their island homeland against clear-cut logging. In 1985, scores of Haida were arrested for blocking a logging road on Lyell Island, one of the area's larger islands. Then, in 1988, the federal and provincial governments agreed to establish a national park reserve. The Haida Nation subsequently negotiated the right to co-manage the area with the federal government, pending settlement of land claims through treaty discussions.

HAIDA CULTURE

HAIDA GWAII, which means "homeland," is the Haida name for the Queen Charlotte Islands. Blessed with a mild climate and abundant food from forest and sea, their island homeland afforded the Haida the leisure they needed to develop a complex culture with a high level of rare artistry. The forest provided woods and other materials for creating elaborate houses, totem poles, and myriad objects for everyday and sacred use.

Once numbering about 10,000, the Haida fell to smallpox and other diseases in the 19th century. But recent years have brought a cultural resurgence. Haida paddlers (right) test a canoe called *Wave Eater*, built in the 1980s using techniques developed by their canoe-making, warrior ancestors. Craftsmen fashioned the 50-foot, seagoing vessel—the first built in many generations—out of a single red cedar log. Objects from

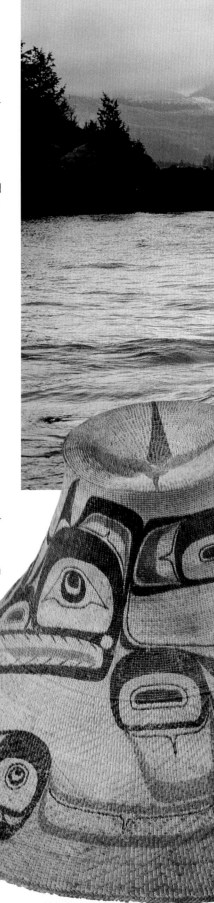

Steller sea lions gather on a rocky islet near Anthony Island. Some 30 percent of British Columbia's

Steller sea lions, along with many other marine mammals, frequent the coastal waters of Gwaii Haanas.

the past reveal how the Haida spiritual pantheon mingles with everyday themes: A stylized mountain goat with prominent horns, painted on a hat of woven spruce roots (left), is perhaps a family crest of the Raven clan. Painted designs and a woven cover transform a cedar food storage box (below) into a work of art; the bear-head rattle (right) served on ceremonial occasions.

Ivvavik

A realm of hummocky tundra, rounded, treeless mountains, and low-lying coastal flats studded with lakes and webbed with braided waterways, Ivvavik has the quiet beauty of vast open spaces. It is a true wilderness preserve in the northwest corner of the Yukon Territory, with no road access or visitor facilities. Most people come with outfitters on organized tours using charter flights from Inuvik, in the Northwest Territories, a distance of some 125 miles from the park's eastern boundary. The most popular activity is white-water rafting on the Firth River, which cuts through the British Mountains and empties into the Beaufort Sea. Otherwise there are few travelers on the boggy tundra, where alder thickets, tussocks of grass or sedge, and squadrons of mosquitoes make walking a nonstop challenge.

Established primarily to safeguard the calving grounds of the Porcupine Caribou Herd, Ivvavik means "a place for giving birth and nursing young." It was the first national park in Canada to be created by a land claim agreement involving negotiations between the federal government and aboriginal people. The Inuvialuit, whose ancestors fished, hunted, and trapped in the area for thousands of years, share in the responsibility for managing the park and are guaranteed the right to practice their traditional lifestyle. Caribou, which have provided food and material for clothing, shelter, and tools, remain central to that subsistence way of life.

A member of the Porcupine Caribou Herd lopes across calving grounds on Ivvavik's coastal plain.

PORCUPINE CARIBOU HERD

ANTLERED HEADS held high, caribou surge across a river during their fall migration. Numbering about 150,000, the Porcupine Herd, named for a tributary of the Yukon River, moves seasonally along ancient migration routes, seeking food and places to calve and raise its young. Caribou paw through the snow for lichens, a staple of their winter diet. During the summer months, the animals usually graze on sedges and grasses.

Ivvavik National Park

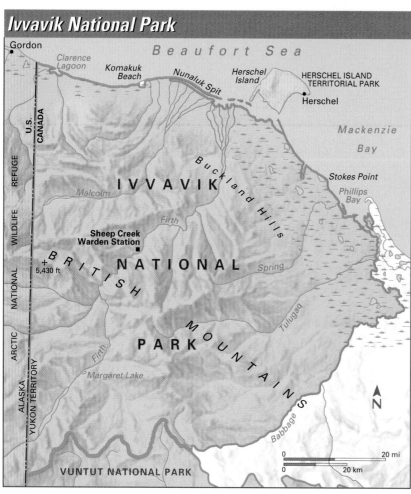

PARK DATA

TERRITORY: Yukon
ESTABLISHED: 1984
AREA: 3,926 sq mi (10,168 sq km)
CLIMATE: Arctic conditions prevailing; light precipitation; temperatures averaging 60°F (16°C) in July and −26°F (−31°C) in January
NATURAL FEATURES: Low, rounded mountains throughout much of the park; a long stretch of coastal plain; permafrost; a few lakes and rivers, including the Firth River, which is favored by white-water enthusiasts

FLORA: In the northern region, tundra vegetation including low shrubs, sedges, and herbs; in the southern region, typical tundra vegetation, as well as stunted white spruces and birches
FAUNA: Porcupine Caribou Herd, which ranges from Alaska's Arctic National Wildlife Refuge to Ivvavik's coastal plain; also Dall sheep, grizzly and polar bears, wolves, arctic foxes, wolverines; beluga and bowhead whales, ringed seals; birds including gyrfalcons and golden eagles

Rapids churn the Firth River, which drains the British Mountains as it flows north into the **Beaufort Sea. On the coast, the Firth fans into a delta, an important wildlife habitat.**

Jasper

The Yellowhead Highway divides the largest of Canada's Rocky Mountain national parks in two. South of the highway, Jasper's natural wonders are accessible via the Icefield Parkway and the Maligne Lake Road. North of the Yellowhead lies a roadless realm of moose, mountain caribou, grizzlies, black bears, and the largest wolf population in the mountain parks. Only one major hiking trail penetrates this remote wilderness.

The Icefield Parkway starts at Lake Louise in Banff National Park and runs northwest 142 miles to Jasper townsite. Just north of the Jasper-Banff boundary, the parkway passes near the toe of the Athabasca Glacier, one of six major outlet glaciers fed by the Columbia Icefield. North America's largest ice field south of Alaska, Columbia covers 125 square miles of a gently undulating plateau surrounded by some of the highest peaks in the Rockies.

Castleguard Cave, the country's largest cavern system with 12 miles of explored passages, probes northwest from Castleguard Mountain into the rock underlying the ice field. The caves are nearly 1,000 feet below the base of the 1,200-foot-thick ice cap.

Farther northwest along the parkway at Sunwapta Falls, the Sunwapta River smashes through a deep, right-angled limestone canyon en route to its meeting with the Athabasca River, which in turn plummets more than 50 feet in a powerful cascade, then roils through a narrow, steep-walled gorge.

As the parkway nears Jasper townsite, a side road switchbacks to the base of Mount Edith Cavell, an 11,033-foot pyramidal peak. Angel Glacier occupies an enormous amphitheater in Cavell's sheer, snow-striated north face and spills over a 1,000-foot cliff in a

PARK DATA

PROVINCE: Alberta
ESTABLISHED: 1907
AREA: 4,200 sq mi
(10,878 sq km)
NATURAL FEATURES:
Rugged mountains,
U-shaped valleys, Devonian
reef formations; Maligne
Karst System, one of
the largest and most
complex karst systems in
North America; ice fields,
glaciers, lakes, rivers,
and waterfalls
FLORA: Engelmann
spruces (oldest specimens
in Canadian Rockies),
alpine and subalpine firs,
lodgepole pines; montane
grasslands; wildflowers
FAUNA: Grizzly and black
bears, elk, moose, caribou,
bighorn sheep, mountain
goats, wolves, cougars,
mule deer; wide variety of
birds; fish including
rainbow, cutthroat, and
Dolly Varden trout
UNIQUE FEATURES:
Columbia Icefield, largest
in the Canadian Rockies;
Maligne Lake, Rockies'
largest glacial water body

Far from the safety
of their usual haunts,
a mountain goat and
her kid head to the
Disaster Point mineral
lick between Talbot
Lake and Pocahontas
Pond in the Athabasca
Valley. Herbivore diets
are low in essential
salts, so mountain goats
and other grazers travel
long distances to find
sodium at licks.

spectacular icefall. Alpine meadows here are ablaze with flowers from mid-July to late August.

The Maligne Lake Road begins northeast of Jasper townsite and winds to the southeast, passing several scenic spots. The first stop is Maligne Canyon, the most impressive limestone slit canyon in the Canadian Rockies. A swirling, churning river has shaped a twisted gorge more than 160 feet deep and, in places, only 7 feet wide.

Farther to the southeast, the Maligne River flows into one end of Medicine Lake, but no waterway flows out. The river's volume decreases each fall, and the lake nearly dries up. It was discovered that Medicine Lake drains through sinks that connect with caverns on at least two levels under the Maligne Valley. The water resurfaces ten miles down the valley and is again called the Maligne River.

The road ends at Maligne Lake, a deep blue, fjordlike finger of water that extends 17 miles into a wilderness of rugged peaks and hanging glaciers. At the lake's midpoint, photographers and

Shaking its head like a wet dog, a moose surfaces after grazing on milfoil and other water plants in Jasper's Maligne Lake. The largest members of the deer family, moose swim well and dive to depths of up to 15 feet.

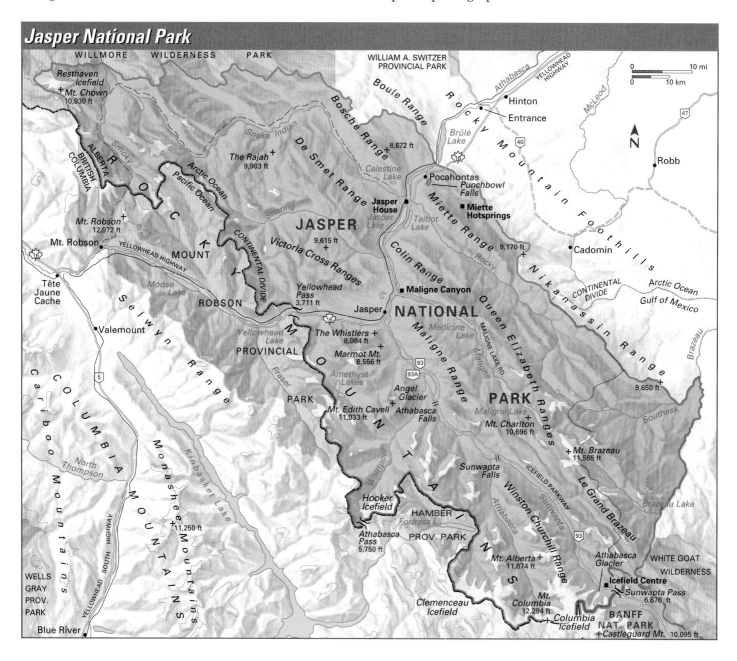

Jasper National Park

60

MOUNTAIN FORMATION

FOLD MOUNTAINS in the Canadian Rockies (right) began forming some 85 million years ago when the North American plate rammed into an island arc on the Pacific plate. The collision rumpled layers of sedimentary rock hundreds of miles inland. Beds of limestone, sandstone, siltstone, and shale (below) arched into giant anticlines, bent into U-shaped synclines, and even contorted into Z-shaped folds.

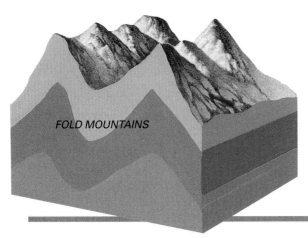

FOLD MOUNTAINS

The Athabasca River washes tons of glacial silt and sand into Jasper Lake each year. In late summer, when the volume of the river decreases, the lake becomes a vast flat dotted with shallow pools. Prevailing westerlies blow exposed silt as far as the foothills. Heavier grains of sand settle out to form shoreline dunes up to a hundred feet high. By late May, the flat is once more a lake.

artists find a favorite subject in Spirit Island, a gravel bar on which a spruce grove grows against the backdrop of massive, glacier-clad Mount Charlton.

The Maligne Valley is home to a population of harlequin ducks, endangered in eastern Canada and declining in much of their western range. After wintering on the Pacific coast, the ducks migrate inland to breed and nest near clean, fast-flowing valley streams. To preserve nesting areas, white-water rafting and other human activities are prohibited along the Maligne River between Maligne and Medicine Lakes from May 1 to July 1.

Elk are the most commonly seen large mammals in the park. They are so accustomed to humans that they graze on roadside grasses, nibble lawns at Jasper Park Lodge, and trim hedges in Jasper townsite. By the turn of the century, overhunting had nearly wiped out the elk in the central and southern Rockies. Most of Jasper's present population (1,000 to 2,000) descend from 88 animals imported from Yellowstone National Park between 1917 and 1920.

PREDATOR CONTROL PROGRAM

CONFLICTS BETWEEN recreation and preservation have generated friction ever since parks were established. Early in this century, parks encouraged wardens to kill "bad" animals—wolves, cougars, coyotes—that preyed on "good" species valued by visitors—elk, deer, and bighorn sheep.

The essence of park policy was that the only good predator was a dead one. Wardens disagreed, however, on the most efficient tools in their arsenal: guns, dogs, poison bait, or traps. A Yellowstone superintendent recommended that Canadians try dynamiting wolf and coyote dens.

Bears were viewed as nuisance animals to be

shot if they interfered with human activities. Photographed in the early 1900s, Jasper wardens stand over "troublesome" grizzlies (above). Otherwise, bears were treated as tourist attractions. Today, Jasper and other national parks take a conservation-driven approach to managing these vast, complex natural areas held in trust for future generations.

Kejimkujik

Set on a chunk of ancestral Mi'kmaq Indian land, this serene place of woods and waters takes its name from Kejimkujik Lake. The name of the lake is thought to have come from a Mi'kmaq word, but its exact meaning is unclear.

Today Kedge (KED-gee), as the park is known, is considered one of Atlantic Canada's best canoeing areas. Here visitors can explore an inland wilderness of lush forests, bogs, and sedge meadows— all watered by a web of rivers and shallow lakes. In some isolated spots, groves of 300-year-old hemlocks can be found.

The park's undeveloped Seaside Adjunct contains 8.5 square miles of Nova Scotia's south shore. Accessible by foot, this pristine wilderness rewards hikers with tidal flats, lagoons, sandy beaches, and headlands carpeted with meadows.

Several species of amphibians and reptiles live in the park. Kejimkujik's birdlife includes the endangered piping plover, which builds its nest on dunes and beaches.

PARK DATA

PROVINCE: Nova Scotia
ESTABLISHED: 1974
AREA: 147 sq mi (381 sq km)
NATURAL FEATURES: Headlands, drumlins, tidal flats; lakes, rivers, lagoons
FLORA: White pines and ancient hemlocks; endangered water pennyworts
FAUNA: 3 turtle species, 7 frog and toad species, 5 snake species, and 4 salamander species; birds including common loons and piping plovers

Night falls on island-studded Kejimkujik Lake, the largest of the park's waters. Once plied by Mi'kmaq canoes, this waterway now affords visitors a fine—but sometimes windy—way to view the wilderness areas surrounding the lake.

Kluane

*L*and of superlatives, Kluane National Park Reserve is home to some of the fastest and longest glaciers, the largest subpolar ice field, Canada's highest mountain, the biggest known concentration of Dall sheep, and perhaps the greatest assemblage of plants and animals in northern Canada.

Located in the Yukon Territory's remote southwestern corner, Kluane showcases an assortment of habitats in one of the world's most pristine wilderness areas. With some 2,000 glaciers on the flanks of the St. Elias Mountains, much of the landscape belongs to a nearly lifeless realm of snow, ice, and rock. But there are also forests crowded with white spruces and gilded with aspens in the fall. There are small glades verdant with prairie grasses, meadows with more than 200 varieties of alpine flora, and landscapes where pioneer plants colonize silt and gravel eroded from valleys and deposited by receding glaciers.

Twin arms of the Kaskawulsh Glacier merge to form a slow-motion river of ice. Rock scraped from the land as the glacier plows downhill produces rubble ridges called moraines. As the ice moves over steep terrain, its surface buckles and fractures.

With keen eyes, a wolf pack leader surveys a forested slope for prey. This predator also relies on acute hearing, a strong sense of smell, and teamwork by its 10- to 15-member pack to bring down larger animals such as moose and Dall sheep.

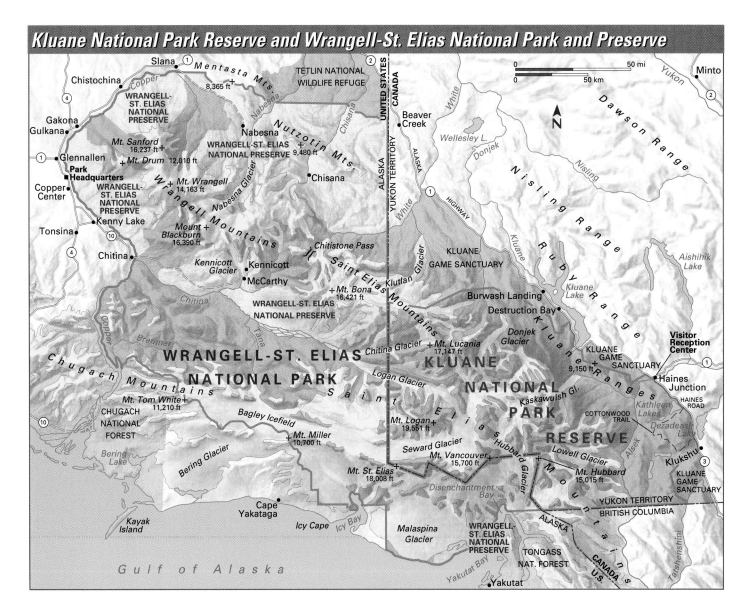

The reserve, which takes its name from a Tutchone Indian word meaning "place of many fish," lures anglers to mountain-framed lakes and glacier-fed streams populated by grayling, trout, and kokanee—Kluane's landlocked variety of salmon. For river runners, the Alsek River offers white-water adventure and a premier wilderness experience. As the scenic waterway rushes through the Kluane Ranges en route to the Gulf of Alaska, it surges past glaciers and carries rafting parties past mountain goats balancing delicately on narrow ledges, grizzly bears raking bushes for berries, and moose foraging on willow shoots.

Experienced, high-altitude mountaineers from all over the world tackle the St. Elias, North America's highest mountain range. Expeditions to 19,551-foot Mount Logan, the highest peak in Canada, must cross heavily crevassed glaciers and meet the challenges created by harsh and rapidly changing weather. Intense snow glare pushes the temperature up to 90°F, but storms bred in the Pacific Ocean can bring sudden winds of more than a hundred miles an hour and sub-zero cold.

For day hikers there are short, pleasant trails near the visitor reception center at Haines Junction, a town of 800 on the Alaska Highway. For

backpackers, longer trails, also on the reserve's eastern fringe, can provide access to the interior. The 53-mile Cottonwood Trail is Kluane's longest. The horseshoe-shaped route winds through forests and alpine meadows and climbs high above the tree line.

On clear days travelers taking the Alaska Highway can glimpse a few of the higher peaks of the St. Elias, but charter planes taking off from the airstrip at Burwash Landing, northwest of Haines Junction, offer larger vistas that capture the grandeur of the named and unnamed peaks and the vast areas of wilderness that make Kluane such a magnificent experience.

PARK DATA

TERRITORY: Yukon
ESTABLISHED: 1972
AREA: 8,500 sq mi (22,015 sq km)
HIGHEST POINT: Mount Logan, 19,551 ft (5,959 m), Canada's highest peak
NATURAL FEATURES: St. Elias Mountains; glaciers, ice fields, lakes, rivers
CULTURAL FEATURES: Alaska Highway; remains of mining camps built during the 1898 Kluane Gold Rush; traditional native villages near the reserve
FLORA: Great diversity of Pacific and Arctic plants, including white spruces, quaking aspens, balsam poplars, dwarf birches, willows, crowberries; wildflowers, mosses, lichens
FAUNA: Dall sheep, grizzly and black bears, moose, mountain goats, wolves, lynx; ptarmigans, peregrine falcons, eagles

Head-to-head combat during the Dall sheep rutting season establishes a pecking order among the rams and gives victors the right to mate. The males, identified by long, curling horns, travel peaceably in bachelor bands for most of the year, leaving protection of the young to the ewes.

SCULPTOR OF THE landscape, Lowell Glacier (left) calves a flotilla of icebergs into the Alsek River. Such icebound rivers and thick continental ice sheets have molded much of the earth's surface at one time or another, scouring out U-shaped valleys and mountainside basins called cirques. Knife-edged ridges and jagged peaks also bear testimony to the cutting power of moving ice. A glacier is spawned when snow piles up year after year and turns into ice. As it moves under its own weight, the ice traps loose rocks that act as rasps. In summer, meltwater drains from the glacier's leading edge into braided streams heavy with glacial debris. When thaw exceeds expansion, the glacier recedes, leaving lakes, gravel deposits, ridges, and dramatic valleys in its wake. The paintings below show how a glacier (upper) carves a U-shaped valley (lower).

GLACIATION

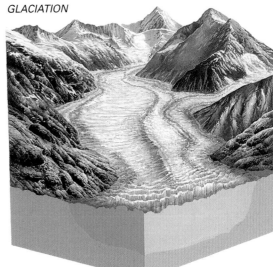

POST-GLACIATION

Kootenay

This long, narrow park on the western slopes of the Rocky Mountains extends for about 5 miles on either side of 65-mile-long Kootenay Parkway, which follows the valleys of the Vermilion and Kootenay Rivers.

Geological forces generated the park's most interesting features. Tokumm Creek, its waters milky with glacial silt, spills over a 70-foot ledge. It froths through Marble Canyon, a 128-foot-deep fault in a formation of gray limestone and quartzite layered with white and grayish dolomite.

The nearby Paint Pots are a series of cold mineral springs stained bright red and yellow by iron oxide. A small creek flows from the springs into a flat area known as the Ochre Beds, which local Indians once excavated to make pigments for war paint, pictographs, and tepee decorations. The beds were also mined commercially.

The parkway angles to the southeast in the shadow of the Rockwall, a sheer limestone escarpment of the Vermilion Range.

Farther south stand the Iron Gates, the first of the towering dolomite cliffs of narrow, sinuous Sinclair Canyon, which was carved by Sinclair Creek. Nearby, the Radium Hot Springs burble from the earth at temperatures higher than 100°F. Some of the water is fed directly into a hot soaking pool, and some is cooled for a swimming pool.

PARK DATA

PROVINCE: British Columbia
ESTABLISHED: 1920
AREA: 543 sq mi (1,406 sq km)
NATURAL FEATURES: Marble and Sinclair Canyons, Vermilion Range, Ochre Beds; Paint Pots, Radium Hot Springs, Stanley Glacier
CULTURAL FEATURES: Sir George Simpson cairn, honoring the governor (1821 to 1860) of Hudson's Bay Company territories
FLORA: Douglas firs, Engelmann spruces, lodgepole pines; asters and black-eyed Susans; prickly pear cactuses
FAUNA: Grizzly and black bears, moose, elk, bighorn sheep, mountain goats, mule deer, white-tailed deer, wolves, cougars, coyotes, hoary marmots, pikas; birds including white-tailed ptarmigans

Dusted by snow, a high, rounded peak in Kootenay's Vermilion Range looms ghostly white beneath a wan winter sun.

Kouchibouguac

A 15-mile rampart of barrier islands shelters the dune-backed beaches, placid lagoons, and salt marshes of Kouchibouguac (koosh-e-boo-gwack). A forest of black spruce and white cedar fills the interior. The park's name, which means "river of the long tides," comes from the Kouchibouguac and other tidal rivers that meander across this low maritime plain.

Park beaches and barrier islands provide nesting sites for endangered piping plovers and the second largest colony of common terns in eastern North America. Lagoons and salt marshes feed and shelter resident seabirds, thousands of migratory water-fowl and shore-birds, and ospreys (the park symbol). Harbor and gray seals feed on fish at the mouth of the St. Louis River, while farther inland, black bears, deer, moose, and coyotes inhabit the dark Acadian forest.

Twenty-seven species of wild orchids fleck bogs and cedar swamps with tiny, colorful blossoms. These wetlands comprise about 20 percent of the park.

Barking, splashing gray seals (above) fight for a flipper-hold on a Kouchibouguac sand-spit. The semipalmated plover (below) is one of many birds seeking food and shelter along the park's shores.

PARK DATA

PROVINCE: New Brunswick
ESTABLISHED: 1979
AREA: 92 sq mi (239 sq km)
NATURAL FEATURES: Barrier islands; wetlands
FLORA: Cedars, pines, birches, and black spruces; wild orchids

FAUNA: Moose, black bears, white-tailed deer, coyotes, beavers; harbor and gray seals; birds including common terns, plovers, red-breasted mergansers, black ducks, ospreys, and warblers

La Mauricie

*T*he lonely cry of the loon; rich autumn hues of scarlet, gold, and green; glacier-scoured bedrock cupping cold, clear lakes—the essence of the Canadian Shield is distilled here in the Laurentian Mountains of southern Quebec.

Conifers of the boreal forest mix with deciduous trees of the Great Lakes-St. Lawrence Lowlands to form La Mauricie's transitional woodlands. Yellow birches and sugar maples grow on sunny, well-drained hillsides with deep soil. The most common birds in these stands are warblers, vireos, and sapsuckers. Pines, spruces, and firs cover valley bottoms and thin-soiled slopes, providing habitats for blue jays, ruffed grouse, chickadees, and finches.

Extensive lakes and streams support 160 beaver colonies, as well as river otters, moose, and waterfowl. About 20 pairs of common loons nest in the park. Twelve raptor species live here, including the broad-winged hawk and barred owl. Black bears range throughout La Mauricie.

PARK DATA

PROVINCE: Quebec
ESTABLISHED: 1970
AREA: 210 sq mi (544 sq km)
NATURAL FEATURES:
Low, rounded hills; rivers, waterfalls, and 150 lakes
CULTURAL FEATURES:
Log hunting and fishing lodges from early 1900s
FLORA: Conifers, birches, and sugar maples
FAUNA: Moose, bears, wolves, beavers; birds including common loons, the park symbol

Fall colors brighten the shores of misty Lake Wapizagonke (left). A billion years of erosion smoothed the contours of forested hills (above) that once rose as high as the Rockies.

Mingan Archipelago

Whether the name "Mingan" comes from an Algonquian word for "wolf" or a Breton word for "rounded stone" is not certain. The archipelago bearing the name, however, reminds most visitors of landscaped rock gardens.

The Mingan isles are scattered across the northern waters of the Gulf of St. Lawrence, near mainland Quebec. Remarkably diverse vegetation thrives here, including some 500 vascular species in 6 distinct plant communities. Arctic-alpine and tundra plants live next to bogs and near boreal forest.

Weather, salt water, and wind sculpture unusual limestone formations called "flowerpots." When cold air moves over the gulf's waters, billowing fog covers the islands, adding a touch of mystery.

Puffins, razor-bills, guillemots, and cormorants nest here; several duck species winter over. Harbor seals breed and whales feed in the vicinity.

PARK DATA

PROVINCE: Quebec
ESTABLISHED: 1984
AREA: 58 sq mi
(150 sq km); 40 main islands
FLORA: Microecosystems that include rare plants
FAUNA: As many as 8 whale species (including blue and humpback) seen near the archipelago; the Atlantic puffin (park symbol) and 208 other bird species reported

Lilliputian gardens of dwarf trees, lichens, and other plants cap eroded limestone formations in the Mingan Archipelago. A wooden walkway on Niapiskau Island (above) protects fragile, often rare plants from visitors' footsteps.

Mount Revelstoke

*I*n 1914, Mount Revelstoke was set aside to protect wildflowers growing on a plateau backed by the Clachnacudainn Icefield and 8,000-foot peaks.

Each summer, from early July to mid-August, riotous colors sweep across alpine meadows. Yellow avalanche lilies and white spring beauties are followed by Indian paintbrushes, yellow arnicas, purple lupines, pink mountain daisies, and red heathers.

By driving the Summit Road from wet woodlands up through subalpine forest, birdwatchers here can sight as many as four chickadee species.

PARK DATA

PROVINCE: British Columbia
ESTABLISHED: 1914
AREA: 100 sq mi (260 sq km)
ELEVATION: As high as 8,500 ft (2,590 m)
NATURAL FEATURES: Subalpine plateau and high, rugged mountains; Clachnacudainn Icefield
FLORA: Conifers; alpine meadows with a variety of wildflowers, including avalanche lilies, arnicas, lupines, spring beauties, Indian paintbrushes, daisies, and heathers
FAUNA: Grizzly and black bears, moose, caribou, mountain goats, wolverines, bats; birds including northern hawk owl, 4 chickadee species (black-capped, chestnut-backed, mountain, and boreal)

Tall trees and snow-capped peaks fill the horizon in Mount Revelstoke National Park. In the foreground, a bed of wildflowers, dense with Indian paintbrushes and purple lupines, splashes color across a meadow.

Nahanni

PARK DATA

TERRITORY: Northwest Territories
ESTABLISHED: 1976
AREA: 1,840 sq mi (4,766 sq km)
NATURAL FEATURES: Rugged mountains, deep canyons, karst landscapes, terraced tufa (calcium carbonate deposits); hot springs; turbulent rivers, including the South Nahanni, which is designated a Canadian Heritage River; Virginia Falls—nearly twice the height of Niagara Falls; extensive wetlands in valley bottoms
FLORA: White and black spruces, lodgepole pines, dwarf birches; grasses
FAUNA: Grizzly and black bears, woodland caribou, moose, mountain goats, Dall sheep, wolves, lynx; birds including breeding populations of trumpeter swans
UNIQUE FEATURE: First natural area to be named UNESCO world heritage site

*T*his preserve protects a long stretch of the South Nahanni, the country's premier wilderness canoeing river, as well as the lower half of a rapid-studded tributary, the Flat River. Legends and tall tales of Indians and prospectors have long fueled Nahanni myths about lost gold mines, gigantic "mountain men," and a tropical valley, but the reality of this remote region is powerful enough.

The South Nahanni flares over Virginia Falls, then slices through the Mackenzie Mountains, carving 4,000-foot-deep canyons. At Rabbitkettle Hot Springs, waters rich in dissolved minerals have built terraced mounds. Along the Flat River, hoodoos cover a mountainside for a mile. North of the river is a karstland of caves, sinkholes, arches, and labyrinthine corridors formed along fault lines and fissures.

A giant pillar of limestone splits the South Nahanni into twin cataracts at Virginia Falls (right). Fiery aspens and birches encircle sinkholes near Yohin Lake (above left).

North Baffin

A treeless land of towering sea cliffs, dramatic fjords, glacier-veined mountains, and lake-dotted tundra, the proposed North Baffin National Park and its food-rich adjacent waters sustain a profusion of wildlife. Marine mammals and birds flourish in astonishing numbers: Thousands of murres, guillemots, and kittiwakes nest in colonies on Bylot Island, which is just off Baffin's northeastern shore. In May, when pack ice begins to break apart, seals, walruses, beluga whales, and spiral-tusked

narwhals congregate in waters teeming with cod. Polar bears prowl the sea ice for prey, pouncing on seals and diving into the sea for fish.

From Pond Inlet, an Inuit settlement on Baffin's coast, visitors can explore the high Arctic with local guides, traveling by dogsled, snowmobile, kayak, or cross-country skis. Outfitters also offer fishing trips, hiking, and wildlife-viewing tours.

PARK DATA

TERRITORY: Northwest Territories
ESTABLISHED: 1992 (agreement to establish)
AREA: 8,538 sq mi (22,252 sq km)
NATURAL FEATURES: Glaciated mountains and steep cliffs; fjords, sea ice
FLORA: Willows, sedges, saxifrages
FAUNA: Polar bears, wolves, caribou; whales, walruses; greater snow geese (35 percent of the world's breeding population)

Glassy calm waters mirror ice floes and the steep slopes of Bylot Island, summer home to myriad seabirds. On Baffin Island itself, tundra regions in the proposed park sustain caribou and wolves.

Pacific Rim

O n the misty western edge of Vancouver Island, Pacific Rim National Park Reserve confronts the sea with lush forests, steep cliffs battered by surf, and secluded beaches strewn with driftwood. In the reserve's rocky coves, the receding tide brings into view seaweeds swaying in the ocean swells and beds of barnacles, clams, and mussels.

Killer whales cruise the dark waters offshore, pursuing sea lions, salmon, seals, and other prey. From the end of February to mid-May, some 18,000 gray whales swim along the coast as they migrate from calving grounds in Baja California to feed in Arctic waters. The sight of these 35-ton leviathans catapulting into the air and crashing back into the sea thrills whale watchers on tour boats and at viewing sites on land. About 40 grays cut short their annual migration and linger near the park throughout the summer.

The park includes three distinct units—Long Beach, the West Coast

Diverse seascapes draw hikers to Long Beach (right), a 15-mile stretch of rocky coves, coastal forests, and secluded beaches in Vancouver Island's Pacific Rim National Park Reserve. At low tide, sea stars (above) cluster on rocks speckled with barnacles. In the shallows, sea anemones retract their tentacles and wait until the tide comes back in.

Shade-tolerant ferns and shrubs crowd a rain forest floor cast in darkness by a canopy of Sitka spruce and western hemlock. The majestic western red cedar also flourishes in these luxuriant woodlands. Moist Pacific winds bring some 120 inches of rainfall each year, encouraging the rampant growth of lichens and mosses, which derive nutrients from the rain and fallen organic matter.

Trail, and the Broken Group Islands in Barkley Sound. The varied habitats offer many activities for visitors.

Boaters can motor or paddle through waterways sheltered from the open ocean by more than a hundred wooded islets in the Broken Group, home to most of the area's bald eagles.

Beachcombers head for the Long Beach Unit, where huge breakers cast driftwood, giant kelp, and Japanese glass fishing floats onto wind-rippled sands. Here, hikers have easy access to the coastal rain forest. Short trails wind past majestic red cedars in woodlands carpeted with velvety mosses and hung with gauzy lichens.

The rugged West Coast Trail Unit offers the only wilderness hike in the park. Built as a rescue route for seamen shipwrecked in the treacherous waters southeast of Long Beach, the grueling 47-mile route, which crosses boggy areas and scales cliffs, is suitable only for experienced backpackers.

PARK DATA

PROVINCE: British Columbia
ESTABLISHED: 1970 (agreement to establish)
AREA: 193 sq mi (500 sq km)
CLIMATE: 120 in (305 cm) of rainfall a year; mild temperatures year-round
NATURAL FEATURES: Islands and narrow coastal strip with cliffs, caves, and beaches of hard-packed sand; streams, waterfalls, and lakes
CULTURAL FEATURES: Shipwrecks dating back to the 19th century in a region known as the Graveyard of the Pacific (southeast of Long Beach); several sites of early Indian habitation

FLORA: Western red cedars and hemlocks, Sitka spruces, and Pacific silver firs; ferns, mosses, and lichens; Indian paintbrushes, yellow monkey flowers, rose-colored beach peas, yarrows, white-petaled wild strawberries, yellow skunk cabbages; seaweeds
FAUNA: Deer, black bears, cougars, otters; seabirds, bald eagles, black oystercatchers, Canada geese and trumpeter swans (in winter only); marine life including whales, sea lions, giant octopuses, wolf eels, sea anemones, purple starfish, mussels, barnacles, sea urchins

Point Pelee

E ach May this tiny, dagger-shaped peninsula brims with a diversity of birdlife rivaled by few other places in North America. Birds congregate at the park, where they rest and feed. Some touch down in vine-hung forests and open fields, others on beaches and a marshland jigsaw of cattails and ponds. At this time of year, bird-watchers can easily sight a hundred species in one day.

In September, as many as 10,000 monarch butterflies may darken hackberry trees near the peninsula's sandy tip. The migratory insects await fair weather before crossing Lake Erie en route to Mexico, where they spend the winter.

PARK DATA

PROVINCE: Ontario
ESTABLISHED: 1918
AREA: 6 sq mi (15.5 sq km)
NATURAL FEATURES: Southernmost point in mainland Canada; freshwater marsh; sand and pebble beaches
FLORA: Red cedar, black walnut, and hackberry trees; prickly pear cactuses; swamp rose mallows (Canada's only wild hibiscus species)
FAUNA: Exceptional spring and fall migration point for birds, monarch butterflies, dragonflies, and bats; reptiles including five-lined skinks and fox snakes

The woodlands, wetlands, and beaches of Point Pelee (right) are welcome havens to migratory birds winging northward across Lake Erie in spring. The scarlet tanager (above) is one of about 350 species recorded here.

Prince Albert

T he park's three main habitats mark the ecological transition from southern to northern Canada. Fescue grasslands in the southwestern corner of Prince Albert, which represent Saskatchewan's northernmost extension of prairie, are home to badgers, ground squirrels, and about a hundred free-ranging plains bison.

Farther north, prairie blends into aspen parkland, a mosaic of aspen groves and pockets of grassland. In this

productive habitat live elk, white-tailed deer, ruffed grouse, beavers, snowshoe hares, and 165 species of nesting birds. The easily excavated, gravelly soil of the Waskesiu Hills makes the hills a favorite denning ground for red foxes and wolves. The park's 60 to 80 wolves move in several packs, covering vast distances in search of moose and other prey.

Aspen parkland gives way to the lake country of the north, land of the loon. (In all, a third of Prince Albert National Park is water.) Bald eagles and ospreys nest in the mixed woodlands and boreal forest fringing the largest lakes—Waskesiu, Kingsmere, and Crean. Lavallee Lake, in the park's northwestern corner, is so remote that the easily disturbed American white

Tendrils of morning mist waft across the placid surface of a remote lake in Prince Albert National Park.

Under a leaden autumn sky, aspens gleam golden amid the dark green spruces edging a reed-filled pond.

pelican breeds freely there in a colony of some 7,000 birds.

Virtually all the park's physical features are legacies of the Ice Age, which ended here about 10,000 years ago. The Waskesiu Hills were formed when a lobe of retreating ice deposited mounds of glacial till. Gravel ridges known as eskers, once the banks of subglacial streams, snake across the countryside. Broad channels that siphoned off torrential meltwater now form outsize valleys for small streams. When chunks of ice buried in glacial till melted, the soils above slumped, creating craters called "kettles." These depressions, usually water-filled, pock the region.

Before the arrival of European fur traders in the late 18th century, native peoples followed a pattern of seasonal movement that probably changed little over centuries. The Cree of the boreal forest summered in small groups along lakes and rivers, fishing, hunting, and trapping. To the south, the Assiniboin spent the warm-weather months on the open prairie, following the great bison

herds. Winter brought these two culturally distinct groups together in the sheltered aspen parkland.

By the late 19th century the fur trade had nearly exterminated beavers in the area. In the fall of 1931, the renowned conservationist, author, and orator Grey Owl moved to a cabin on Ajawaan Lake and worked to help stabilize the park's beaver population. Grey Owl lived in isolation with his wife, Anahareo, and Jellyroll and Rawhide, two orphaned beavers immortalized in his writings.

After a grueling speaking tour in 1937, an exhausted Grey Owl returned to Ajawaan Lake. The following spring he died, and the next day an exposé in the *North Bay Nugget* revealed that Grey Owl, who wore buckskins and long black braids, was not a Canadian Indian. He was an Englishman named Archibald Stansfeld Belaney, who had come to Canada as a young man. Despite his deception, Grey Owl is still honored for his passionate advocacy of native peoples and wildlife.

Prince Edward Island

Marram grass waves atop dunes backing long, pink-sand beaches. Red sandstone cliffs rise beside the sea, their scrubby blufftops yielding to woods and fragrant meadows punctuated by ponds and salt marshes.

In literature, this is the realm of the irrepressible Anne of Green Gables.

Prince Edward Island National Park faces the Gulf of St. Lawrence. Here, along 25 miles of shore, are some of the finest beaches in eastern Canada. Beyond the beaches, a line of stunted spruce trees protects forests and fields from winds and salt spray.

At the park's western end, the Green Gables House carefully preserves the turn-of-the-century world of fictional Anne Shirley. The property had once belonged to elderly cousins of the author, Lucy Maud Montgomery, and it was in this now restored farmhouse that she found inspiration for her many novels.

PARK DATA

PROVINCE: Prince Edward Island
ESTABLISHED: 1937
AREA: 12 sq mi (32 sq km)
NATURAL FEATURES: Sandstone cliffs; marshes; *barachois*—landlocked, coastal freshwater ponds
FLORA: Spruces; grasses
FAUNA: Foxes, muskrats, minks; common and arctic terns, guillemots, ospreys, piping plovers, blue herons

Ragged red sandstone cliffs, sculptured by the warm waters of the Gulf of St. Lawrence, limn the western stretch of Prince Edward Island National Park. Gulf waters wear the soft stone into sand grains, which build barrier islands, sandbars, beaches, and dunes.

Pukaskwa

*T*his isolated park in southern Canada protects a wild stretch of Lake Superior shoreline—a vast, pristine place of austere beauty. Along Pukaskwa's northern boundary, the White River tumbles through rugged uplands of the Canadian Shield en route to the greatest of the Great Lakes. Nearly 50 miles to the south, the Pukaskwa River churns through a narrow canyon at Schist Falls before emptying into Superior.

Between these two rapid-choked rivers stand ranks of obdurate granite headlands separating coves and bays rimmed by sand or pebble beaches. Franklin's lady's slippers, encrusted saxifrages, pearlworts, northern twayblades, and other Arctic and alpine plants thrive in cool lakeside microclimates far south of their normal range.

In exposed locations along the coast, ancestors of the Ojibwa built more than a hundred of the so-called Pukaskwa Pits. Low, rough stone walls enclose circular areas ranging in size from several to hundreds of square feet. The pits—some more than 2,000 years old—may have been used in vision quest ceremonies for fasting boys seeking guidance from powerful spirits.

This storm-hammered shoreline is backed by 725 square miles of virtually impenetrable wilderness, where scores of rivers and streams run in zigzags through a hummocky, severely faulted plateau. The landscape is dominated by Tip Top Mountain, which rises 2,099 feet above sea level.

Moose, black bears, wolves, red foxes, lynx, deer, and woodland caribou range dense forests of spruce, fir, and cedar mixed with aspen and birch. Deep, spongy mosses carpet the woodland floor, where swards of ferns, blue asters, and other shade-tolerant plants grow amid the ancient rocks.

Ten thousand years of
pounding waves have
not softened a shoreline
of huge granite
boulders marbled with
minerals and splotched
with lichens.

Riding Mountain

Riding Mountain hovers like a hazy blue mirage at the horizon, teasing you as you head across the farmland of southern Manitoba. But it is no mirage. Neither is it a mountain, though it seems like one in comparison with the flat terrain around it. In geological terms, Riding Mountain is an escarpment that pushes more than 1,200 feet above the plains. It is a welcome surprise: an island of wilderness and abundant wildlife in a sea of intensely cultivated prairie.

Nearly 2,700 lakes, ponds, and winding streams water the Riding Mountain area, and a complex mix of boreal forest, meadowland, and prairie intermingles here.

The region was left largely alone when surrounding lands at lower elevations fell to settlers' plows, but by the early part of this century logging and hunting had taken a toll. Bison and woodland caribou were long gone, and other animal populations were dwindling. To protect what remained, a national park was established in 1929.

Autumn tinges hardwoods near Lake Audy, and a stream snakes across a low meadow (left). An early snow frosts shrubs along the shores of a small lake (above). Almost 2,000 lakes and ponds and nearly 700 streams lie within park boundaries. No one knows exactly how the name Riding Mountain evolved. Perhaps early fur trappers called it that as they abandoned canoes for horses to traverse this high country.

Many large mammals flourish here now, including a few bison, which roam an enclosed area where visitors can observe them. Trails in the park reveal many aspects of Riding Mountain's complex ecology. The Burntwood Trail, for example, shows how fire shapes vegetation patterns. The Arrowhead Trail offers a taste of tranquil wilderness solitude.

Riding Mountain has a dual character: The townsite where most visitors go, Wasagaming on Clear Lake, seems more bustling resort than parkland. Yet for those who want to go farther afield there is plenty of backcountry. One of the most beautiful areas is Birdtail Valley, in the park's western reaches, where streams loop through lush meadows and forests.

PARK DATA

PROVINCE: Manitoba
ESTABLISHED: 1929
AREA: 1,148 sq mi (2,973 sq km)
NATURAL FEATURES: Escarpment rising more than 1,200 ft (366 m) above the surrounding prairie; 667 streams and 1,942 lakes and ponds
FLORA: Diverse ecological niches, from boreal forest to rough fescue prairie and eastern deciduous forest
FAUNA: Deer, beavers, wolves (more than 50); high density populations of black bears, moose, and elk; a demonstration herd of 25 to 40 reintroduced bison; more than 260 bird species, including the great gray owl, Sprague's pipit, chestnut-sided and golden-winged warblers; fish including rainbow, lake, and brook trout

Beaver lodge emerges from a pond. By building dams, the park's 14,000 beavers transform the terrain. Studies indicate they help create prairie habitat for such animals as elk.

St. Lawrence Islands

Known to the region's Algonquin Indians as the Garden of the Great Spirit, the Thousand Islands are strewn along the upper portion of the St. Lawrence River for more than 35 miles. Canada's smallest national park includes a riverside headquarters and all or part of 21 islands—the tops of granite hills rising above a flooded landscape.

Remarkably diverse flora and fauna are due to the park's location in a transitional zone. Here, southern trees mix with northern species. A relatively mild climate and a watery environment nurture a variety of amphibians and reptiles.

Twin sloops lie at a sheltered anchorage off Camelot Island in the middle of the Thousand Islands archipelago. Pleasure craft share waters near the park with Great Lakes freighters that glide through channels of the St. Lawrence Seaway.

Terra Nova

Legacy of the Ice Age, countless inland lakes fill depressions left by retreating glaciers. Visitors to Terra Nova can camp at secluded sites and take nature walks in a lush forest.

*T*hree long fingers of the North Atlantic Ocean reach deep into the landscape of Canada's eastern-most park. Scraped and gouged for thousands of years by glacial ice, this rugged preserve of boreal forest, lakes, bogs, and barrens on Newfoundland's east coast offers a fine vantage point for watching icebergs out in the ocean and whales in Bonavista Bay.

Many large and small mammals live in a thick forest of spruce and fir that covers much of the park, and some 63 nesting bird species find sanctuary here.

PARK DATA

PROVINCE: Newfoundland

ESTABLISHED: 1957

AREA: 154 sq mi (400 sq km)

ELEVATION: From sea level to 656 ft (200 m)

CLIMATE: Annual average rainfall 50 in (127 cm)

NATURAL FEATURES: Remnants of ancient Appalachian Mountains; numerous lakes and streams; Bonavista Bay

FLORA: Boreal forest of black spruce and balsam fir

FAUNA: Moose, caribou (a unique subspecies), black bears, lynx, beavers, snowshoe hares; 63 nesting bird species, including the bald eagle and osprey

Vuntut

Some 30,000 years ago most of Canada lay under vast glaciers. But Vuntut, in the Yukon's northwest corner, remained ice free and open to nomadic bands hunting mammoths and other Ice Age megafauna. On the Old Crow Flats, archaeologists have found bone scrapers that may have been used by North America's earliest inhabitants.

Today, Vuntut is a major waterfowl area, as well as a thoroughfare for caribou herds that move from the Ogilvie Mountains to summer calving areas on the coast.

PARK DATA

TERRITORY: Yukon
ESTABLISHED: 1995; Vuntut Gwitchin people co-managers of the park
AREA: 1,699 sq mi (4,400 sq km)
NATURAL FEATURES: Ogilvie Mountains, wetlands, Old Crow River
CULTURAL FEATURES: Archaeological sites along the Old Crow River
FLORA: Stunted white and black spruces; willows; sedges
FAUNA: Grizzly, polar, and black bears; moose, caribou, muskrats, wolves, foxes, lynx, wolverines; Canada geese, tundra swans, ravens, owls, ptarmigans, gyrfalcons

Old Crow Flats owes its waterlogged look to permafrost that extends from a few inches below the surface of the ground to depths of about 1,000 feet. Unable to drain away, meltwater accumulates in bogs, ponds, and shallow lakes.

Waterton Lakes

D ubbed "land of shining mountains" by Indians who once lived in its valleys, Waterton Lakes National Park boasts vistas of wild beauty. Tucked into the southwest corner of Alberta, this Rocky Mountain playground embraces sparkling lakes and ponds that reflect the mountain-ringed wilderness. These waters also provide rest stops for Canada geese, tundra swans, and ducks as they wing southward in autumn.

Forests so thick with evergreens that trees brush against each other in the wind ascend mountain slopes, where they give way to flower-filled alpine meadows. Golden eagles soar overhead, searching the uplands for marmots and other prey. An estimated 20 to 25 grizzlies forage for food in the high country. To prevent bear incidents, wardens monitor the animals and, if necessary, close hiking trails to keep people at a safe distance from them. Visitors are warned to store food away from campsites.

The park is also the meeting place of mountains and prairie, and in summer the short grasses ripple with the pastel hues of prairie roses, lupines, and asters. This pocket prairie provides grazing for a herd of 20 bison kept in a paddock. Another treeless habitat, the wetlands, produces cattails and other aquatic plants that draw moose, minks, and muskrats.

A network of 48 hiking trails and three roads with pull-offs and exhibits

Glacier-carved mountains surrounding Upper Waterton Lake dwarf the chalet-style Prince of Wales Hotel, built in the early 1900s to draw visitors to the national park. The hotel sits atop sand, gravel, and other materials deposited in the valley by melting Ice Age glaciers.

give visitors access to the diverse scenic wonders of the park. Hikers as well as motorists can enjoy views of 9,645-foot Mount Blakiston, the park's highest peak. It towers over Red Rock Canyon, where minerals have painted steep rock walls in vibrant colors. The Akamina Parkway and several footpaths skirt Cameron Lake, a blue mirror for Engelmann spruce forests and beargrass meadows that explode with white flowers in early summer.

Among the longer walkways is the Tamarack Trail, which runs 22 miles along the park's western boundary. After passing a series of waterfalls, the route climbs to alpine highlands of stunted trees and rugged cliffs, where nimble Rocky Mountain bighorn sheep seek safety from cougars.

The Crypt Lake Trail offers one of the most unusual excursions in the Rockies. A series of switchbacks leads hikers through a forest and up a ladder.

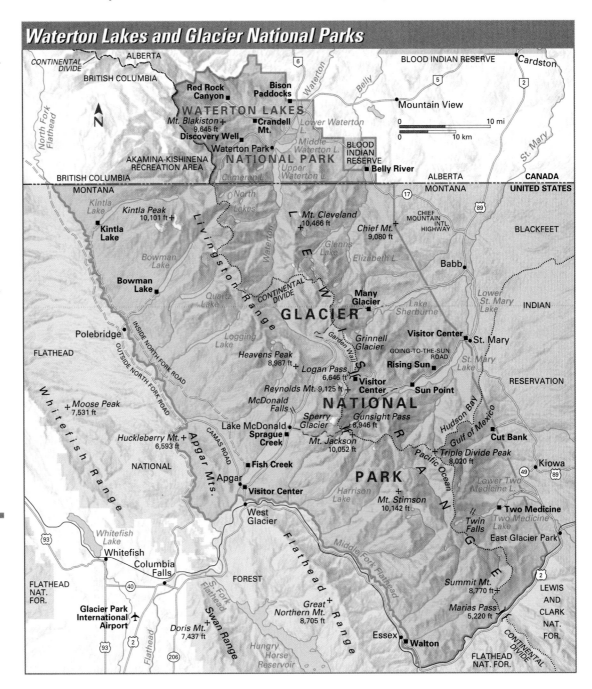

Waterton Lakes and Glacier National Parks

At the top is a tunnel that exits onto a narrow ledge. From there the trail, equipped with a cable banister, drops gently to Crypt Lake, which is set in a glistening, glacier-carved amphitheater occupied by furry marmots and white mountain goats.

The park remains open during the winter months, and when the deep snow in the valleys is patterned with the hoofprints of elk, deer, and moose, conditions may be excellent for cross-country skiing on the two designated ski trails. The area, however, is often subject to warm, dry chinook winds, which bring sudden changes in weather and a rapid melting of snow even in the middle of winter.

Only a couple of lodges are open year-round. In summer, the Prince of Wales Hotel provides luxurious accommodations, but most visitors stay in the park's three main campgrounds.

Despite its large size and lumbering walk, the grizzly bear can sprint more than 30 miles an hour if threatened. Grizzlies usually feed on roots, berries, ground squirrels, and other small mammals.

INTERNATIONAL PEACE PARK

WORKING TOGETHER, Canadian wardens and United States rangers practice a rescue operation in Waterton-Glacier International Peace Park. The Canadian park and its U.S. neighbor, Glacier National Park, in Montana, were joined in 1932 to celebrate friendship between the two nations. Two staffs cooperate in managing this pristine wilderness, sharing common goals that include protection of its diverse wildlife. A gash cut through the forest still marks the international boundary, but park jurisdictions occasionally overlap. The staffs coordinate studies and lead walks across the border.

Wood Buffalo

S pilling across Alberta's northern border into the Northwest Territories, Wood Buffalo encompasses a large area of the subarctic plain. It is a huge national park, certainly the largest in Canada and one of the largest in the world. The park extends 176 miles at its greatest length and averages about 100 miles in width, taking in more than 17,000 square miles—an area five times that of Yellowstone.

Except for some small uplands, the terrain here seems more waterscape than landscape. Countless ponds and lakes dot the vast expanse, and serpentine rivers and streams crisscross it. The park is largely roadless: Only about 150 miles of roads connect Fort Smith to Peace Point and to Pine Lake and other recreation areas. In winter, an ice road links Fort Smith and Fort Chipewyan, the sites of the park's two offices. Motorized boats or canoes provide access in the delta area.

A closer look reveals attributes that gained Wood Buffalo UNESCO world heritage status. Most of the 1,700-square-mile Peace-Athabasca Delta, a complex drainage system of ponds, lakes, and rivers, lies within park boundaries. Four major North American flyways converge here, and perhaps a million waterfowl touch down to rest and feed during migration. Here also is some of the most extensive karst topography in North America. As groundwater dissolves the underlying gypsum and limestone, the surface collapses into craterlike sinkholes. Some fill with

A bison bull browses in Wood Buffalo's forest. About 2,000 bison— Canada's largest free-ranging herd—live in this vast park.

Salt-tolerant samphire adds crimson bands to monochromatic salt flats. After passing through layers of salt deep below the surface, underground springs and streams deposit salt crystals when they emerge above ground. Sometimes several feet thick, the salt deposits have long lured animals to the site and, more recently, people.

water to form ponds; others shelter lush vegetation. Azure-tinted Pine Lake formed when water-filled sinkholes connected with each other. And there are eerie plains where saltwater springs and rivers well up from below, frosting the surface with thick layers of salt.

As Wood Buffalo's name suggests, bison have an important place here. Even as the plains bison were nearly exterminated farther south, a small herd of wood bison—a larger, darker variety—survived in northern Alberta. By 1893 even that herd had dwindled to a few hundred animals. In order to preserve them, a reserve was established. The animals thrived, and by the time

PARK DATA

PROVINCES: Alberta and the Northwest Territories
ESTABLISHED: 1922
AREA: 17,300 sq mi (44,802 sq km); Canada's largest national park
ELEVATION: As high as 3,130 ft (954 m) in the Caribou Mountains
NATURAL FEATURES: Peace-Athabasca Delta one of the world's largest inland deltas; salt plains; karst landscape

CULTURAL FEATURE: Fort Chipewyan—Alberta's oldest continuously inhabited settlement, historic center of fur trade, home to Cree and Chipewyan
FLORA: Boreal forest and sedge meadows
FAUNA: Bison, wolves, black bears, lynx; white pelicans, whooping cranes, peregrine falcons; most northerly known range for red-sided garter snakes

Wood Buffalo was established, in 1922, they numbered 1,500. In the meantime, plains bison in smaller preserves farther south were outgrowing their ranges. Several thousand were shipped north and released in Wood Buffalo, where they multiplied rapidly, interbreeding with the northern herd. They also brought diseases. Some ranchers now advocate destroying the herd, claiming that the animals pose a threat to their livestock. Other people oppose the harsh solution, saying there is little or no threat to livestock. DNA testing indicates that wood and plains bison may not be separate subspecies but merely distinct strains that developed as a result of different environmental conditions. Whether or not they are two subspecies or simply varying

FIRE AND THE BOREAL LANDSCAPE

A MOSAIC OF VARYING greens reveals fire's artistry on Wood Buffalo's boreal landscape. Surprisingly, in this boggy, poorly drained region, fires, usually ignited by lightning, often sweep through.

Depending upon many factors, including moisture, wind, and when a fire last burned, a swath of trees of one species and height may grow right next to another of different species and height. From the air the impact is particularly visible (below): Dark bands in the flourishing forest are black spruces, and the lighter colored conifers are white spruces. Yellow leaves indicate the deciduous aspens and poplars.

Dry and volatile, some black spruces explode into flames (right).

Devastating as fires may be, they are part of a natural dynamic that results in healthier forests and more diverse wildlife habitats. Fire crews now let flames run their course, except when they threaten people or other jurisdictions.

strains, they are Canada's largest free-ranging herd.

The bison are not the only species to find refuge here. Discovered by chance in 1954, in a series of shallow ponds in a remote part of the park, was the last natural nesting ground for the endangered whooping crane. With nurturing, its numbers have now increased and stabilized.

A wide array of other animals also live in the park: black bears, moose, wolves, lynx, fishers, martens, foxes, and beavers; some of the most northerly species of amphibians and reptiles; bald eagles, peregrine falcons, white pelicans, and many other birds.

People in the region still depend on these animals. When Wood Buffalo was established, it was unique among the parks in permitting traditional hunting and trapping activities. That policy continues. Now the park is in the process of settling native land claims. The Fort Chipewyan Cree land settlement allows the Cree hunting, trapping, and guiding rights in large tracts of the delta. Negotiation continues on other land claims.

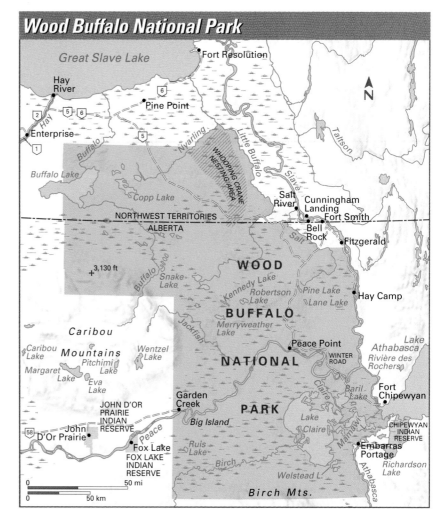

Wood Buffalo National Park

Yoho

*I*cy lakes, waterfalls, and snow-frosted peaks await visitors to Yoho National Park in the Rocky Mountains. Named for a word that Cree Indians used as an expression of awe, Yoho boasts natural wonders such as a rock bridge over the Kicking Horse River and fascinating formations called hoodoos—boulders balanced on columns of glacial silt. The park protects the Burgess Shale, an outcrop of rock with fossils of sea creatures 515 million years old. Though bisected by the Trans-Canada Highway and the Canadian Pacific Railway, the park remains unblighted and breathtaking.

PARK DATA

PROVINCE: British Columbia

ESTABLISHED: 1886

AREA: 507 sq mi (1,313 sq km)

ELEVATION: Some 30 peaks higher than 9,800 ft (2,987 m)

NATURAL FEATURES: Rugged peaks, rock walls, unique igneous rock formations, Burgess Shale; ice fields, waterfalls, lakes, Kicking Horse River (a Canadian Heritage River)

CULTURAL FEATURES: Examples of Canada's first railroads; Canadian Pacific Railway's spiral tunnels

FLORA: Engelmann and white spruces, subalpine firs, jack pines

FAUNA: Bighorn sheep, moose, elk, deer, mountain goats, bears; white-tailed ptarmigans and other birds

From a perch high above Lake O'Hara, hikers pause to take in a view of Yoho's craggy mountains, hanging glaciers, and evergreen forests. Silty meltwater from glaciers flows into the lake. On steep slopes, treeless patches mark the paths of avalanches that have stripped the land bare.

NATIONAL PARKS OF THE

United States

ISLE ROYALE NATIONAL PARK
Lake Superior
MICHIGAN
Lake Michigan
Lake Huron
Lake Ontario
Lake Erie
Lansing
Detroit
Chicago
MAINE
Bangor
Augusta
ACADIA NATIONAL PARK
Montpelier
VERMONT
NEW HAMPSHIRE
Concord
Boston
Albany
MASSACHUSETTS
NEW YORK
Providence
Hartford
RHODE ISLAND
CONNECTICUT
New York
PENNSYLVANIA
Harrisburg
Trenton
NEW JERSEY
Philadelphia
OHIO
Columbus
Ohio
INDIANA
Indianapolis
ILL.
Dover
DELAWARE
Washington, D.C.
Annapolis
MARYLAND
WEST VIRGINIA
SHENANDOAH NATIONAL PARK
Charleston
Frankfort
Louisville
Richmond
VIRGINIA
KENTUCKY
ATLANTIC OCEAN
MAMMOTH CAVE NATIONAL PARK
NORTH CAROLINA
Raleigh
Nashville
GREAT SMOKY MOUNTAINS NATIONAL PARK
TENNESSEE
APPALACHIAN MOUNTAINS
SOUTH CAROLINA
Columbia
Atlanta
MISS.
ALABAMA
GEORGIA
Montgomery
Tallahassee
FLORIDA
Tampa
OF MEXICO
EVERGLADES NATIONAL PARK
Miami
BISCAYNE NATIONAL PARK
BAHAMAS
DRY TORTUGAS NATIONAL PARK
TROPIC OF CANCER
CUBA
0 200 mi
0 200 km
ATLANTIC OCEAN
U.K.
U.S.
Tortola
St. Thomas
St. John
VIRGIN ISLANDS NATIONAL PARK
U.S. VIRGIN ISLANDS
0 15 mi
0 15 km
18° N
Caribbean Sea
St. Croix
65° W
THE UNITED STATES AND OUTLYING AREAS
0 1000 mi
0 1000 km
ARCTIC CIRCLE
CANADA
ATLANTIC OCEAN
THE 48 CONTIGUOUS STATES
U.S. VIRGIN ISLANDS
TROPIC OF CANCER
60°
MEXICO
Caribbean Sea
90° W

To American settlers bound for the Far West in the mid-1800s, wilderness encountered along the way was a feared obstacle—or land waiting to be tamed for the good of civilization. In 1849, prospectors who narrowly avoided death among the shimmering white-sand dunes of a California desert would curse it with a name it bears to this day: Death Valley.

Not until the frontier was closed around the 1850s did admiring accounts begin to circulate of the magnificent scenery, natural wonders, and abundant wildlife of such places as Yosemite Valley and Yellowstone. Worried that these wild vistas might cede to progress, as many already had, visionary conservationists such as John Muir led a fight for their protection. Inspired descriptions, paintings, and photography—a brand-new medium—persuaded Congress and President Ulysses S. Grant to create the world's first national park at Yellowstone in 1872. Others followed. In 1916, in the dark days of World War I, the National Park Service was founded, relieving the U.S. Army from the task of guarding the nation's wild heritage.

Democratically committed from their origin to the enjoyment of all, national parks have grown in number to more than 50 today. Whole ecosystems have been targeted for inclusion in most cases. Native animal and plant life are the objects of protection and research. Latter-day conservationists' anxieties focus on overcrowding and pollution that could yet undermine what has been called "the best idea America ever had."

Acadia

*T*he Abenaki Indians called it Pemetic—"the sloping land." When French explorer Samuel de Champlain happened on this bare-topped, rockbound island off the coast of present-day Maine in 1604, he called it l'Isle des Monts-déserts—"the island of barren mountains"—Mount Desert. In this magnificent and moody land of Acadia, the highest mountain on the eastern seaboard meets the ocean in a panoply of islands, headlands, coves, and bays.

Since the park's founding in 1919 (originally under the name Lafayette, changed to Acadia in 1929), it has grown piecemeal to 35,000 acres, most of it situated on Mount Desert Island. The rest includes 3,000 of the park's least developed acres on remote

Isle au Haut—"high island"—to the southwest, and 2,000 acres on the dramatic, bouldered tip of easterly Schoodic Peninsula, the only mainland portion.

While national parks are usually carved from public lands with public funds, Acadia, the first national park east of the Mississippi, was created solely through the efforts and donations of private citizens—both residents and "summer people" who built their vacation mansions, or "cottages," in Bar Harbor and other enclaves of New England society. The result is a patchwork of public and private lands.

Surrounding the park, seaside villages on Mount Desert range from rustic to chic, and visitors can find all the hallmarks of Down East Maine: lobster traps, weathered gray shacks, foggy harbors, and ruddy-faced, gum-booted fishermen.

The land itself was shaped by glaciation. About 20,000 years ago, great tongues of ice crept across the then continental highlands of Mount Desert, rounding the granite peaks and gouging valleys, lakes, and passes. As the ice melted, the ocean rose, flooding the lowlands and girdling this mountainous, lake-studded island,

In open woodland near Sand Beach, firs and spruces mingle with birches and a soft ground cover of ferns and grasses.

whose indented shoreline boasts the only fjord on the U.S. east coast.

Behind the jagged coast, with its rocky beaches and pink granite cliffs, lie silent woodlands that abound in hiking trails. Sylvan carriage roads —commissioned by John D. Rockefeller, Jr.—connected by romantic stone bridges wind free of motor traffic in the park. Scenic Park Loop Road offers spectacular ocean views, culminating in a panorama of Frenchman Bay from the top of Cadillac Mountain. In season, wildflowers, blueberries, and cranberries color the slopes. The sea provides constant drama to these vistas, whether grayed by mist and fog or reflecting the deep blue of the sky on a crystalline Maine day.

Acadia National Park

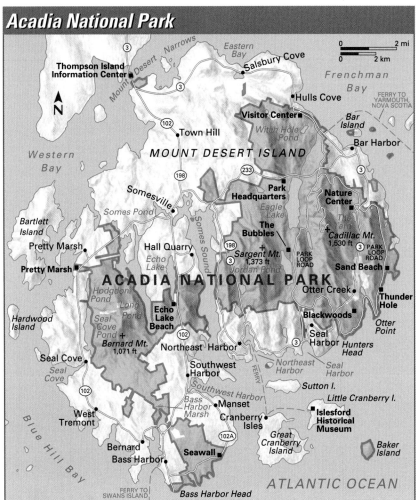

TIDE POOL LIFE

BETWEEN LAND and sea is a tidal zone, twice daily covered by water and then exposed to air again. The receding tide strands pools of seawater in rock basins. These are fragile marine microhabitats, where specially adapted animals and plants—such as periwinkles, mussels, and rockweed (left), which cannot survive out of water—wait for the high tide. Adversity —too much heat or rain, or too little oxygen—limits growth and controls a pool's population.

STATE: Maine

ESTABLISHED: 1919

AREA: 35,000 acres (14,164 ha); mostly on Mount Desert; sections on smaller islands reachable by boat; mainland section on Schoodic Peninsula

HIGHEST POINT: Cadillac Mountain, 1,530 ft (466 m), the highest point on the U.S. Atlantic coast

NATURAL FEATURES: Thunder Hole, a cleft in coastal rocks where surf can produce a thunderous roar; glacially rounded twin hills called The Bubbles, with a glacial erratic—Bubble Rock— teetering on the edge of the southern one; Somes Sound, the only fjord on the U.S. east coast

CULTURAL FEATURES: Two museums housing artifacts from Indian times and from island life of the 19th to early 20th century

FAUNA: Seals, crabs, other marine life; 300 species of birds, including cormorant and common eider, an oceanic duck

Low tide exposes a mass of sea-worn and algae-covered granite boulders at Otter Point. A hidden ledge off the point grounded Samuel de Champlain in 1604— the first of countless nautical mishaps along this rocky, often fog-bound coast before lights and foghorns were installed.

Arches

"Ten thousand strangely carved forms. Rocks everywhere...," wrote explorer John Wesley Powell in 1875, describing this magnificent, otherworldly land of sculptured red rock perched high above the Colorado River in southern Utah.

Established in 1971, Arches National Park belongs to the vast, semi-arid Colorado Plateau known as canyon country—a geologically spectacular region boasting more than 20 national parks and monuments. Permanent as this rugged land appears —its origins date back some 300 million years—it is, in fact, constantly being reshaped by wind, water, and extremes of heat and cold.

Arches resembles an extraterrestrial rock garden filled with fantastical formations: towering spires and pinnacles, whimsical balanced rocks, slickrock domes, sheer walls, and mazes of massive stone fins. The more notable landforms have inspired such names as Marching Men, Park Avenue, Eye of the Whale Arch, Three Gossips, Tower of Babel, Parade of Elephants, Fiery Furnace, and Dark Angel.

What sets this park apart, though, is the feature for which it is named—its arches. The world's greatest concentration of these natural spans, ranging in length from 3 to 306 feet and standing free or rising from buttresses, is found within these 73,379 acres.

The high desert here supports more than 375 well-adapted plant species. Scrubby piñon pines and juniper trees mingle with blackbrush, wildflowers, cactuses, grasses, lichens, and ferns.

Delicate Arch, best known arch in the park, perches on slickrock at the rim of a canyon.

Animals, most of them nocturnal, include mule deer, coyotes, foxes, and porcupines; jackrabbits and cottontails; kangaroo rats and other small rodents; reptiles and insects; and eagles, hawks, and a variety of other resident and migratory birds.

Signs of human life at Arches go back to 8000 B.C. In the 1800s, Mormon missionaries established settlements in the area, including Moab, five miles south of Arches. The first settlers, Civil War veteran John Wesley Wolfe and his son, arrived in 1888; remnants of their primitive cattle ranch stand preserved within the park.

PARK DATA

STATE: Utah
ESTABLISHED: 1971
AREA: 73,379 acres (29,695 ha)
NATURAL FEATURES: More than 2,000 natural stone openings formed in brilliant orange-, red-, and salmon-colored Entrada sandstone; spires, pinnacles, balanced rocks

CULTURAL FEATURES: Anasazi, Fremont, Ute and Barrier Canyon-style pictographs and petroglyphs; 19th-century Wolfe Ranch
FLORA: Piñon-juniper forest; sandy surface of high desert stabilized by a fragile cryptobiotic crust made up of algae, mosses, fungi, lichens, and bacteria—

easily destroyed by off-trail footsteps; wildflowers
FAUNA: Mule deer, coyotes, foxes, desert cottontails; lizards and snakes
UNIQUE FEATURE: Greatest concentration of arches on earth in such a small area—many visible from park road but some requiring a hike

CREATION OF AN ARCH

DEEP UNDERGROUND, earth and salt movements crack overlying layers of sandstone. As cracks are exposed on the surface, rainwater dissolves the calcium carbonate "glue" between sand grains, widening the cracks and creating isolated "fins." Water also seeps into horizontal cracks, where it freezes and expands. When this happens in a vulnerable spot at the base of a fin, an opening results.

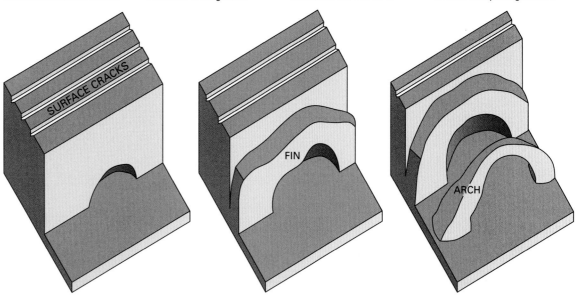

Landscape Arch (above), the park's longest freestanding arch, appears to defy gravity with its thin, 306-foot-long span. But, as slabs of rock flake off and fall, the danger of collapse becomes more likely. Since the mid-1970s, 42 arches have toppled.

ANCIENT PICTOGRAPHS

FOR THOUSANDS of years, Indians have drawn and painted on rock walls. Evidence of early humans at Arches includes these figures, painted in the Barrier Canyon style on the Lower Courthouse Wash wall. The shieldlike circles were superimposed on some of the figures by an unknown hand.

Having survived centuries of exposure to the elements, the pictographs were nearly obliterated in minutes by modern vandals and cannot be restored. This photograph predates the damage.

Badlands

*A*t first sight from the road, the distant, tawny "Wall" breaking the prairie expanse registers as a mirage. Suddenly, the gentle grasslands yield to a stark, tortured moonscape: the Badlands. Water, wind, and frost created this geological anomaly out of the South Dakota landscape, scouring and sculpturing the soft rock into fluted ridges, pinnacles, knobs, and gullies and baring sedimentary rock layers as much as 65 million years old.

Established as a national monument in 1939, Badlands, which consists of North and South Units, was made a national park in 1978. The sprawling South Unit, located on Oglala Sioux land, was acquired in 1976. It contains Stronghold Table, where the last Ghost Dance was held in 1890, just before the slaughter of more than 200 Indians by U.S. Army troops at Wounded Knee, 25 miles to the south.

The park encompasses both badlands and prairie in western South Dakota. Distinct striations in the rock reveal the region's geologic history: Black shale, once the bottom of an ancient sea, is topped by layers from the Eocene, then the Oligocene epoch. These rich, fossil-laden beds prove the abundance and extraordinary variety of animals that once inhabited the plains.

Badlands preserves a remnant of the great grasslands that once covered nearly a fourth of the country, stretching from Canada almost to Mexico and from the Rockies to Indiana. Among the most impressive sights here is that of majestic bison once again roaming their native range in the Sage Creek Basin. Pronghorn, bighorn sheep, mule deer, prairie dogs, and reintroduced black-footed ferrets also frequent this wilderness area, affording excellent opportunities for wildlife viewing.

PARK DATA

STATE: South Dakota
ESTABLISHED: 1978
AREA: 243,303 acres (98,461 ha); two units, the North Unit containing park facilities and the 64,144-acre (25,958-ha) Badlands Wilderness Area; the South Unit, part of the Pine Ridge Reservation, remaining largely undeveloped
CULTURAL FEATURES: "Badlands" name from French fur trappers calling them "bad lands to travel across"; Stronghold Table —place where the Sioux held Ghost Dances
FLORA: Mixed-prairie grassland; scattered wildflowers; few trees
FAUNA: Deer, pronghorn, bighorn sheep, bison, coyotes, prairie dogs; rattlesnakes; grouse, eagles
UNIQUE FEATURE: Great variety of mammal fossils found in Oligocene strata here, leading to designation of the epoch as the Golden Age of Mammals

Great Wall of Badlands interrupts the dry South Dakota plains in a tumult of banded peaks, spires, and ridges. Layers of sand, silt, clay, and volcanic ash expose this land's geologic story.

Big Bend

*T*he Indians of the region knew that the geology of Big Bend was complex. According to their tradition, when the Great Creator had finished making the earth, the heavens, and all therein, there was a jumble of stony debris left over. Tossed away, that became Big Bend.

Here the Rio Grande cuts between the southern Rockies and Mexico's Sierra Madre, carves through canyons, and takes a sweeping turn northward around a huge, isolated expanse in the wilds of West Texas. In Big Bend, Chihuahuan Desert—formed from ancient seabeds and then tilted, uplifted, and folded—meets the Chisos Mountains, raised by cataclysmic volcanic events.

El Despoblado—the uninhabited land—is what early Spaniards called the region. Over several millennia Indians did live here, however. And later other arrivals paraded through—desperadoes, Comanche marauders, ranchers, and hardscrabble farmers. Call it isolation, call it desolation, this is remote country; often the only sound car radios pick up is static, or perhaps the faint notes of a mariachi band from south of the border. And some days the air is so clear that, from a high vantage point, you can see a hundred miles into Mexico. By 1944, because of their scenic grandeur, the area's southernmost reaches had gained the designation of Big Bend National Park.

Variations in elevation and terrain create remarkable diversity here: ecological niches for more than 1,000 types of flowering plants, about 450 species of birds, and numerous other animals. The park divides roughly into three natural zones: the river, the desert, and the mountains. Winding 107 miles along the park's U.S.-Mexico border, the river cuts through three

PARK DATA

STATE: Texas
ESTABLISHED: 1944
AREA: 801,146 acres (324,213 ha), 97 percent of it being Chihuahuan Desert surrounding Chisos Mountains terrain
HIGHEST POINT: Emory Peak, 7,835 ft (2,388 m)
CLIMATE: Summers rainy and very hot, with desert temperatures sometimes exceeding 110°F (43°C); winters mild; mountain temperatures cooler
NATURAL FEATURE: Chihuahuan Desert—a young desert, possibly only 8,000 years old
FLORA: Chiefly desert species; trees in moister, cooler upper elevations; endemic species—Chisos oak, Chisos agave, and drooping juniper
FAUNA: In the desert, jackrabbits, coyotes, roadrunners, golden eagles; a birder's paradise—some 450 species found here, a national park record

Sotol spikes aim skyward at Sotol Vista, overlooking the desert wilderness that forms much of Big Bend National Park. Roasted sotol hearts provided a mainstay for Mescalero Apache in the area.

major canyons: Santa Elena, Mariscal, and Boquillas, walled in by cliffs rising some 1,500 feet.

Chihuahuan Desert vegetation—mostly creosote bushes, lechuguillas, cactuses, yuccas, and agaves—occupies fully 97 percent of the park. Wildlife often gathers around desert springs or rock pools, called tinajas. At higher elevations in the Chisos Mountains, desert plants mingle with junipers and piñon pines, and even some oak trees.

Surrounded by high, craggy promontories, the Chisos Basin at 5,400 feet offers a scenic oasis and welcome relief from the scorching summer heat at lower elevations. A gentle walk in the basin at sunset brings visitors to The Window, a spectacular view over the desertscape below. An easy day's ride on horseback—or a long trek on foot—to 7,400-foot South Rim culminates in another panoramic vista.

The park has numerous interpretive trails. More strenuous expeditions take experienced hikers into wilderness areas such as the Dead Horse Mountains. In the backcountry or on the trails, visitors may catch glimpses of wildlife such as the javelina—a piglike animal—or the elusive mountain lion, which locals call the panther.

Sheer walls mirror themselves in glass-smooth waters of the Rio Grande near the mouth of Santa Elena Canyon (above right). Splendid views greet boaters who float through 17-mile Santa Elena—one of three major gorges along the river in Big Bend.

Crimson blossoms of a claret cup cactus (right) belie its formidable exterior, protected by a battery of spines. More than 60 kinds of cactuses grow in the park. "Each plant in this land is a porcupine," observed an early visitor. "It is nature armed to the teeth."

Biscayne

*A*zure waters, balmy breezes, deserted subtropical islands, right in metropolitan Miami's backyard? Biscayne National Park is a surprise. It encompasses much of Biscayne Bay off southeast Florida, some of the longest stretches of undeveloped shoreline in the East, and the northernmost coral reefs in the mainland U.S. The endangered manatee, the American crocodile, and rare sea turtles find refuge here.

Biscayne gained national park status in 1980. Beyond the mangrove-fringed mainland where park headquarters stand, islands act as stepping-stones to a watery world: Meadows of turtle grass and bowers of mangrove roots hide jewel-hued fish, spiny lobsters, and myriad other exotic creatures; forests of elkhorn and staghorn and delicate sea fans cap boulders of brain coral.

PARK DATA

STATE: Florida
ESTABLISHED: 1980
AREA: 181,000 acres (73,248 ha); 95 percent underwater, with 45 islands and a stretch of mainland shore; (map on page 149)
FLORA: Mangrove shoreline an important habitat for fish and birds
FAUNA: More than 200 kinds of fish along park reefs; many coral species and other invertebrates

Dubbed "walking trees" for gangly roots by which they spread across the water, red mangroves shelter many young sea creatures. A queen conch's golden-pink shell and delicious flesh make it a target for collectors.

Bryce Canyon

A silent city...organ pipes by the thousand...hooded monks... a sinking ship...church spires or minarets...Queen Victoria. Like a Rorschach test in rock, the eroded limestones of Bryce Canyon National Park suggest a world of forms limited only by the beholder's imagination.

To the Paiute of southwestern Utah, the formations were the Legend People, quasi-human animals frozen in stone as punishment for their bad deeds. To 19th-century Mormon pioneer Ebenezer Bryce, whose name has endured long past his time, the region was "a helluva place to lose a cow!"

Today, Bryce's towering rock pillars are known simply as hoodoos, a word derived from voodoo. Water, not wizardry, carves them during rock-splitting "freeze-thaw" cycles that occur more than 200 times a year on south-facing slopes; this continuous process crumbles old hoodoos at the same time that it creates new ones. The rock's luminous pinks, purples, and browns result from the inner glow of iron and manganese oxides, enhanced by the clarity of light more than a mile above sea level.

Bryce's elevation, which ranges up to 9,100 feet, also gives the air year-round crispness. Unlike some southwestern parks, Bryce draws a preponderance of its many visitors in summer, as it has since the early 1900s.

Despite the park's official name, Bryce is not really a single canyon. It is a series of amphitheaters scoured by erosion from the eastern edge of the Paunsaugunt Plateau. These geological features make Bryce, by far the smallest of Utah's national parks, perhaps also its most accessible, with trails that reward even the most casual stroller with spectacular scenery.

New snow dusts the Table Cliffs Plateau beyond Bryce's rock spires in this view from Sunset Point. The hoodoos' seeming "snowcaps" are really a topping of dolomite and calcium carbonate.

Canyonlands

erspective fades as the eye grapples with the dizzying panorama of bare rock that is southeastern Utah's Canyonlands. In 1869, explorer John Wesley Powell came upon "a wilderness of rocks—deep gorges where the rivers are lost below cliffs and towers and pinnacles, and ten thousand strangely carved forms in every direction, and beyond them mountains blending with the clouds."

And so Canyonlands remains to this day. Water and wind continue to sculpture the 300-million-year-old Colorado Plateau sandstone, as they have for eons. Primary mover, the Colorado River carries off three cubic miles of rock each century. Where its main tributary, the Green, meets the Colorado, the Y-shaped river system slices the park into three distinct areas that share a wild and untrammeled character.

To the north, Island in the Sky, a broad mesa, floats 2,000 feet above the glinting rivers. The Maze, to the west, takes its name from a 30-square-mile labyrinth of canyons; it ranks among the most inaccessible places in the U.S. To the east, The Needles describes a landscape of 100-foot pinnacles, banded in red and white, and a multitude of other bizarre natural shapes.

PARK DATA

STATE: Utah
ESTABLISHED: 1964
AREA: 337,570 acres (136,610 ha)
CLIMATE: Hot summers with low humidity
NATURAL FEATURES: 300-million-year-old rocks exposed by river action in Cataract Canyon; banded spires in The Needles
CULTURAL FEATURES: 2,000-year-old life-size figures painted on rock in Horseshoe Canyon; 900-year-old Fremont culture pictographs in Salt Creek; Tower Ruin and other Anasazi dwellings and rock art
FLORA: Cactuses, piñons, junipers in arid areas; cottonwoods, willows, hanging gardens along river
FAUNA: Bighorn sheep, deer, coyotes, bobcats, small mammals; snakes, lizards; migratory birds

Viewed from Dead Horse State Park (foreground), the Colorado loops around the Goose Neck and along the rocky ramparts of Canyonlands (at rear).

Trickling groundwater (left) draws a chipmunk and a sparrow to a hanging garden alcove.

Capitol Reef

Nineteenth-century pioneers aboard their prairie schooners likened these nearly impassable cliffs in south-central Utah to an ocean reef. A highway now pierces the 2,300-foot-high rampart, but its parallel rows of rock breakers still create a formidable barrier. Stretching 100 miles north to south, this immense monocline, the Waterpocket Fold, defines Capitol Reef National Park.

Originally level, the area was flexed into a giant fold as the uplift of the Colorado Plateau began 65 million years ago. Over time, erosion carved the Entrada sandstone into today's colorful chaos of cliffs, spires, snaking canyons, towering monoliths, and massive white rock domes that reminded early visitors of the Capitol dome in Washington, D.C. Early explorers named Waterpocket Fold after natural catchment basins in the rock.

A free-flowing source of water, the Fremont River is a fountain of life in the park's midst. Instead of stunted junipers, piñons, and other desert plants, willows and wildflowers line its banks; one sees there not only kangaroo rats, lizards, and other hardy desert denizens, but unexpected visitors ranging from ducks to mule deer.

Along the river, humans have left a varied legacy. Petroglyphs of human figures and bighorn sheep survive the Fremont people, who mysteriously disappeared after 1250. Six centuries later, their abandoned fields were cleared by Mormon pioneers who planted orchards that still thrive. The park purchased the last private homes in the 1960s. Remains of the Mormon village of Fruita, including a one-room log schoolhouse, now the park's visitor center, and several other structures stand in the shadow of red-rock cliffs.

PARK DATA

STATE: Utah
ESTABLISHED: 1971
AREA: 241,904 acres (97,895 ha)
CLIMATE: Less than 8 in (20 cm) rainfall; summer thunderstorms, temperatures in 90s °F (30s °C); spring and fall milder
NATURAL FEATURE: Among the largest and best exposed monoclines in North America
CULTURAL FEATURES: Fremont Indian petroglyphs and pictographs; remains of pioneer Mormon fruit-farming community
FLORA: Cottonwoods, willows, ashes, wildflowers along river; junipers, piñons, cactuses in desert
FAUNA: Along river—mule deer, marmots; songbirds, migratory ducks; in desert—bighorn sheep, kangaroo rats; lizards, toads; golden eagles

Halls Creek Canyon threads a remote region near the park's southern boundary—a wilderness area frequented by backpackers. Alcoves containing hanging gardens of monkey-flower and maidenhair fern dot the canyon's walls.

Carlsbad Caverns

A hushed crowd gathers just before sunset on clear summer evenings near the yawning mouth of Carlsbad Caverns. A few bats straggle out. Then comes a great *whoosh* as thousands upon thousands of Mexican free-tailed bats burst forth into the twilight. At a rate of about 5,000 a minute, they pour into the night skies over southern New Mexico to hunt a meal of moths and other insects.

Prehistoric Indians sheltered in Carlsbad Caverns more than a thousand years ago and left paintings at the entrance. But it was the daily exodus of clouds of bats that led to the present-day discovery of the caverns. When Texas cowboy James Larkin White first noticed the outer cave in 1901, he thought the clouds must be billowing smoke from a volcano. "I'd seen plenty of prairie whirlwinds—but this thing

PARK DATA

STATE: New Mexico
ESTABLISHED: 1930
AREA: 46,766 acres (18,926 ha)
CLIMATE: Caverns a constant 56°F (13°C), providing refuge from summer temperatures in the 90s °F; (30s °C); mild winters

NATURAL FEATURES: Caves carved in limestone reef from an ancient inland sea; same reef exposed as part of the Guadalupe Mountains
FLORA: Cactuses, other Chihuahuan Desert plants; Douglas firs, ponderosas

FAUNA: Some 17 bat species, but Mexican free-tailed bats most numerous from May through October, peaking at one million; mule deer, bobcats, foxes, small mammals; rattlesnakes, lizards; cave swallows and other birds

RESIDENTS OF BAT CAVE

RADIOCARBON DATING documents bats at Carlsbad 17,000 years ago. By far the most numerous species, from spring into autumn, is the Mexican free-tailed bat.

After spending the day in the cave, the bats stream out to feed at night and consume nearly their own weight in insects. The baby bats, born in early summer, remain behind clinging to the wall. If a young bat falls, it will land on the guano below, where predatory insects wait to attack. By midsummer the young will release hold of their ceiling roosts to fly and hunt on their own.

From an estimated eight million in 1936, the bat population at Carlsbad has dwindled to one million. Researchers blame this decline on the falloff in numbers of insects due to the use of pesticides—which also poison the bats' food supply and may fatally affect young bats.

Mexican free-tailed bats fill the air at Carlsbad (opposite).

Crevasses (left) provide roosts for young bats. Females bear a single baby in June. By July or August it can fly. In winter, all head to Mexico.

didn't move...," he reflected later. "I watched it for perhaps a half-hour." After investigating, White realized that the cloud was formed by millions of bats spinning upward out of the cave. "Any hole in the ground which could house such a gigantic army of bats must be a whale of a big cave," he said.

White had stumbled upon a vast underground world—what would later be known as the Big Room, measuring at its maximum 1,800 feet long by 1,100 feet wide, and other places that would later bear such names as Queens Chamber, Kings Palace, Green Lake Room, Hall of Giants, Painted Grotto, and the Temple of the Sun.

In a rococo vision, fanciful rock sculptures adorn nearly every cranny and chamber of the huge complex. Stalagmites rising from the floor, stalactites dropping from the ceiling, and numerous other formations with names such as corolloids, helictites, and flowstone tease the imagination.

White and other entrepreneurs soon found a profitable use for the cave— the mining of tons of bat guano for use as fertilizer. Taking delight in showing off his "glittering underground palace," White lowered curious visitors 170 feet in a bucket—once used to haul out guano—to explore Carlsbad's depths. By comparison, today's tourists travel in style along a walkway that spirals gently into the heart of the main cavern, one of 81 known caves in the park. Or elevators whisk visitors to the main chambers and back.

For more venturesome spirits, the park provides guided tours down a steep, sometimes slippery trail into the Slaughter Canyon Cave. Opened to the public in 1973, this cave offers such formations as the graceful Christmas Tree and the sinister-looking Klansman. In 1986, the discovery of vast unexplored areas in Lechuguilla Cave provided new realms for expert spelunkers to investigate. Lechuguilla is in the park's designated wilderness area.

LECHUGUILLA CAVE

WIND BLASTING out of surface rubble provided the clue in 1986 to locating extensive additional chambers at Lechuguilla, one of Carlsbad's caverns.

Like its prickly namesake plant, Lechuguilla does not invite easy access. Entry requires a rope descent of nearly 100 feet. Evocative names bestowed by cavers give an idea of the difficulties encountered once there: Freakout Traverse, Hard Daze Night Hall, Death Pit. Others reveal sublime sights—Firefall Hall, Chandelier Ballroom, Rainbow Room—that make Lechuguilla for some people the most beautiful cave in the world.

Painstaking exploration and mapping continue. So far explorers have penetrated 84.3 miles into Lechuguilla. No one knows how much farther they can go. One concern is the damage visitors may inflict on this pristine underground wilderness. Body heat, for instance, can cause fragile, 30-foot-long "angel hair" crystals to sway.

Lamp of a spelunker's helmet illuminates the passageway toward YO Acres in Lechuguilla Cave. Only members of scientific expeditions may enter this part of Carlsbad.

UNDERGROUND WONDERLAND

SPIRALING BELOW the surface of the Guadalupe Mountains in southern New Mexico, the explored part of Carlsbad Caverns plunges more than 1,000 feet. The cave complex may extend much farther.

Perhaps 250 million years ago a limestone reef, formed from the remains of algae, sponges, and seashells, developed here in a shallow Permian sea. Cracks allowed acidic water to penetrate, beginning the hollowing-out process.

Some 20 million years ago, an uplift created the Guadalupe Mountains, dropped the water table, and allowed air into the caverns. In a process that continues today, calcite-bearing water seeped down, drop by drop, building mineral deposits that grew into the caverns' exuberant decorative features.

Carlsbad Caverns National Park

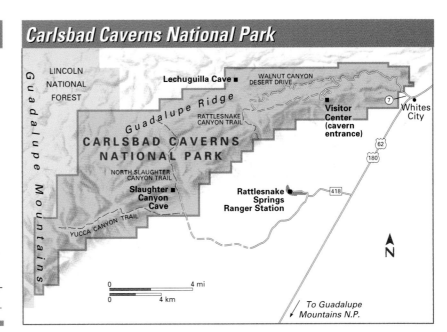

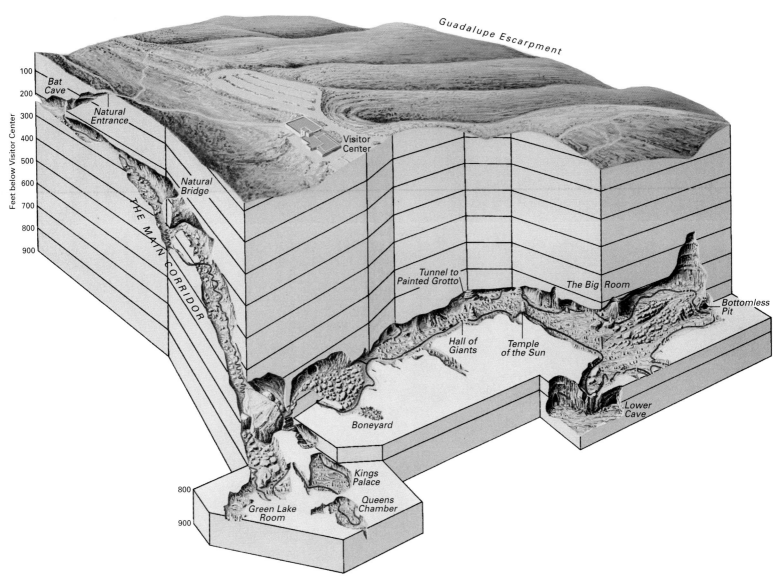

Channel Islands

*E*leven miles of open water buffer Anacapa Island (nearest point to the mainland in Channel Islands National Park) from southern California, creating a world apart.

In past centuries, native peoples, fur traders, and others settled these five rugged islands. A park since 1980, the islands and offshore waters teem with a vast array of animals, ranging from the planet's largest, the blue whale, to microscopic plankton.

Blossoms of the giant coreopsis (above), or "tree sunflower," brighten windswept island crags only briefly each spring.

A garibaldi (right) plucks a purple sea urchin from its lair in an offshore kelp forest.

PARK DATA

STATE: California
ESTABLISHED: 1980
AREA: 248,515 acres (100,571 ha), including seafloor extending 1.15 mi (1.8 km) from each island
CULTURAL FEATURES: Hundreds of largely undisturbed archaeological sites
FLORA: Some 85 endemic plant species; giant kelp
FAUNA: Cat-size foxes; whales, seals, sea lions; endangered brown pelicans, seabirds, songbirds

Crater Lake

*L*ike an immense sapphire, 21-square-mile Crater Lake in southern Oregon sparkles with the deepest colors of the sky on a sunny day. Steep cliffs rise nearly 2,000 feet from its cool waters, and wind-whipped evergreens ring the caldera of Mount Mazama, a dormant volcano.

About 7,700 years ago this tranquil setting witnessed one of North America's most violent geologic episodes as Mount Mazama erupted, hurling volcanic ash miles into the sky. Forty-two times more severe than Mount St. Helens's eruption in 1980, Mount Mazama's blast ejected so much of its mass that its peak collapsed, creating a smoldering cauldron up to six miles across and 4,000 feet deep. Continuing geothermal activity pushed up the volcanic cone known as Wizard Island and sealed the cracked floor of the basin. Snow, rain, and springwater eventually filled the caldera, creating the lake. Forests of fir, hemlock, and pine colonized the rock on the crater's rim.

Testing found that Crater Lake was more than 1,900 feet deep, making it the deepest lake in the United States.

Each winter decks Wizard Island and the rim of Crater Lake with an average of 45 feet of snow. Because of its immense volume, the lake rarely freezes over.

Packed parking lot at Rim Village in the 1940s reveals the popularity of Crater Lake in winter.

Death Valley

Death Valley is a place of paradox, both harsh and beautiful. Superlative in more ways than one, it is the hottest and driest spot on the continent and the lowest point in the hemisphere. The former national monument became the largest national park in the lower 48 states on October 31, 1994. Most of it lies in California.

Barricaded by mountains that hold the heat and bar the rain, the valley—a sunken chunk of the earth's crust—harbors a huge salt pan, sand dunes, stark canyons, a volcanic crater, and rainbow-hued—"painted"—rocks. A date-palm grove thrives at Furnace Creek oasis, and spring rains splash the desert with wildflowers.

Abandoned mines and other landmarks tell of the parade of Native Americans, pioneers, borax miners, and mule skinners who passed this way. The valley's name is the legacy of some forty-niners who barely survived.

PARK DATA

STATES: California and Nevada

ESTABLISHED: 1994, part of California Desert Protection Act

AREA: 3,367,627 acres (1,362,831 ha)

HIGHEST POINT: 11,049 ft (3,368 m)

CLIMATE: Hottest, driest desert in North America

CULTURAL FEATURES: Scottys Castle, mansion named for a flamboyant prospector; adobe ruins of borax mining works

FLORA: Bristlecone pines more than 3,000 years old; 21 endemic plant species

FAUNA: Including endangered pupfish descended from Ice Age species

UNIQUE FEATURE: Location of lowest point in Western Hemisphere— −282 feet (−86 m)

These eroded mud hills at Zabriskie Point were once the bed of an ancient lake.

Denali

*O*n a clear day, the peak of Alaska's Mount McKinley seems to scrape the top of the sky. Most often, North America's highest peak shrouds itself in mystery, drawing a mantle of clouds around its sheer-walled magnificence. Few mountains so confuse the division between earth and sky. Yet even when obscured, the 20,320-foot mountain exerts a strong presence. From the 2,000-foot-high lowlands near Wonder Lake, McKinley shoots up 18,000 feet, a greater change in vertical relief than Mount Everest. No wonder the native Athapaskans named the mountain Denali, "the high one."

The southern half of the park protects McKinley and a swath of the Alaska Range, a 600-mile, arc-shaped mountain chain that divides south-central Alaska from the interior plateau. Carved into sharp knifepoints by glacial action, many of these peaks remain nameless and unclimbed. They range from 7,000 to 9,000 feet high, except for a cluster including McKinley and Mount Foraker, which stand head and shoulders above the rest. Avalanches, grinding glaciers, and stiff winds regularly scour these rugged mountains in an inhospitable land where temperatures sometimes dip to 95° below zero Fahrenheit.

The park's northern portion consists of taiga and tundra, a nearly flat sub-arctic landscape that also feels the bitter winds and heavy snows of winter. Rivers course through these lowlands, often changing direction and character. Their waters are milky from suspended sediments known as glacial flour.

Surviving the harsh winters puts severe strains on all life here: On the tundra grow energy-efficient dwarf shrubs and miniature plants. Tiny

wildflowers produce delicate blooms during short growing seasons.

Despite these austere conditions, the land supports North America's largest mammals: grizzly bears, moose, caribou, Dall sheep, and wolves. All of

these mammals have evolved at least one of several metabolic and physical adaptions to cope with the weather: broad feet and longer legs to walk in snow, a thick coat for insulation or all-white for camouflage, and the ability to hoard food and hibernate.

Even today, park rangers rely on the strength and instincts of sled dogs for winter patrols. Few parks remind us so powerfully and completely that we humans are only visitors to this land.

Denali's Wonder Lake reflects the image of Mount McKinley, the towering, massive centerpiece of Alaska's most visited park.

NATURE'S BALANCE

VISITORS TO DENALI see wildlife that haunts the imagination: the lumbering form of a massive grizzly bear, a moose (opposite) browsing at lakeside, or a pack of wolves loping easily across the tundra.

It was not Mount McKinley but the preservation of the park's population of large mammals that created the basis for the area's designation as a national park in 1917. In fact, until 1980, the park did not include the entire McKinley massif. In 1980, Denali tripled in size to six million acres, encompassing the wintering and calving grounds of its caribou herd and enabling the park's large mammals to coexist in a sustained natural balance.

The vast expanse of tundra and taiga maintains important predator-prey relationships as wolves and bears feed on moose, Dall sheep, and caribou, thereby weeding out sick and feeble animals. Foxes, weasels, wolverines, lynxes, martens, snowshoe hares, and hoary marmots make up part of the remainder of Denali's 37 mammal species.

Denali National Park and Preserve

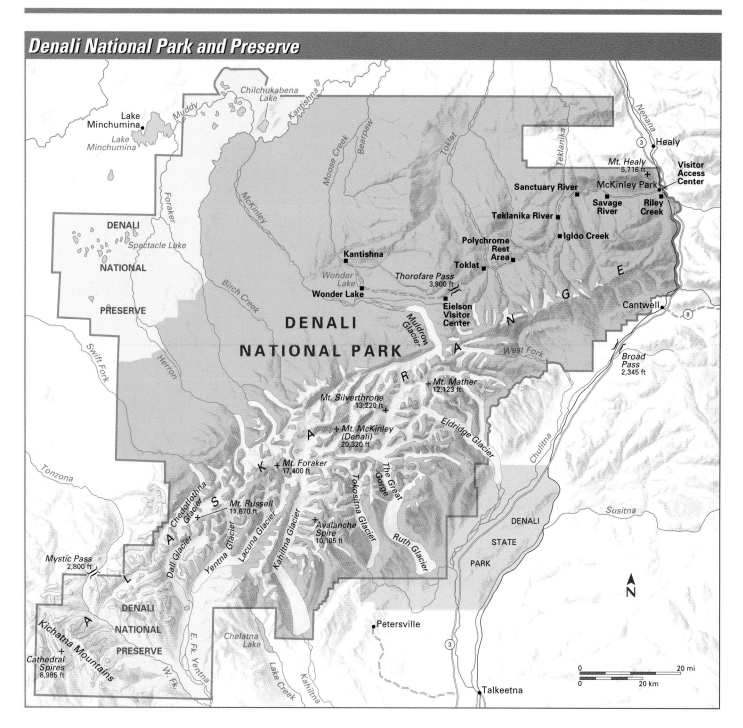

SCALING MOUNT McKINLEY

LOOMING PRISTINE and awesome, 20,320-foot-high Mount McKinley tests many of the world's foremost mountaineers every year. Although some routes are not technically difficult, North America's tallest mountain offers more than enough challenge. Avalanches and crevasses aside, altitude, bone-chilling temperatures, and fierce winds gusting up to 100 miles per hour create one of the earth's most hostile environments. Successful climbers, weakened by exhaustion, lack of oxygen, and fear of worsening weather conditions, rarely stay long on the summit.

A foursome of tough miners known as the "Sourdoughs" made mountaineering history in April 1910, when two of them sprinted the final 8,500 feet up North Peak and back down in a single day. Although later climbers conquered McKinley's true summit, South Peak, noth-ing will ever diminish the Sourdoughs' heroic feat.

Since then, established routes and innovations in equipment have helped thousands of climbers conquer McKinley. However, increased traffic has resulted in overcrowding and many accidents—more than 70 climbers have lost their lives. Despite perils, the sheer flanks of Mount McKinley still lure those wishing for one of the world's premier climbing experiences.

PARK DATA

STATE: Alaska

ESTABLISHED: 1917; expanded in 1980 to become Denali National Park and Preserve; designated a UNESCO international biosphere reserve

AREA: 6,028,091 acres (2,439,484 ha)

ELEVATION: From nearly sea level to 20,320 ft (6,194 m)

CLIMATE: Summer temperatures from 35° to 75°F (2° to 24°C); windy; possi-bility of snow year-round

FLORA: Taiga—spruces, aspens, birches, alders, poplars; tundra—dwarf willows, birches, fire-weeds, mosses, fungi, lichens; more than 650 flowering plant species

FAUNA: 37 large and small mammal species; 159 species of birds

UNIQUE FEATURE: Mount McKinley, at 20,320 ft (6,194 m) North America's highest mountain

Dry Tortugas

*I*n the clear, shimmering waters of the Gulf of Mexico 70 miles west of Key West lie seven tiny sand-and-coral islands—the real end to the Florida Keys. One of the slivers of land contains the abandoned hulk of mid-19th-century Fort Jefferson. Its remoteness, which led to the fort's abandonment, today protects one of the least disturbed coral reef ecosystems in North America and the nesting grounds for loggerhead turtles, frigate birds, and terns.

PARK DATA

STATE: Florida
ESTABLISHED: 1992
AREA: 64,657 acres (26,166 ha); less than one percent dry land
FLORA: Few land plants, chiefly mangroves
FAUNA: Sanctuary for thousands of migrating birds; 442 species of fish

Fort Jefferson (top) stands silent vigil over Garden Key. Bush Key (foreground) is a prime sooty tern nesting site.

Everglades

At first glance, the saw grass expanse of the Everglades resembles the Old West prairie. A closer look reveals that this prairie has very wet feet. Indians referred to the Everglades as Pa-hay-okee, "the grassy waters." In the 1940s writer Marjory Stoneman Douglas coined the evocative and apt name "River of Grass."

Indeed, the original Everglades encompassed flowing water, a sheet 50 miles wide moving unimpeded, almost imperceptibly, across marsh, swamp, and mangrove from Lake Okeechobee into Florida Bay. The region teemed with huge flocks of birds and other wildlife. By the 1930s, however, populations of many bird species had plummeted, as they were slaughtered

for their plumes. And this intriguing ecosystem, where temperate vegetation and animals mingle with the subtropical, was fast being drained for development.

The southern end of the Everglades was set aside as a national park in 1947. Divided roughly into three zones and sprawling across a million and a half acres, the park embraces perhaps a tenth of the original Everglades. Here are the true glades—the freshwater saw grass marshes; dense tangles of coastal mangroves; and the shallow, island-scattered waters of Florida Bay.

At first the flatness may seem monoto-nous. A closer look reveals that a few inches, a foot or two, of variation in elevation signal subtle worlds of difference. Clumps of bay trees claim slightly higher terrain in the sea of grass. With still more elevation, tree islands of subtropical hardwoods form. On the highest, driest limestone ridges, four or five feet above sea level, grow stands of native pine.

Everywhere there is life. A look into the clear water reveals spongy algae called periphyton, an essential link at the bottom of the food chain. At the top lurks the alligator. Dragonflies swoop; kingfishers dive;

Waves of saw grass ripple over the watery world of the Everglades. The shallow, slow-moving sheet of water once flowed across most of southern Florida. Now only a portion remains protected in the park.

anhingas preen; roseate spoonbills, ibis, and several kinds of herons feed in tidal waters. More difficult to spot is a bittern or a green tree frog against the saw grass background or jewel-like tree snails on hardwood bark. The list goes on, but there is growing concern for the Everglades. Wading bird populations and other wildlife have declined drastically in recent years. Changes in the water flow have been blamed.

MARJORY STONEMAN DOUGLAS

"THERE ARE NO OTHER Everglades in the world," Marjory Stoneman Douglas began her 1947 book, *The Everglades: River of Grass*—an eloquent defense of that remarkable environment. Well beyond her 100th year, she exam- ines blades of saw grass (right) typical of the Everglades. Though she never spent much time in the glades, Mrs. Douglas understood the ecosystem's importance to southern Florida's water supply and devoted much energy to promoting its preservation.

She likened the Everglades to "a set of scales on which the forces of the seasons, of the sun and the rains, the winds, the hurricanes, and the dewfalls, were balanced so that life of the vast grass and all its encompassed and neighbor forms were kept secure." Her work has gained her a respected place among the luminaries of conservation.

BIRDING IN THE EVERGLADES

SKIES "DARKENED BY great flocks of birds of gorgeous plumage," a writer in the 1920s described the Everglades before plume hunters decimated bird populations. The protection of birdlife provided a major impetus to the park's founding. The region still draws birders to more than 300 species, including wading birds such as the tricolored heron (right). Breeding wading birds have declined 90 percent since the 1940s. Researchers think erratic water flow may interrupt nesting and disturb food sources.

WATER MANAGEMENT PROBLEMS

WATER IS KEY in the Everglades: the salt water of Florida Bay; the mangrove-fringed brackish waters (above) that provide nursery habitat for fish, shrimp, and birds; and the freshwater glades and sloughs farther inland. And the Everglades supplies southern Florida with fresh water by replenishing the Biscayne Aquifer.

Though rainfall is copious, averaging 60 inches a year, there is little natural storage in this flat terrain. Generations of Floridians have attempted to solve that problem by building 1,400 miles of canals, levees, and spillways—to drain areas for housing, to irrigate farmland, or simply to get rid of excess water.

The result has been an interruption in the historical cycle of water flowing across the Everglades. At the lower end of the watershed, the park has been flooded out in wet years and parched in dry ones. It was long thought that a regular amount of fresh water entering the park was the answer. In recent years, however, animal populations have dwindled, vegetation has changed, and the Everglades has become one of the most endangered U.S. parks. Scientists now aim to achieve adequate water quantity while correcting subtle changes wrought by improper timing, location, and quality of delivery.

In an attempt to restore the patterns of natural flow, researchers are testing computer models, hoping to engineer technical manipulations that will simulate as closely as possible the original cycle.

PARK DATA

STATE: Florida
ESTABLISHED: 1947
AREA: 1,506,539 acres (609,708 ha); UNESCO world heritage site and international biosphere reserve
ELEVATION: Highest point in park 8 ft (2.4 m)
CLIMATE: Hot, humid in summer with many thunderstorms; winter drier and cooler
FLORA: Meeting point of temperate and subtropical vegetation; mangroves; tree islands called hammocks—high, drier ground caused by protrusions in the bedrock and populated by hardwood trees; epiphytes (aerial plants)—bromeliads, orchids
FAUNA: Rare Florida panthers, deer; manatees, bottlenose dolphins; more than 300 species of birds, including nesting groups of ibis, herons, roseate spoonbills, anhingas—and endangered wood storks and snail kites; alligators, endangered crocodiles, snakes, turtles; abundant mosquitoes in wet season

ALLIGATORS TOP THE FOOD CHAIN

ITS POWERFUL JAWS boasting some 70 teeth, an alligator devours a red-bellied turtle. In addition to topping the food chain, the gator acts as "chief engi-neer of the Everglades," as one naturalist puts it. To cool body temperature, the huge reptiles use pools and muddy wallows, which they keep clear of vegeta-tion. These oases—gator holes—become important to the survival of other ani-mals such as turtles, vari-ous water snakes, frogs, otters, and birds that gravi-tate to them during the dry season. Concentrated at low water, fish and other gator hole creatures be-come easy prey.

Fearsome as they may be, female alligators are extremely good mothers, tending their eggs care-fully and protecting their young for more than a year after hatching.

Biscayne and Everglades National Parks

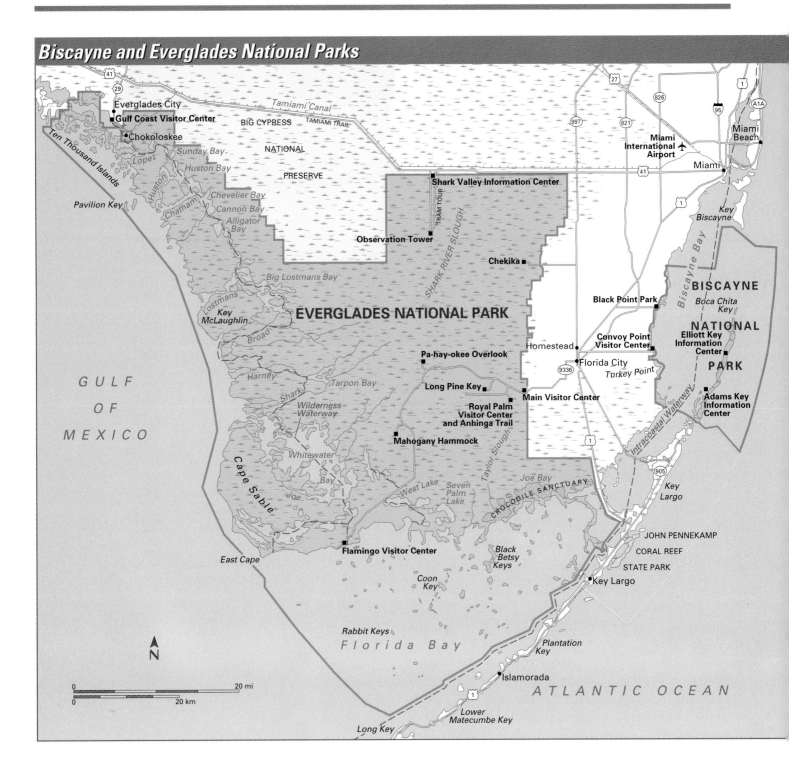

Gates of the Arctic

Gates of the Arctic National Park and Preserve is the very essence of wilderness. Located entirely above the Arctic Circle, the park enfolds the heart of the jagged Brooks Range. Here, the northernmost reaches form a staircase that rises from foothills to 7,000-foot peaks on the Arctic divide and then reverses itself to descend toward the vast tundra—and beyond park boundaries, to the Arctic Ocean. Six National Wild and Scenic Rivers, along with uncounted other waterways, pour forth through Gates of the Arctic from headwaters on the Arctic divide.

The park's treeless tundra, lichen-covered slopes, and plunging valleys are home to grizzlies and black bears, wolves, moose, Dall sheep, and wolverines. A major share of the Western Arctic caribou herd's range is contained within the park's 8.5 million acres, which adjoin vast federal preserves to east and west.

The area's immensity, and its blankness on the map, first drew conservationist Bob Marshall in 1929 to what would become his most cherished wilderness. On one of his frequent hikes along the North Fork of the Koyukuk River, Marshall named two peaks, Frigid Crags and Boreal Mountain—and described the pair evocatively as "Gates of the Arctic."

Topographic maps name few landmarks in the central Brooks Range. But both the name Marshall gave the region and his vision survived him at the park's creation in 1980. Protection of this untouched Arctic environment was the chief mandate. Gates of the Arctic has only one visitor center and few facilities of any kind. It has no trails and no year-round road. There is a single Nunamiut village, Anaktuvuk Pass, within park boundaries.

Gates of the Arctic is accessible only by air taxi or on foot; river travel within the park is popular. Extremely challenging terrain can slow the going to five miles a day, even for veteran backpackers. But for their troubles, visitors reap countless rewards, perhaps none greater than a sense of the immensity of nature's creation.

PARK DATA

STATE: Alaska

ESTABLISHED: 1980

AREA: 8,500,000 acres (3,439,831 ha)

HIGHEST POINT: Mount Igikpak, 8,510 ft (2,594 m), highest peak in central Brooks Range

CLIMATE: Short, mild summers, with lowland temperatures rising to around 80°F (27°C); highlands cooler; August very rainy; Arctic winter temperatures from −20° to −50°F (−29° to −46°C)

NATURAL FEATURES: Arrigetch Peaks—dramatic region of black granite spires that intrudes into limestone of Brooks Range; clear rivers fed by pristine lakes; glacier-carved landscape, but few glaciers left owing to insufficient snowfall

CULTURAL FEATURES: Local subsistence activities of native peoples and others still pursued in park

FLORA: Boreal white spruce, aspen, and birch forests; black-spruce taiga; tree-line birches, alders, willows; alpine tundra of fragile lichens and mosses

FAUNA: Grizzly and black bears, caribou, moose, Dall sheep, wolves, wolverines; migratory bird species from around the world; graylings, sculpins

Mist froths the John River at sunrise. From its trickling headwater at Anaktuvuk Pass, the John gathers strength as it flows south through alpine and later lowland forest before joining the Koyukuk River outside the park.

Glacier

Rising sharply above the plains in northwestern Montana, Glacier National Park has long inspired superlatives. Naturalist John Muir recommended an extended stay amid "the best care-killing scenery on the continent," a world of hoary peaks, turquoise lakes, alpine meadows, and other tonics for the ills of civilization.

To the 19th-century explorer George Grinnell, Glacier was the "crown of the continent." He meant the accolade literally: The Continental Divide winds along ridgetops of the Lewis Range through the center of the park. The divide splits not only headwaters but Glacier itself into distinct regions. To the west, mild, moist Pacific fronts favor slopes cloaked with cedars and hemlocks, while a drier, windier, and more severe environment prevails to the east. Glacier's topography and natural history link it closely to its adjacent sister park in Canada—Alberta's Waterton Lakes National Park.

Some 50 small glaciers glint in the dazzling summer sunshine. The park owes its name, however, to the vast Ice Age glaciers that once lapped at its highest peaks and sculptured its contours. Quarrying and plucking as they advanced and retreated, the glaciers created U-shaped valleys, knife-edged arêtes, cirque lakes backed by 3,000-foot headwalls, and horn-shaped peaks.

Initially inhospitable to plant and animal life, the glacier-carved landscape now harbors an abundance of both, including more than 1,250 plant species and 272 bird species. Among its 63 native mammals are thousands of mountain goats, hundreds of bighorn sheep, elk, moose, mountain lions, wolverines, gray wolves, and about 200 grizzlies—the densest concentration of these bears in the lower 48 states.

PARK DATA

STATE: Montana

ESTABLISHED: 1910; joined in 1932 with Waterton Lakes N.P., Canada, as Waterton-Glacier International Peace Park; designated a biosphere reserve by UNESCO

AREA: 1,013,572 acres (410,178 ha)

CLIMATE: Summer temperatures ranging from 30° to 90°F (–1° to 32°C); winter lows in the –40s °F (–40s °C)

NATURAL FEATURES: Some of the oldest exposed sedimentary rock layers in the U.S.—more than a billion years in age; fossils of colonial blue-green algae visible in rock; 6 peaks more than 10,000 ft (3,048 m) tall

FLORA: More than 1,250 plant species; park renowned for the variety and beauty of its wildflowers

FAUNA: All 63 mammal species native; many of 272 bird species migratory; 5 amphibian and 2 non-poisonous snake species

Reynolds Mountain, shadowed by thunderheads, cups a steep-walled cirque at its base. Pyramid-like rock faces result from glacial sanding on several sides.

GLACIER PARK LODGE

CAPPED BY Ionic "scrolls," columns hewn out of Douglas fir soar above the smart set at rest in Glacier Park Lodge, shortly after its opening in 1913.

Advertising Glacier as the "Switzerland of America" and the railroad as the "National Park Line," the Great Northern Railway transported tourists to its complex of hotels, chalets, and luxury campsites connected by roads and trails.

However, the short tourist season limited Great Northern's return on its investment, and eventually the line withdrew as a developer at Glacier.

Glacier and Waterton Lakes National Parks

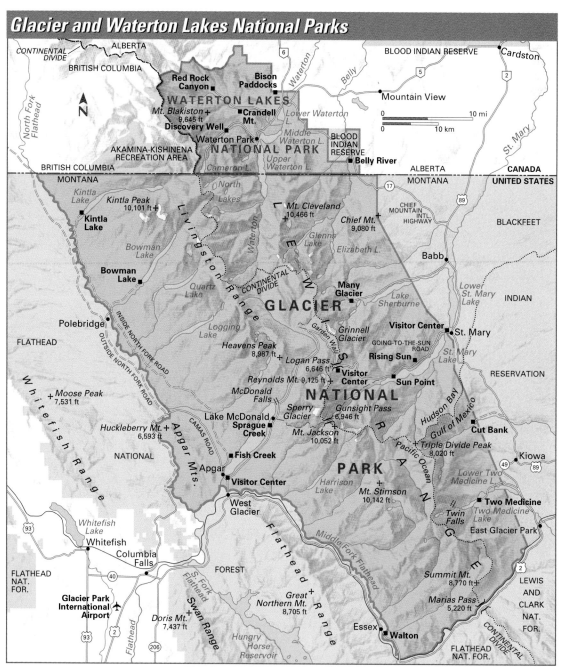

WATERTON-GLACIER PEACE PARK

A CLEAN CUT ALONG the 49th parallel, the U.S.-Canada boundary transects not only Waterton Lake but the natural unity of an entire glacier-carved mountain system. But, thanks to the efforts of Rotarians in both countries, Waterton-Glacier International Peace Park has since 1932 knit landforms, ecosystems, and some park administrative functions together in a unique goodwill gesture.

In more recent years, pressures around their perimeters—ranging from amusement parks to seismic blasting—have further united the two parks in a shared search for solutions.

Beyond a watery mirror (opposite), Avalanche Creek pours through walls softened by moss and reddened by iron-bearing hematite.

Glacier Bay

Regularly the cool stillness of Glacier Bay in southern Alaska shatters with a thunderous explosion. Immense blocks of ice as tall as 200 feet break off the sheer-walled glaciers and crash into the sea, creating a sound that the Tlingit Indians called "white thunder." Johns Hopkins Glacier calves so many massive icebergs that cruise ships can approach no closer than a mile.

These calving glaciers mark the rapid retreat of a little ice age that began 4,000 years ago. When Capt. George Vancouver sailed into Icy Strait just over two centuries ago, the area known today as Glacier Bay lay buried under glacial ice several miles wide and some 4,000 feet thick. By 1879, when John Muir visited that area, the glacier that would eventually bear his name had receded 48 miles up the bay. In its wake lay a barren and mountainous landscape of rock rubbed smooth by the immense weight of the ice. Today, these hundreds of cubic miles of ice have receded 65 miles, representing the fastest glacial retreat on record.

As the ice retreated, tidewater filled in the narrow, deep fjords. Plant life reclaimed this land long asleep, and a spruce-hemlock rain forest now thrives at the southern end of the bay. In newly vegetated areas, wildlife now includes wolves, moose, and bears. Bay waters teem with salmon, harbor seals, harbor porpoises, and humpback, minke, and killer whales.

To scientists, Glacier Bay remains a laboratory for global climate change as they puzzle over the remarkable speed of glacial retreat. For the time being, the fast retreat has slowed: Of the seventeen glaciers that reach tidal waters, three are retreating, six are advancing, and eight are stable.

PARK DATA

STATE: Alaska
ESTABLISHED: 1980
AREA: 3,280,198 acres (1,327,450 ha)
ELEVATION: From sea level to highest point, Mount Fairweather, 15,300 feet (4,663 m)
NATURAL FEATURES: Four mountain ranges in the park that spawn more than a hundred glaciers
FLORA: Park a natural laboratory for the study of plant succession on newly created land—from algae, then moss; through dwarf fireweeds, alders, and willows; to mature forests of spruce and hemlock

McBride Glacier (below) slowly retreats from Muir Inlet, revealing a scoured landscape lost to the world for 4,000 years.

Lituya Bay's steep-walled mountains and rounded boulders (opposite) attest to the grinding power of the receding glaciers.

Grand Canyon

There are many ways to obtain a panoramic view of the magnificent Grand Canyon—carved deep into the Colorado Plateau in northern Arizona and stretching 290 miles to the horizon. But there is no way to take it all in at once.

Theodore Roosevelt, overwhelmed when he visited the canyon for the first time in 1903, began a move to preserve this natural wonder. The park was finally established in 1919, becoming one of the most visited in the system.

Though characterized by Roosevelt as "the one great sight every American...should see," the Grand Canyon is really many sights and experiences. It is "a composite of thousands, of tens of thousands, of gorges," Civil War veteran and explorer Maj. John Wesley Powell said. "Every one of these...is a world of beauty in itself.... Yet all these canyons unite to form one grand canyon...."

Standing at Hopi Point on the brink of this yawning abyss, you feel all sound engulfed by the immense silence beyond. Tier upon tier of flat-topped buttes recede, bearing exotic names bestowed in another era: Confucius Temple, Shiva Temple, Tower of Ra. In late afternoon, the setting sun paints canyon walls in a fading rainbow of colors.

To the northeast winds the Bright Angel Canyon. A trail from Grand Canyon Village on the South Rim switchbacks eight miles down to the creek that cut this canyon. Here the scent of cottonwoods and willows floats on the air a mile below the rim at river's edge. In fern-filled side canyons waterfalls splash into azure pools, and river rafters head past into white water. To hike the vertical mile back to the canyon rim is like a trip

Early morning light bathes O'Neill Butte, part of the Supai sandstone formation. The South Kaibab Trail to the canyon bottom winds nearby.

through ecozones from Mexico to Canada. In the canyon depths, the riverside willows, cottonwoods, shrubs, and wildflowers are surrounded by dry desert scrub. A woodland of piñon and juniper climbs the slopes above, mingling at the rim with the dominant ponderosa pine.

During the past ten million years or so—a mere blink in the geological scheme of things—the Colorado River cleaved the Kaibab Plateau into two parts, dividing the North Rim from the South Rim. The five-hour drive between the two sectors takes visitors from the lower, milder, drier climate of the South Rim to the higher, cooler, moister North Rim. Open all year, the South Rim receives most of the park's nearly 5 million annual visitors.

For several months of the year the North Rim is closed in by snow. But skiers can then taste the exhilaration of traversing its winter snowpack. Again and again this crown jewel of national parks reveals another facet.

THE LIFE CYCLE OF A CANYON

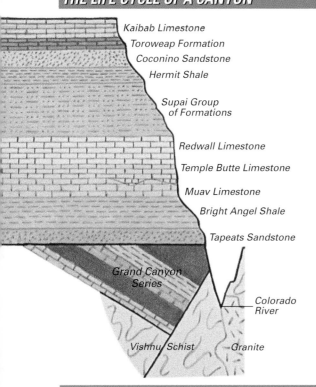

Kaibab Limestone
Toroweap Formation
Coconino Sandstone
Hermit Shale
Supai Group of Formations
Redwall Limestone
Temple Butte Limestone
Muav Limestone
Bright Angel Shale
Tapeats Sandstone
Grand Canyon Series
Colorado River
Vishnu Schist
Granite

THE SAGA OF geological formation is perhaps nowhere so clearly illustrated as on the Colorado Plateau, shown in cross section below. Multicolored strata reveal evidence of layers building up and wearing down, of land lifting and subsiding, of volcanoes erupting with cataclysmic force, of water carving inexorably through rock.

Once there were high mountains, deserts, and shallow seas here. The diagram at left shows formations laid down by

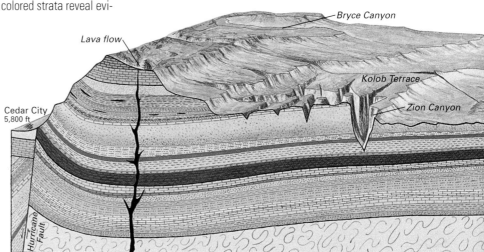

Lava flow
Bryce Canyon
Kolob Terrace
Zion Canyon
Cedar City 5,800 ft
Hurricane Fault

those events.

The top layer, Kaibab limestone, is about 240 million years old. The sea has invaded at least five times, as shown by the limestones of the Kaibab, Toroweap, Redwall, Temple Butte, and Muav formations. There were river deltas, too, as indicated by the Supai group and Hermit shale.

Below, several rivers and creeks slice into layers of rock, though none probes as deep as the Grand Canyon, at right. Younger gorges expose only the more recent formations, while the Grand Canyon reaches Precambrian rock 1.7 billion years old. As the erosional process continues, the Colorado and its tributaries constantly wear down this ancient landscape.

A redbud tree clings to the sinuous wall of a side canyon carved by Deer Creek. The force of water continues to shape such idyllic oases in the park.

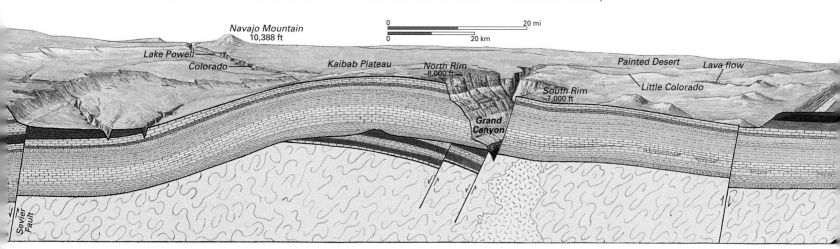

Navajo Mountain
10,388 ft

Lake Powell
Colorado
Kaibab Plateau
North Rim
~8,000 ft
South Rim
~7,000 ft
Grand Canyon
Painted Desert
Lava flow
Little Colorado

0   20 mi
0   20 km

Sevier Fault

"YOU CANNOT SEE the Grand Canyon in one view…you have to toil from month to month through its labyrinths," noted Maj. John Wesley Powell some time after his two grueling expeditions on the Colorado River. Though humans had ventured here for thousands of years—more than 2,700 archaeological sites have been located—Powell's trips, in 1869 and 1871, marked the first systematic exploration of the Grand Canyon.

Shown here in 1871 with a Paiute Indian called Tau-gu, one-armed Powell, along with his men, braved ferocious white water in fragile wooden boats. Sheer walls, such as this 3,000-foot-high sandstone face at Toroweap Overlook (right), precluded a change of heart once they had begun their journey "down the Great Unknown."

VARYING IN elevation and moisture and stretching over a vast area, the Grand Canyon has developed many distinct ecological niches. Some unique species have evolved, such as the salmon-hued Grand Canyon rattlesnake, which blends with canyon walls.

Over time, the gap between the North and South Rims has widened as the Colorado has carved ever deeper. Larger animals such as deer, foxes, and bobcats cross this gap. Smaller species with confined ranges and specialized diets often do not. Distinct variations have sometimes emerged.

The two subspecies of tassel-eared squirrels were once a single species. Both kinds of squirrels depend for food on the ponderosa pine, which grows on either rim but not in the arid inner canyon. Isolated from one another, the two populations have developed different characteristics. Though closely resembling the Abert squirrel, its South Rim cousin, the Kaibab squirrel (right) sports different tail and belly markings.

Grand Canyon National Park

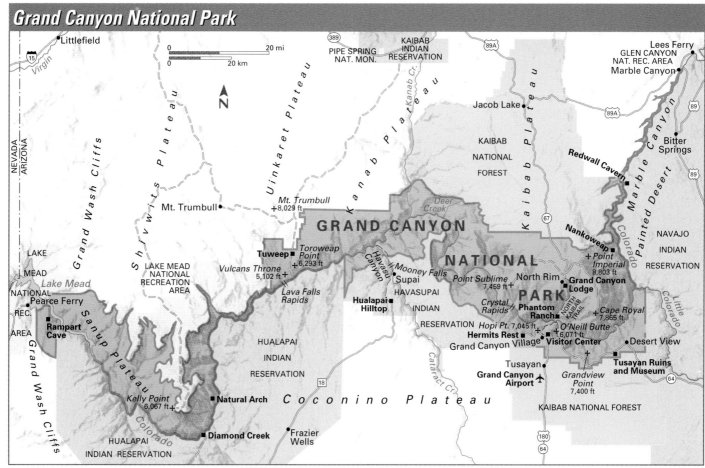

Grand Teton

F ault movement began shaping the Teton Range some five to ten million years ago. The earth cracked; as one side tilted upward, the other sank down. Scientists believe movement has recurred periodically since then and could happen again. The resulting view is like no other in North America—a sudden, 7,000-foot vault from the sunken side, the valley of Jackson Hole, to the pinnacle of the high side, the Teton Range.

Upon this 40-mile-long block of upheaved rock, the forces of grinding glaciers, freeze and thaw, wind and rain, have worked for that geologically brief five to ten million years. These are young mountains, the youngest in the Rockies. They remain rough-cut jewels—set off by plunging canyons, bedecked with glaciers and snowfields, strung with lakes at their feet—and they delight the eye from every aspect. They fill a panoramic lodge window, riveting the loungers. They slow motorists rolling through the valley. They lure climbers, step by weary step. They present a changing tableau to rafters on the Snake River. At dawn the peak tips fire up, kindled by a sun yet unseen in the darkness of the valley.

What most park visitors do not see is a landmark image resembling female breasts—the image, conjured by French fur trappers, that gave its name to the range. Perhaps the lonely wilderness fueled their imagination; more likely they beheld the mountains from the west side, approaching from Idaho. There the resemblance does not seem so far-fetched. At all events, a magnificent view of the three Tetons—South, Middle, and Grand—may be enjoyed from the heights of Targhee National Forest. Along the west side, also, runs the popular Teton Crest Trail, with

PARK DATA

STATE: Wyoming
ESTABLISHED: 1929
AREA: 310,000 acres (125,453 ha)
ELEVATION: Total of 12 peaks above 12,000 ft (3,658 m)
CLIMATE: Winter weather, with deep snows on the range for more than half the year
NATURAL FEATURES: Textbook geology featured in Teton Range and surrounding formations—absence of foothills evidence of uplift of mountain block along a deep fault; Oxbow Bend, cutoff meander of the Snake River, comprising a rich habitat
CULTURAL FEATURES: Homestead remains at Mormon Row; Plains Indians art in museum at Colter Bay Visitor Center
FLORA: Varied plant communities ranging from alpine to coniferous; streamside cottonwoods
FAUNA: Moose, elk, deer, pronghorn, bears, smaller mammals; birds including bald eagles, ospreys, great blue herons, trumpeter swans; 17 fish species

Beyond a beaver dam, an unruffled side channel of the Snake River reflects the cool majesty of the soaring Tetons at sunrise.

access to Alaska Basin and its famed wildflower display in late summer.

The mountain spectacle from Jackson Hole inspired a Gothic imagery. Within a span of four miles rises the tight cluster of spires called the Cathedral Group, consisting of the Grand Teton, Mount Owen, and Teewinot Mountain. All of them tower more than 12,000 feet.

Many a visitor eyeing the Grand Teton, 13,770 feet high, aspires to scale that summit. Novices, however, would be wise to take some training and join a guided climb. In past years the park registered summit climbers, but it no longer does so. Too many failed to check back in, triggering searches. Sometimes rangers discovered overdue mountaineers quaffing restorative potions at a bar in nearby Jackson.

The park tallies more than 3.5 million visitors annually. The number includes many people traveling a major highway through park territory, bound for Yellowstone, to the north, or points east. Airline jets deposit and pick up passengers at the only commercial airport inside a national park, a distinction that park officials would gladly forgo. Powerful local voices insist that safety and Jackson's growth require an expanded airport at its present site.

Travelers merely passing through account for some two-thirds of the visitor total. That leaves more than a million people a year who come to fill the campgrounds and lodges, to hike the 230 miles of trails, to hear the elk bugling in autumn. Increasingly, winter visitors accept the harsh challenge of the backcountry. Among the most devoted, in all seasons, are many locals who repair to this national treasure as to a favorite neighborhood park.

Some 3,000 elk summer in the park and winter at the National Elk Refuge. An annual hunt aims to limit herd size.

Great Basin

*S*equestered in the high, lonesome country just inside Nevada's eastern frontier, this park takes its name from the vast, arid hinterland known as the Great Basin. Sheer bigness defines every aspect of this untamed landscape sprawled between the Rockies and the Sierra Nevada, where all the rivers flow inland. Alternate pitched peaks and broad valleys, running generally north and south, comprise a major ecosystem called the Basin and Range Province.

Great Basin park was established in 1986 in the remote South Snake Range to preserve a sample of this ecosystem. The park contains most of the main plant communities found in the province, from dusty sagebrush desert to alpine meadows and tundra. In between grow stands of piñon pine and juniper. Above these rise Englemann spruces, limber pines, firs, and aspens, and higher still, mountain mahoganies.

Inhospitable as it may appear, Great Basin harbors an array of wildlife, from rodents to bighorn sheep, brightly colored songbirds to birds of prey, and a variety of snakes and lizards.

The park's main attractions are Lehman Caves, formerly a national monument, known for its magnificent limestone formations; and 13,063-foot Wheeler Peak, pinnacle of the Snake Range, boasting a glacial cirque and the region's only glacier. Near tree line stand twisted bristlecone pines, the world's oldest living trees, many of which date back more than 3,000 years.

As part of its founding legislation, Great Basin permits cattle grazing and unpatented mining within its boundaries. This departure from normal park legislation reflects not only a compromise between conservationists and local ranching and mining interests but also larger issues concerning wilderness preservation and land use.

Pockets of sandy desert (left) attest to the region's aridity. Most clouds here, their moisture wrung out over the Sierra Nevada, do not presage rain.

Ancient bristlecone pines (above), the oldest living tree species, have weathered millennia on **Wheeler Peak,** thanks to their resinous, rot-resistant wood.

*I*t is a relief to leave the urban jumble of Gatlinburg, Tennessee, or Cherokee, North Carolina, and enter the cool, lush verdure of Great Smoky Mountains National Park. Most people know that this park draws more visitors than any other U.S. park—nearly ten million a year—a result no doubt, of its location within easy driving distance of dense population centers. Traffic can clog the park's 270 miles of roads, especially when deer or black bears appear at road's edge; or during spring wildflower and autumn leaf pilgrimages; or when rhododendrons bloom on high meadow "balds."

But Great Smokies also embraces pristine corners, rugged wilds, some of the highest peaks in the Appalachian range, and some 800 miles of trails. The largest stands of old-growth forest in the eastern U.S. blanket a fifth of the park's half million acres. And the park boasts the richest diversity of flora in any comparable area in temperate North America—1,500 different species of flowering plants and 130 kinds of trees. Glaciers of the Ice Age never reached this far south, allowing many northern species to retreat south and survive here as relicts that mingle with more southerly species.

That Great Smokies became a national park at all is due in part to Horace Kephart, who came here from St. Louis in 1904. He became enchanted with the region and its people and wrote a classic work, *Our Southern Highlanders.* After loggers devastated much of his "superb forest primeval," he became a dedicated national park advocate. Others joined the cause.

The land was largely in private hands. Money had to be raised to buy it. Eventually, in the 1930s, all but a few families sold out. Though much of the soil was depleted, it was a bittersweet end for these resilient mountaineers. A few chose to remain in Cades Cove on agricultural leases.

Forest again cloaks much of Great Smokies. Now it faces new dangers: an invasion of exotic insect pests, such as the balsam woolly adelgid; and acid rain and other pollutants that diminish water, soil, and air quality.

PARK DATA

STATES: North Carolina and Tennessee
ESTABLISHED: 1934
AREA: 520,409 acres (210,602 ha)
ELEVATION: From 855 ft (261 m) to 6,643-ft (2,025-m) Clingmans Dome; 16 peaks rising more than 6,000 ft (1,829 m)
CLIMATE: Precipitation ranging from 55 in (140 cm) a year near Gatlinburg to 85 in (216 cm) at higher elevations
NATURAL FEATURE: Ancient mountains, part of Appalachian chain
CULTURAL FEATURE: Cades Cove, containing one of the nation's finest collections of log houses, farm buildings, and other accoutrements
FLORA: Most extensive stands of forest in the eastern U.S. untouched by loggers; richest biodiversity in temperate North America, with 1,500 flowering plant species and 130 kinds of trees
FAUNA: Red wolves being reintroduced, perhaps as predators for exotic wild hogs; black bears, bobcats; foxes and other small mammals; reintroduced river otters; 200 species of birds; amphibians including 27 salamander species

Cave salamander—one of a remarkable variety that flourishes here—adds a vivid touch to the mossy forest floor.

Lush vegetation along the Oconaluftee River displays a rich diversity. Great Smokies gained its UNESCO biosphere reserve designation as "perhaps the best example of undisturbed hardwood forest in the United States."

Mist-veiled ridges stretch to the horizon in Great Smokies. The Cherokee, who came here for game and medicinal plants, called the region Shaconage, or "place of blue smoke," for its characteristic haziness. Current thought credits the interaction of water vapors and hydrocarbons with sunlight.

RED WOLF REINTRODUCTION

A NEW DAY MAY BE coming for red wolves in Great Smokies. The park, together with adjacent forest reserves, may provide tracts of wilderness large enough for reintroduction of the endangered red wolf —which once ranged here and farther south.

Chris Lucash, biologist with the U.S. Fish and Wildlife Service (right), prepares to set loose a female red wolf after an unsuccessful earlier release. "Some captive-born wolves need a few tries to perfect wild

behavior," he says.

The wolf program, begun in 1991, raises controversy among area farmers. Opponents fear calf losses and a heavy toll on deer. The program pays restitution for valid livestock claims. Wildlife specialists are working out management systems to protect vulnerable newborn stock. Researchers hope the wolves eventually will prey on exotic hogs, which destroy park vegetation and compete with native wildlife for nuts and berries.

Great Smoky Mountains National Park

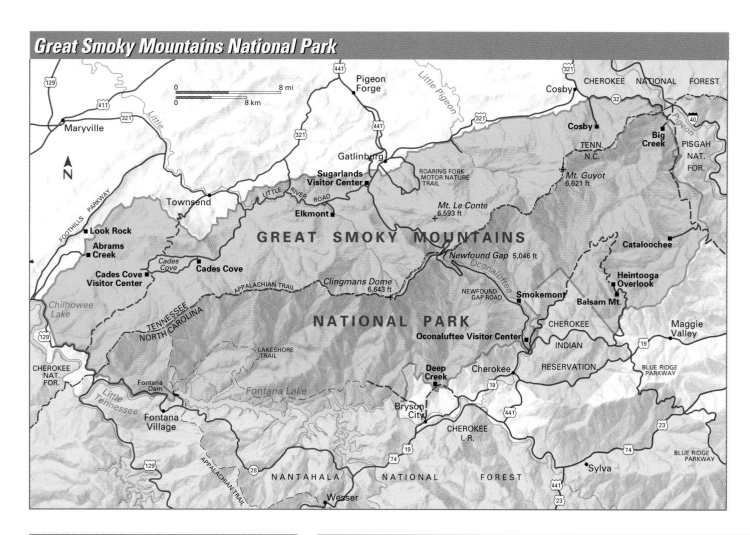

THE LAST FAMILY IN CADES COVE

AS THE SUN SETS in Cades Cove, Lois and Kermit Caughron contemplate the end of an era on lands their ancestors first settled nearly two centuries ago. When Great Smokies was created they were among several thousand owners holding 6,600 parcels of land. Most of the 100 or so Cades Cove families sold out and relocated. The Caughrons are the last of a handful that remained in Cades Cove on agricultural leases.

In the 1960s (above), they raised their children and ran cattle—furthering park goals to keep the cove from reverting to forest and to present a living reminder of the self-reliant mountain families that once filled these valleys.

Guadalupe Mountains

L ike the prow of a gallant ship, El Capitan, southern bluff of the Guadalupe Mountains, seems to cut through waves of gleaming gypsum sands. It is a moment to remember, that first glimpse of the massive escarpment rising 5,000 feet above the sere Chihuahuan Desert in West Texas.

The towering ramparts of the Guadalupes harbor many other surprises: well-watered side canyons where bright maples and oaks flourish —trees normally found much farther east; high meadows dotted with northerly Douglas firs and pines; madronas, relicts of the last ice age; shimmering dunes of gypsum sand 50 feet tall.

About 250 million years ago, the Guadalupes were a barrier reef at the edge of a Permian sea. Later the land tilted upward to form the present escarpment. In the 1920s, New York geologist Wallace E. Pratt found the area a likely prospect for oil exploration. He fell in love with McKittrick Canyon. So enchanted was he with the lush beauty of the little gorge that he bought the land, built himself a stone cabin, and in 1957 donated 5,632 acres to the U.S. government. It became the nucleus of Guadalupe Mountains National Park, which was established in 1972. Other lands were acquired from local supporters of the idea of a national park.

McKittrick is still a star attraction, especially in fall when the maples and oaks take on vivid hues. The canyon's sheltering walls help visitors escape the park's fierce winds. They also expose a fossil record of life that once flourished in the ancient Permian sea.

A strenuous hike up a steep incline leads to moderate walks along ridges into The Bowl—a lush subalpine meadow. More than half of the park is designated a wilderness area.

PARK DATA

STATE: Texas
ESTABLISHED: 1972
AREA: 86,416 acres (34,971 ha)
ELEVATION: From about 3,650 ft (1,113 m) to 8,749-ft (2,667-m) Guadalupe Peak, the highest mountain in Texas
CLIMATE: Renowned for violent winds and extremely changeable weather conditions
NATURAL FEATURE: The 50-mi-long (80-km-long) mountain range, formerly a Permian barrier reef
CULTURAL FEATURES: Ruins of The Pinery, a stage station on the Butterfield Overland Mail Line; Pratt's stone cabin; Williams and Frijole Ranches, early 20th-century homesteads
FLORA: Range in vegetation as elevation climbs from Chihuahuan Desert to subalpine meadow
FAUNA: Elk, mule deer, mountain lions; 260 species of birds

Wind-lapped sea of gypsum sands undulates toward El Capitan. Driven by the wind, the sands are shifting ever closer to the massive escarpment at the southern end of the Guadalupe Mountains.

Haleakala

Growing in dense clumps, this bamboo, introduced to Maui from Asia during the last century, now threatens many endemic species.

The view from Haleakala's 10,023-foot summit on the Hawaiian island of Maui is otherworldly and magnificent. In the distance, volcanoes Mauna Loa and Mauna Kea reach through the clouds, while nearer by yawns what seems to be a 19-square-mile volcanic crater.

From its floor rises a host of symmetrical cinder cones up to 600 feet tall, streaked red, yellow, gray, and black.

Not a crater at all, the park's centerpiece is actually a great basin carved over hundreds of thousands of years by torrential rains. It filled with cones and a thick layer of ash and pumice during volcanic eruptions that burst from its vents. For the time being, the volcano is dormant.

With the sun high and the clouds low, hikers near the rim of the huge bowl may chance to see the famous Brocken specter —their shadows silhouetted on the cloud bank below and ringed with rainbow colors. With such sights, it's no wonder that the 33-mile-long volcano figured in early Polynesian legend. Its name Hale a ka Lā, or House of the Sun, comes from the story of the demigod Maui, who roped the sun from the summit, forcing it to move more slowly and give the earth longer days.

Perhaps one of the world's steepest gradients for cars, the park road to the volcano's summit is a white-knuckle experience. Leaving the cane and pineapple fields near sea level, it switchbacks steeply up nearly 10,000 feet, reaching Haleakala's rocky peak after 38 miles. Along the upper reaches of the road, footpaths descend into the Haleakala wilderness area.

A contrast to the inner volcano's subalpine environment, the verdant rain forest of Kīpahulu Valley constitutes the park's other major attraction. This steep, wooded cleft, which runs down the southeast flank of the volcano to the sea, is drenched each year by 250 inches of rain. While the forests of the upper valley remain closed to protect rare indigenous species, visitors can drive down to where Kīpahulu meets the sea. Here, along the Palikea Stream, are sparkling pools, misting waterfalls—including 400-foot Waimoku Falls—and a 50-foot stand of introduced bamboo that creaks mysteriously in the breeze.

PARK DATA

STATE: Hawaii

ESTABLISHED: 1916

AREA: 28,655 acres (11,596 ha); on Maui

ELEVATION: Highest point Pu'u 'Ula'ula summit, 10,023 feet (3,055 m)

CLIMATE: Summers warm and dry; clear weather at volcano rim early morning and late afternoon; 250 in (635 cm) annual rainfall in Kīpahulu

NATURAL FEATURES: Haleakala currently dormant, but may not yet be extinct; Maui shifted by Pacific plate a short way from the volcanic hot spot that created in turn each Hawaiian island

CULTURAL FEATURES: In lower Kīpahulu Valley, remains of traditional Hawaiian taro patches, stone walls, temple sites

FLORA: 80 species of rare native plants endangered by aggresssive spread of imported exotics

FAUNA: Nene, a Hawaiian goose, and other endangered bird species protected in the park; native mammals—hoary bat and monk seal; introduced pigs, goats, mongooses, now feral, a threat to unique endemic species

Thriving where few plants survive, on the subalpine slopes of Haleakala volcano, the rare silversword (foreground) may live for two decades—yet blooms only once, then dies.

Hawaii Volcanoes

E arth in the making and remaking is the spectacle of Hawaii Volcanoes National Park. Among the world's most active volcanoes, 13,677-foot Mauna Loa and 4,078-foot Kilauea crown seafloor magma vents some 18,000 feet below the island of Hawaii. Mauna Loa, the largest mountain on earth, last erupted in 1984.

Kilauea's rocketing lava fountains still gouge new craters, and lava flows build up its slopes. Molten rivers roll over roads and older lava to meet the Pacific in great bursts of steam. Where the flow stops, new land is created.

The hiss of steam vents, the smell of sulphur, and the tremors of a jittery seismic zone are constant reminders of Kilauea's activity. So is the succession of plants—from algae and lichens to sword ferns and eventual rain forest—that have recolonized devastated areas.

Pahoehoe lava, hardening into smooth, ropy coils or billows, flows more frequently from Hawaii's volcanoes than rough-edged 'a'a lava. Seeing a similarity in black satin, introduced in the 19th century, Hawaiians called it pahoehoe as well.

STATE: Hawaii

ESTABLISHED: 1916

AREA: 229,177 acres (92,745 ha)

ELEVATION: From sea level to 13,677 ft (4,169 m)

CLIMATE: Lava fields very hot; sea level temperatures averaging from the upper 70s to the lower 80s °F (26° to 28°C), with little precipitation; Kilauea Caldera cooler, with frequent rainfall

NATURAL FEATURES: Mauna Loa, "long mountain," less than a million years old; taller than Mount Everest, when measured from base 18,000 ft (5,486 m) below sea level to 13,677-ft (4,169-m) summit; Thurston lava tube —a natural tunnel created when pahoehoe crust cooled while molten lava was still flowing inside

CULTURAL FEATURES: Ancient Hawaiian petroglyphs at Pu'u Loa; remains of 13th-century open-air temple, Waha'ula Heiau

FLORA: On Mauna Loa, kipuka—patches of older land isolated by lava flows —that preserve upland forests containing native Hawaiian plants such as koa and 'ohi'a trees, maile vines (protected here, but harvested elsewhere to make leis), and ferns

FAUNA: Birds including white-tailed tropic birds, Hawaiian honeycreepers; some 120 nene, the endangered Hawaiian goose

UNIQUE FEATURE: Mauna Loa, earth's most massive mountain—some 10,000 cu mi (41,682 cu km)

THE GENTLE VOLCANOES

HAWAII'S SHIELD volcanoes may be the only volcanoes on earth that offer a relatively safe and easily accessible ringside view of their eruptions.

Most volcanoes erupt violently—unleashing huge explosions, poisonous gases, rains of rock, and other terrors. Kilauea has erupted explosively only twice in recorded history. Much more often, lava bubbles quietly and slowly from volcanic vents. Though capable of burying homes, roads, and forests, the lava flows can generally be predicted.

What distinguishes Hawaii's gentler eruptions is the nature of the lava itself. High temperatures and a low, 50-percent silica content make Hawaiian lava extremely fluid. This allows gases to escape easily, rather than build up explosive pressure within the lava. The high fluidity produces a rapid rate of lava flow—miles in one day here as opposed to feet in other locations.

Lured by a pyrotechnical outburst, a geologist gathers lava spatter at Mauna Ulu, or "growing mountain." Beginning in 1969, five years of eruptions along Kilauea's east rift zone layered enough lava to raise this satellite shield 400 feet tall.

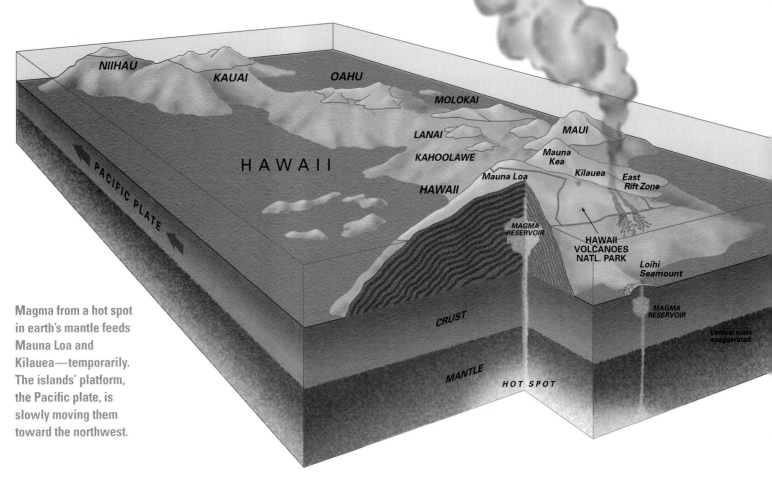

Magma from a hot spot in earth's mantle feeds Mauna Loa and Kilauea—temporarily. The islands' platform, the Pacific plate, is slowly moving them toward the northwest.

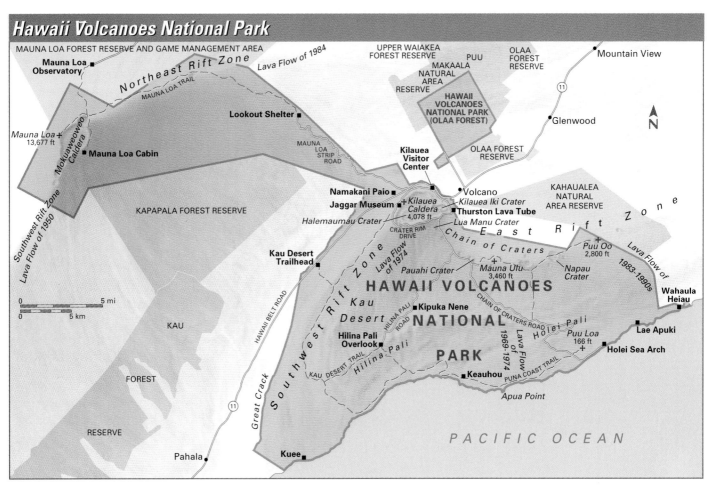

Hawaii Volcanoes National Park

Hot Springs

*I*n spring the scent of magnolia blossoms permeates the air in Hot Springs, Arkansas. Ghostly echoes of fashionable folk who once flocked Bathhouse Row to take the curative waters seem to mingle with steam billowing from springs that gush out of Hot Springs Mountain.

In 1832, to protect the popular thermal complex, President Andrew Jackson designated it a reserve. In 1921 this mix of small-town charm and natural beauty gained national park status. The grande dame of the old bathing houses, the Fordyce, now holds park headquarters and a museum. At the nearby Buckstaff, visitors still gather to "take the waters."

PARK DATA

STATE: Arkansas
ESTABLISHED: 1921
AREA: 5,549 acres (2,246 ha); smallest U.S. national park
NATURAL FEATURE: Hot Springs Mountain the source of 47 springs that gush 850,000 gal (3,217,600 l) a day
CULTURAL FEATURES: Turn-of-the century bathhouses, such as Spanish Renaissance-style Fordyce; DeSoto Rock honoring the reputed visit of explorer Hernando de Soto; stone quarries where Indians mined novaculite for spearpoints and arrowheads

Youngster tests steaming spring waters at a Hot Springs fountain. Visitors take away jugs filled with mineral-laden water.

Isle Royale

Named centuries ago in honor of a French king, it remains a royal isle for those who prize the wild sound and light of the north woods—the calls of loons and eagles and ospreys; the summer serenades of winter wrens and white-throated sparrows; the howl of wolves; the fiery shimmer of northern lights.

For decades scientists have studied the predator-prey interactions of wolves and moose here. Wolf numbers fell from 50 to 12 in the 1980s; disease may have been a factor. In the mid-1990s they seem to have stabilized at around 14 in three packs. With the decline in the wolf population, the number of moose has increased to some 2,400 today.

Native lake trout thrive in waters adjacent to the park. Popular with fishermen, the hardy trout escaped local ravages of the exotic sea lamprey.

Stretching for the high end, a bull moose munches on birch.

Ample fare includes aquatic plants in beaver ponds and lakes.

Joshua Tree

E erie forests of giant tree yuccas march across the high western half of Joshua Tree National Park in southern California. Their angular branches, tipped with spiny masses, rise as much as 40 feet into the desert sky. Legend says that Mormon pioneers saw in the shaggy limbs the beckoning arms of the Prophet Joshua. Growing only above elevations of about 3,000 feet, Joshua trees define the southern boundaries of the high Mojave Desert, which ranges in elevation from 3,000 to 5,000 feet. Bighorn sheep and nocturnal bobcats roam these highlands, and golden eagles soar overhead.

As part of the California Desert Protection Act, Joshua Tree, along with Death Valley, was upgraded from national monument to national park on October 31, 1994. In the process, both parks acquired new acreage. Joshua Tree is prized for its unique transition zone between two desert ecosystems: the high Mojave in its western half and the low Colorado in the east, part of the Sonoran Desert. Low desert hallmarks are ocotillos, ironwoods, and fuzzy-looking Bigelow—"jumping"—chollas, whose barbed spines constitute a booby trap for unwary hikers. Despite the heat and aridity, vast Pinto Basin in the east harbors a variety of wildlife, from roadrunners to tortoises, snakes, and small rodents.

A third ecosystem exists at some five oases in Joshua Tree, where stately fan palms shade moist green havens for plants and wildlife.

Rock piles of pinkish monzogranite boulders dot the upland desert, and mountains rim the park. Hidden Valley and other locations offer such a wealth of challenges for rock climbers that the park has become one of the most popular in the country for this sport.

PARK DATA

STATE: California
ESTABLISHED: 1994, as part of the California Desert Protection Act
AREA: 793,000 acres (320,916 ha)
CLIMATE: Average temperatures in 60s °F (16° to 21°C); sparse rainfall
NATURAL FEATURES: Park straddling division between high Mojave Desert—at elevations above 3,000 ft (910 m)—and low Colorado Desert, a subdivision of the Sonoran; igneous rock piles such as Jumbo Rocks formed underground; groundwater, seeping down joints, split and rounded the rock, which weathered further after surface soil eroded
FLORA: Ocotillos and brittlebushes on low hills and slopes; after spring rains in low desert, vivid bloom of annuals whose seeds lie dormant until moisture and warmth trigger growth

A young Joshua tree bristles with spines near weathered Jumbo Rocks. These relatives of low-growing yuccas usually reach 30 to 40 feet in height.

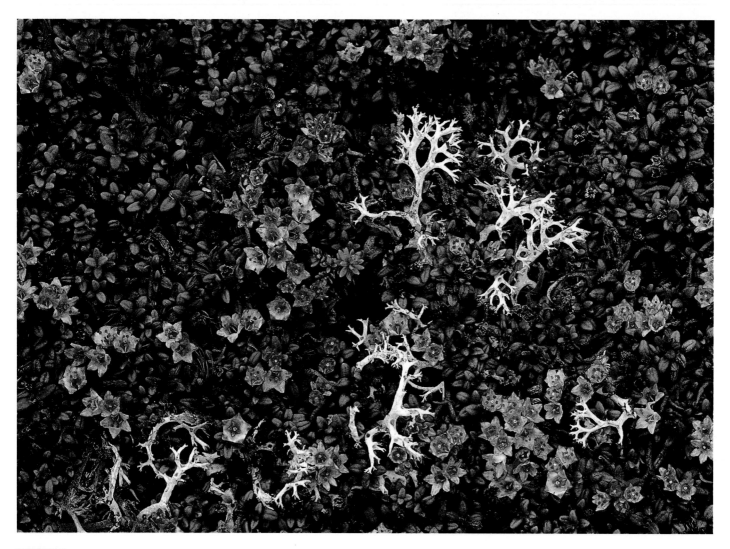

*K*atmai National Park and Preserve represents the epitome of North American wilderness. Located at the base of the Alaska Peninsula, this wild, sweeping land encompasses three distinct regions: In the west, treeless tundra drops to forests, then to island-studded lakes and white-water streams thick with salmon and trout. To the east towers a line of steaming volcanic peaks—part of the Aleutian Range—cloaked with ancient glaciers. Beyond the mountains lies a rugged shoreline, its bays cut by steep-sided fjords.

Most visitors experience only the western section of the park. Floatplanes bring them in summer to the main staging area at Brooks Camp. From here, some fly north to fishing lodges on Grosvenor or Nonvianuk Lakes. Others venture into wilderness country with backpack or kayak. But the park's most popular attraction involves its 1,500 or so Alaskan brown bears—the largest protected population of these animals in North America.

In July millions of sockeye salmon flood into Bristol Bay, west of Katmai. Some swarm upstream to Brooks River in the park, where the huge bears lie in wait for salmon leaping Brooks Falls. A

Summer on Katmai's spongy tundra brings tiny, vibrant blooms of alpine azalea (above) amid branching stalks of reindeer moss.

At Brooks Falls, the park's prime bear-viewing facility, three Alaskan brown bear cubs (opposite) watch intently as their mother fishes for salmon.

viewing platform allows spectators a ringside seat for this annual feast as the bears fatten up for next winter's hibernation.

The park's only road leads 23 miles from Brooks Camp to the Valley of Ten Thousand Smokes. Here, the Ukak River carves deep gorges into layers of volcanic ash deposited by the cataclysmic eruption of Novarupta on June 6, 1912—a blast ten times stronger than that of Mount St. Helens in 1980. The valley floor was riven by thousands of steaming fumaroles that have disappeared since. A 1916 expedition to the site, sponsored by the National Geographic Society, led to the original designation of Katmai as a protected area.

PARK DATA

STATE: Alaska
ESTABLISHED: 1980
AREA: 4,090,000 acres (1,655,165 ha)
HIGHEST POINT: Mount Denison, 7,606 ft (2,318 m)
NATURAL FEATURES: One of the most active volcanic areas in the world— 10 major eruptions in the last 7,000 years; 15 still active volcanoes within the park, part of the volcanic Ring of Fire that rims the Pacific
CULTURAL FEATURES: Three important archaeological sites dating back some 6,000 years; reconstructed semisubterranean house at Brooks Camp
FLORA: Green vegetation around Brooks Camp area built up since Novarupta eruption; Valley of Ten Thousand Smokes still virtually barren because of thick, sterile ash layer
FAUNA: Bears, moose, caribou, various small mammals; sea lions, sea otters, hair seals; beluga, killer, and gray whales in Shelikof Strait; 40 species of songbirds, tundra swans, ducks, loons, arctic terns, bald eagles, other raptors, many seabirds

Kenai Fjords

Finger of black rock, polished by glaciers, stretches into a park fjord. The landscape is a mountain range that is slowly sinking into the Gulf of Alaska.

*C*apped by an immense ice field and deeply carved by dozens of active glaciers, Alaska's Kenai Fjords National Park stretches over a spectacular coastal labyrinth of steep-sided bays, coves, inlets, and lagoons. These narrow bodies of water are flooded valleys of the Kenai Mountains, which are gradually sinking into the Gulf of Alaska. The jade green fjords, with their high walls of jagged, grayish rock, were once spacious, U-shaped valleys hollowed out by glaciers. The offshore islands were summits, and the half-moon bays glacial cirques. All were dragged under the waves by a tectonic plate collision off the southern coast of Alaska that continues to this day. In this sunken world, seals and porpoises cavort where eagles may have flown.

Though in the process of submerging, much of the range still reaches some 5,000 feet above sea level. Winter storms drop 35 to 65 feet of snow along its crest, replenishing the region's vast Harding Icefield, a 300-square-mile wilderness of ice and snow that buries all but the highest peaks. More than 30 large glaciers and many smaller ones flow down from the ice field in all directions. A few reach the sea as tidewater glaciers, calving icebergs into the fjords with a tremendous boom.

In the narrow life zone between sea and ice grow mature rain forests of hemlock and spruce. Mountain goats amble along the cliffs. Bears, moose, and wolverines roam the headlands. Humpback, gray, and minke whales surface in the fjords. Sea otters dive for crabs, and harbor seals and Steller sea lions keep a sharp lookout for pods of killer whales. More than 65 species of seabirds nest along the coast, including puffins, rhinoceros auklets, and fork-tailed storm-petrels.

PARK DATA

STATE: Alaska
ESTABLISHED: 1980
AREA: 670,000 acres (271,140 ha), with 600 mi (966 km) of coastline; remote areas reachable only by boat or plane; smallest national park in Alaska
CLIMATE: Summers cool and rainy with temperatures from 50° to 65°F (10° to 15°C)
NATURAL FEATURES: Mile-high (1.6 km) Kenai Mountains cloaked by 300-sq-mi (777-sq-km) Harding Icefield; from here ice flows down to form 8 tidewater glaciers, such as those in Aialik Bay, which calve into the sea; Palisade Peak waterfall 900 ft (274 m) tall
CULTURAL FEATURES: Native American archaeological sites and historic gold mine locations
FLORA: On land exposed by glacial retreat, plant succession, from pioneer species to mature forests
FAUNA: Moose, black bears; harbor seals, sea lions, whales; puffins, bald eagles

Kobuk Valley

PARK DATA

STATE: Alaska
ESTABLISHED: 1980
AREA: 1,750,000 acres (708,200 ha); one of least visited U.S. national parks
CULTURAL FEATURE: Onion Portage, a gold mine of Arctic archaeology, with strata 10,000 years old
FLORA: Boreal forest, taiga, tundra vegetation
FAUNA: Moose, caribou, grizzly and black bears, wolves; salmon, char

No roads, no campgrounds, and— around the summer solstice—no night. Fly in, float in, walk in. After spring ice-out, the Kobuk River makes a fine scenic highway; most boaters put in at Kiana or Ambler. Kobuk's 33,000-year-old sand dunes—45 miles north of the Arctic Circle—invite a detour and a climb to hundred-foot-high crests. In late summer and fall, thousands of migrating caribou swim the Kobuk at Onion Portage, where Inuit hunters await them. Here their forebears built hearths and worked stone weapons as they stalked caribou and other game 10,000 years ago.

Great Kobuk Sand Dunes, formed by wind-driven debris from melting Ice Age glaciers, gain an inch a year on encircling spruces.

Lake Clark

Rugged, mountainous, and incredibly diverse, Lake Clark National Park and Preserve embraces nearly every vista and landscape Alaska calls to mind. Active volcanoes rise 10,000 feet from the icy waters of Cook Inlet, where beluga whales and seals break the surface. Immense glaciers drape the jagged Chigmit Mountains, which tower over forests of Sitka spruce, open tundra, and sparkling lakes. Wild rivers rage across the land toward Bristol Bay, the world's largest sockeye salmon fishery. Large bears roam the park, along with restless herds of caribou and white Dall sheep.

PARK DATA

STATE: Alaska
ESTABLISHED: 1980
AREA: 4,044,000 acres (1,636,550 ha)
NATURAL FEATURES: 2 Pacific Rim volcanoes
FLORA: Sitka and white spruces, birches; Arctic tundra sedges, wildflowers
FAUNA: Bears, caribou, moose, wolves, Dall sheep; puffins, cormorants, kittiwakes; salmon, trout

Early morning mists hang over spruce-girt Lake Clark at the base of Alaska's Chigmit Mountains.

Lassen Volcanic

ollowing 150 preliminary blasts, the May 1915 eruption of California's Lassen Peak, the world's largest plug dome volcano, hurtled a mushroom cloud of debris some seven miles skyward. It left a tortured, desolate landscape of lava pinnacles and jagged craters. Life slowly has reasserted itself, and now hot springs, boiling mud pots, and steaming sulphur vents mingle with meadows and evergreens.

PARK DATA

STATE: California
ESTABLISHED: 1916
AREA: 106,366 acres (43,045 ha), with a scenic road looping around three sides of Lassen Peak
FLORA: Spring meadows teeming with wildflowers
FAUNA: Deer, bears, mountain lions; 200 bird species in area

Heat-tolerant bacteria created sulphuric acids that carved Bumpass Hell, a volcanic rockscape of hot springs, steam vents, and other geothermal features.

Mammoth Cave

H idden beneath the wooded hills of south-central Kentucky, Mammoth Cave is a vast, rambling network of interconnected passageways, enormous caverns, and giant vertical shafts hollowed out of limestone bedrock by subterranean rivers. Dark, damp, cool, alien yet strangely inviting, this sinuous, multi-level labyrinth extends for about 360 miles and ranks as the longest known cave system in the world.

For thousands of years, people have descended into Mammoth's dank chambers to admire its cascades of flowstone, delicate gypsum crystals, bizarre cave animals, and underground rivers and lakes. Ancient artifacts such as woven sandals and mummified human remains indicate that people have been present here for at least 4,000 years. But this park offers more than a window on the netherworld.

Its diverse woodlands include a remnant of Kentucky's old-growth forest of immense white and black oaks, tulip poplars, and sugar maples. Pileated woodpeckers hammer the tree trunks, and white-tailed deer pause among the flowering dogwoods. Green River—broad, lazy, and rich in aquatic life—bends through the hills.

The park lies in the midst of one of the world's greatest cave regions, a classic karst landscape of sinkholes and deep gullies, springs, underground rivers, and hundreds of gaping cave entrances.

Mammoth Cave itself began forming millions of years ago, as ancient subterranean rivers wore away at cracks between rock layers and carved out the cave's long, horizontal passages. Flowing ever downward, the waters created five interconnected levels. Emerald streams still flood the cave's

PARK DATA

STATE: Kentucky
ESTABLISHED: 1941; named a UNESCO world heritage site in 1981 and designated an international biosphere reserve in 1990
AREA: 52,830 acres (21,380 ha)
CULTURAL FEATURES: Ruins of a saltpeter mine run by slaves during the War of 1812; stone huts of a tuberculosis hospital abandoned in 1843
FLORA: Mountain laurels, white dogwoods; birdfoot violets, butterfly weeds; wetland flora; open barrens of prairie wildflowers and grasses
FAUNA: Small mammals such as squirrels, chipmunks, raccoons, skunks; reptiles including poisonous copperheads and timber rattlesnakes; woodpeckers, kestrels, wild turkeys; catfish, bass, bluegills, trout, 50 freshwater mussel species
ENDANGERED SPECIES: Kentucky cave shrimp; Indiana bat, gray bat

Immense, curving walls and arched ceilings of brown and gray limestone typify much of the subterranean landscape found in Mammoth Cave National Park.

deepest passages and continue to carve channels through the rock 360 feet below the earth's surface.

Because most of the water flowed horizontally, Mammoth contains few travertine formations, such as stalactites and stalagmites, which build up when water carrying dissolved limestone flows vertically. Extravagant exceptions to the rule are found in the cave's Frozen Niagara section, where a 75-foot drip-castle column of orange-white flowstone seems to ooze from the roof of the cavern.

More than 200 species of animals use the cave to some degree, but perhaps the most fascinating are the dozens of permanent cave dwellers, such as eyeless fish, that have adapted to a world with no light and a scant food supply. Part-time residents include 12 species of bats, two of which are listed as endangered.

LIVING IN THE DARK

THE DIVERSITY OF cave animals at Mammoth rivals that of any caveland region in the world. They divide into three broad classes.

Troglobites live exclusively within the cave. Troglophiles can spend their entire lives in the cave or on the surface. Trogloxenes commute, passing their days inside the cave but foraging on the surface at night.

Twelve of Mammoth's 42 species of troglobites are found nowhere else. Trapped between glacial advances 10,000 years ago, troglobite species such as the eyeless cave fish and eyeless crayfish (both at right) genetically phased out the development of eyes and coloration because they have use for neither. Instead, they developed other sensory organs, such as antennae, to detect predators and prey. Troglobites also have longer life spans and lower metabolic rates than their surface counterparts—adaptations to the cave's scarce, intermittent food supply.

A type of grasshopper, the graceful cave cricket (top right) is a trogloxene that uses its long antennae to navigate the cave's dark passages and hunt for food. Once on the surface, eyes help it to locate food and avoid predators, such as salamanders.

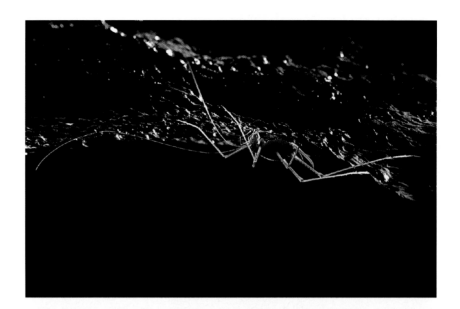

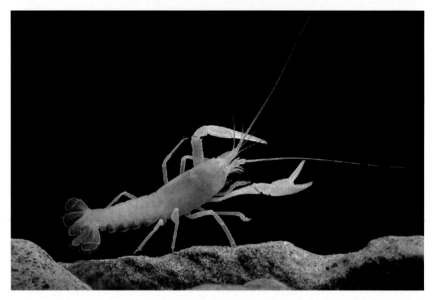

Visitors squirm through narrow passages (above) on Mammoth's Wild Cave Tour. For those who would rather not muck their way through Mammoth on hands and knees, the park offers several other, less arduous tours of the cave's interior, including one route suitable for wheelchairs. In the 1930s, visitors could drift in a flatboat (right) on subterranean Echo River, one of 20 known rivers in the cave complex.

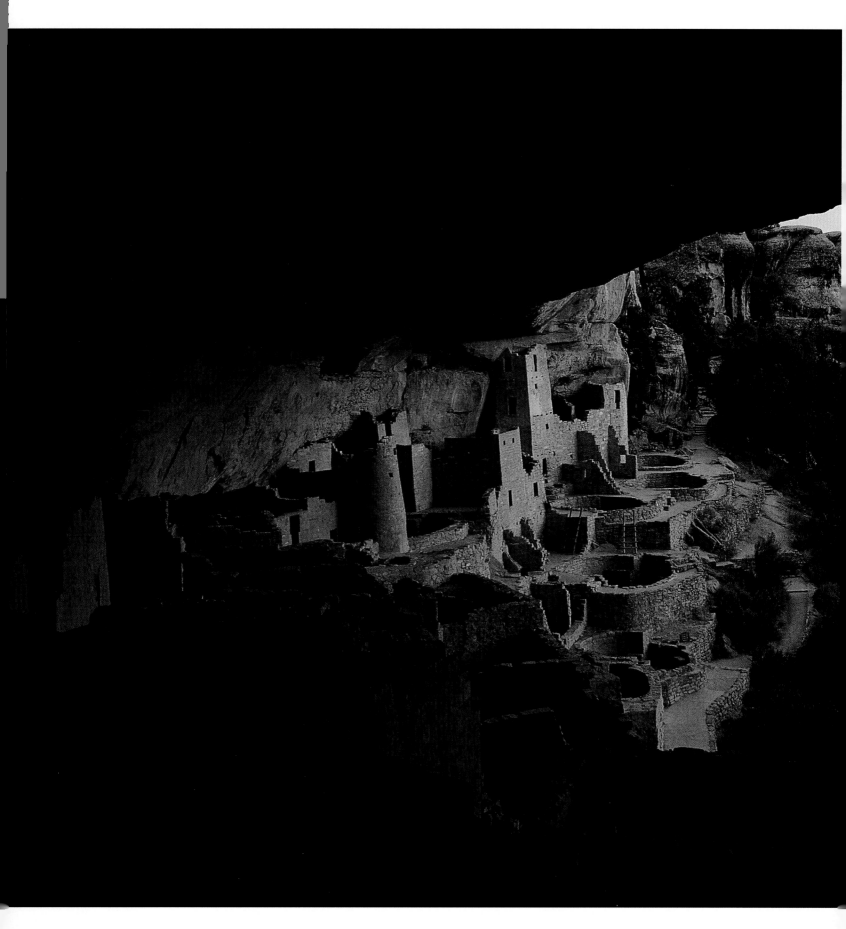

Mesa Verde

*I*ts Spanish name is Mesa Verde—the great "green table" that looms at first sight like an earthen citadel, sharp-edged against the big southwestern Colorado sky. It was the home of part of a group of prehistoric Indians whom archaeologists call the Anasazi, from a Navajo word meaning "ancient ones."

The Mesa Verde branch of this widespread southwestern people inhabited the high Colorado Plateau of southwestern Colorado and southeastern Utah from about A.D. 550 to 1300. Here the group flourished, dry farming the mesa tops and building stone dams and reservoirs to conserve rainwater. Then, during the late 13th century, the Anasazi abandoned the plateau, perhaps due to drought, depleted resources, and overpopulation. Archaeologists speculate that they resettled among the upper Rio Grande Anasazi, where their descendants, the Pueblo Indians, still reside.

Sheer sandstone canyons cut this vast mesa (measuring some 15 miles long by 18 miles wide and rising 2,000 feet above the surrounding plateau) into narrow tablelands, scattered with piñon and juniper trees. Atop these cliffs or ingeniously wedged into cliffside alcoves are the ruins of prehistoric Anasazi structures, a fascinating record of their long presence here. More than 4,000 sites, ranging from early pit houses to multistoried cliff pueblos, farms, ceremonial shrines, and petroglyphs, illustrate the Anasazi's cultural evolution from nomadic hunter-gatherers to architects of one of the greatest ancient civilizations north of Mexico. Nothing on the scale of their apartmentlike dwellings appeared in the United States until the late 1800s—some 700 years later.

PARK DATA

STATE: Colorado
ESTABLISHED: 1906
AREA: 52,074 acres (21,074 ha)
HIGHEST POINT: Park Point, 8,571 ft (2,612 m), affording views of whole Four Corners region
NATURAL FEATURE: Alcoves in which cliff houses were built formed by water seeping into soft, porous sandstone, splitting away sections of rock
CULTURAL FEATURES: Human remains and traces of mesa-top crops of corn, beans, and squash found among the ruins
FLORA: Douglas firs, ponderosa pines on northern elevations; junipers, piñons on mesa tops; cottonwoods, grasses in canyons; wildflowers in bloom from spring to fall
FAUNA: Bighorn sheep, mule deer, coyotes; rabbits and other small mammals; more than 160 species of birds, including wild turkey

Exemplar of ancient urban planning, Mesa Verde's Cliff Palace shelters under the sandstone brow of an alcove on Chapin Mesa. North America's largest cliff dwelling, Cliff Palace once held 23 kivas and 217 rooms.

The first reports of ruins at Mesa Verde came in 1874. Then, in 1888, while searching the mesa for stray cattle wintering on Indian lands, a couple of local cowboys named Richard Wetherill and Charles Mason stumbled on two spectacular cliff ruins: Cliff Palace, the park's largest ruin, and Spruce Tree House, the third largest. News of the finds spread fast, prompting an increase in visits to the ruins. While the Wetherill family kept records of their amateur excavations, countless untrained investigators ravaged the sites and carried off artifacts.

In response to protests by local residents, Mesa Verde National Park was established in 1906 during President Theodore Roosevelt's term of office. Its chief purpose was to act as an archaeological bank safeguarding the ruins, and it remains the only national park dedicated entirely to the preservation of man-made works. The park contains one of the most complete existing records of Anasazi culture, with more and better preserved cliff dwellings than anywhere else in the Southwest.

While the building ruins are the main draw, they represent only the last chapter in the local Anasazi's long story. The park's Chapin Mesa Museum presents the whole picture, including displays of exceptional basketry and weaving—hallmarks of the earlier Anasazi.

The park contains some 40 excavated pueblos and cliff dwelling sites, chief among them Cliff Palace, Spruce Tree House, and Balcony House. Park Point offers visitors a 360-degree panorama from the mesa top. And at Petroglyph Point, a 12-foot-wide panel of rock bears one of Mesa Verde's largest inscriptions made by the ancient Anasazi.

LEGACY OF THE ANASAZI

THE ANASAZI developed a complex Stone Age culture, accumulating a remarkable body of traditions and skills—in building, art, farming, and hunting—which they passed down for generations. Their influence persists today in the modern Pueblo cultures.

When they abandoned the plateau in the late 13th century, they left behind a rich material legacy, from tiny artifacts to cliff cities—archaeological clues to their daily and religious life. The Anasazi had a keen aesthetic sense. The objects they created —whether for work, ornament, or ritual—showed fine design and craftsmanship. These deer-bone scrapers (below), five inches long and handsomely inlaid with turquoise and jet, show superior quality, suggesting the owner was a person of rank. Ceremonial objects, such as a stylized, 25-inch wooden altar effigy (left) made around A.D. 1350, resemble images still used in Pueblo religion today.

Pottery, the Anasazi's chief artistic legacy—made by the women and still fashioned by Pueblo Indians—varied regionally in style. A black-and-white design—a typical Anasazi combination—adorns this Tularosa jar (opposite, below). Macaw symbols, on Kayenta Anasazi ware (below), reflect the importance of these birds and their bright plumage in trade and ritual.

The circular courtyard at Spruce Tree House (right) was one of eight spiritual and social centers of Anasazi life here. Rituals took place underground in a ceremonial chamber, or kiva, accessible by ladder through a small opening in the roof, which also served as the courtyard floor.

Mesa Verde National Park

Mount Rainier

Mount Rainier, an immense volcanic dome gleaming with ice and snow, bursts from a sea of evergreen forests in western Washington. Its 14,410-foot summit, the highest of the Cascades, rises an astonishing 8,000 feet above its surroundings and shares the sky with nothing but the clouds, the moon, and the stars. It forms the central feature of the nation's fifth oldest national park and caps a spectacular landscape of mossy old-growth forests, deeply glaciated valleys, knife-edged ridges, waterfalls, river gorges, ice caves, and radiant wildflower meadows.

One of the world's most massive volcanoes, Mount Rainier stands along the Ring of Fire—the line of volcanic mountain ranges that nearly encircles the Pacific Ocean. It is a composite cone made up of fragmented rock, lava, and ash that began spewing from a vent in the earth's crust about one million years ago. It has been 2,000 years since its last major eruption, but it spurted pumice and ash as recently as 1894. Dormant, but not extinct, it still releases enough heat to cut a maze of steam tunnels and caves into the ice pack occupying its summit craters.

Twenty-six named glaciers radiate from Rainier's summit like the spokes of a wheel, covering a 35-square-mile area and forming the largest glacial system found on any single peak in the contiguous United States. The glaciers are responsible for massive avalanches

PARK DATA

STATE: Washington
ESTABLISHED: 1899
AREA: 235,612 acres (95,349 ha); 96 percent designated wilderness
NATURAL FEATURES: Near-Himalayan climbing conditions; training site for first American team to climb Everest
CULTURAL FEATURES: Longmire, site of Mineral Spring Resort, now a museum; Paradise Inn, built in 1917
FLORA: Lowland forests containing 35 species of deep-shade flowers and 150 species of fungi; a variety of spruces, firs, cedars, hemlocks, pines
FAUNA: Mountain goats, elk, black bears, black-tailed and mule deer, mountain lions, bobcats, coyotes; foxes, beavers, other small mammals; hawks, owls, woodpeckers

Park visitors of the 1920s explore an ice cave inside Paradise Glacier. These caves have collapsed in recent years.

Snowy ramparts of Rainier shine over a subalpine meadow of lupines blooming in the park's Paradise area.

Black-tailed deer, one of two deer subspecies at Mount Rainier, roam below tree line. They feed on meadow plants, ferns, berry bushes, and shrubs such as vine maple.

of ice, snow, and rock as well as devastating mudflows.

Much to the chagrin of visitors intent on actually catching sight of Rainier, clouds often hide the peak, which wrings amazing amounts of rain and snow from wet air masses flowing inland from the Pacific. An average of 51 feet of snow falls every winter on subalpine meadows surrounding the park's Paradise area, which holds the world's record for annual snowfall: 93.5 feet in 1971-72.

Mount Rainier's slopes rise through four major vegetational zones. Lower elevations include a rare inland example of a temperate rain forest—Sitka spruce on Carbon River, where the rainfall is heaviest—and lavish lowland forests of cedar, hemlock, and Douglas fir trees 500 to 1,000 years old. Higher up spread silver fir forests, then the open meadows and clustered trees of the subalpine level, and, finally, a vast realm of snow and ice arching 8,000 feet above tree line.

North Cascades

Set high in the wild Cascade Range, northwest Washington's North Cascades National Park sprawls over a glorious tangle of dark, toothy peaks and knife-edged crests that rise abruptly from ancient rain forests. Countless waterfalls spill from the cliffs, and more than 300 glaciers gnaw away at the park's mountains. Fed by heavy snowstorms that sweep in from the Pacific, they represent more than half of all the glaciers in the contiguous United States.

The spine of the Cascades forms a startling climatic divide that splits the park into two weather zones. The west side catches most of the moisture and supports misty, old-growth forests of cedar, hemlock, and Douglas fir. On the much drier east side grow open forests of drought-resistant ponderosa pine, sagebrush, and grass.

More than 1,700 species of vascular plants live in this diverse climate. So do wolves, mountain goats, cougars, bears, deer, bald eagles, and many smaller creatures.

PARK DATA

STATE: Washington

ESTABLISHED: 1968, including two adjoining national recreation areas: Lake Chelan and Ross Lake

AREA: 684,237 acres (276,901 ha) in park and recreation areas; 93 percent wilderness

CLIMATE: Considerable variation in precipitation— 110 in (279 cm) on west side, 35 in (89 cm) on east side; heavy snowfall

NATURAL FEATURE: Lake Chelan, 1,529 ft (466 m) deep, located in a glacial trough, its bed 426 ft (130 m) below sea level

CULTURAL FEATURE: Stehekin, a remote community on Lake Chelan

Climbers approach the 8,236-foot summit of Mount Challenger.

Heavy snowfall feeds the many glaciers that drape the park's peaks.

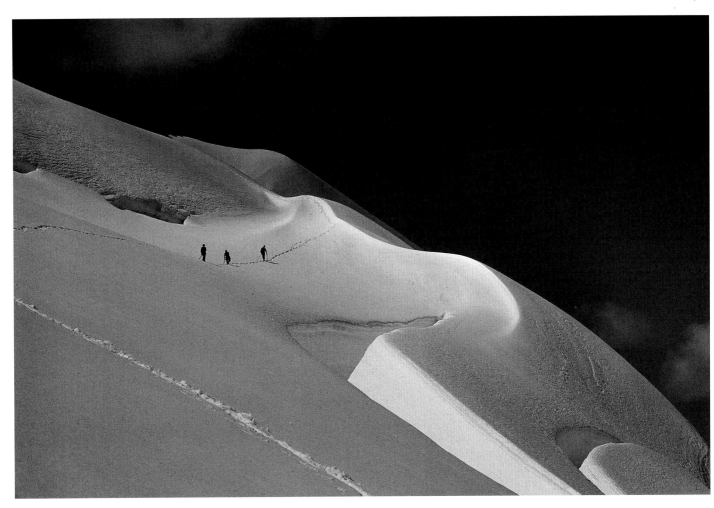

Olympic

Visible for more than a hundred miles, the snowcapped peaks of Washington's Olympic Peninsula rise nearly 8,000 feet from the crashing surf of the Pacific Ocean. Both the mountains' wilderness core and a long strip of unspoiled coastline lie within Olympic National Park, an awesome preserve of stunning diversity.

Here, misty rain forests thick with mosses and ferns sprawl a few thousand vertical feet beneath long tongues of glacial ice and treeless crags. River canyons bite into the mountains, funneling cascades of fresh water to the sea. Miles of cliffs, log-strewn beaches, and detached columns of rock called sea stacks harbor varied marine life.

Sustained by more than 12 feet of precipitation annually, Olympic's lush, temperate rain forest contains one of the world's largest areas of living, standing biomass.

During the Ice Age, glaciers a mile thick isolated the Olympic Peninsula by carving out the Strait of Juan de Fuca, Puget Sound, and Hood Canal. That isolation spurred the evolution of 16 unique species of plants and animals. It also seems to have prevented 11 mammal species—including grizzly bears and mountain sheep found in the nearby Cascades and Rockies—from establishing themselves here.

The park's moist western side encompasses the greatest remaining true wilderness forest in the contiguous United States. It extends from the fog-shrouded coast to the tree line and comprises four major types: lowland, montane, subalpine, and—most important—Olympic's temperate rain forest. This last is thought to be one of the finest in the world. Intimate and tranquil, it is a spongy realm where chartreuse light filters through the emerald fuzz of moss-laden branches, and massive trunks of Sitka spruce, hemlock, red cedar, and bigleaf maple tower over a verdant crush of sorrel, vine maple, trillium, huckleberry, and licorice fern.

STATE: Washington

ESTABLISHED: 1938, enlarged 1953; both a UNESCO world heritage site and an international biosphere reserve

AREA: 922,000 acres (373,120 ha)

CLIMATE: Wettest climate in the lower 48 states

NATURAL FEATURES: 60 glaciers, 13 rivers, waterfalls, hot springs; the westernmost point in the contiguous United States

FLORA: World's largest Alaska cedar, western hemlock, and Douglas fir; fungi, mosses, lichens, ferns

FAUNA: Roosevelt elk, black-tailed deer, black bears, mountain lions; bald eagles, many seabirds

UNIQUE FEATURES: Endemic species, including Olympic chipmunk and marmot; Beardslee and Crescenti trout; Flett's violet, Piper's bellflower

AN IMMENSE RAIN TRAP

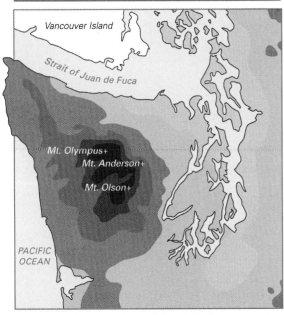

Vancouver Island

Strait of Juan de Fuca

Mt. Olympus+
Mt. Anderson+

Mt. Olson+

PACIFIC
OCEAN

Average Annual Precipitation

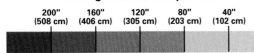

| 200" (508 cm) | 160" (406 cm) | 120" (305 cm) | 80" (203 cm) | 40" (102 cm) |

DAMP AIR FLOWING inland surges against the western slopes of the Olympic Mountains, then rises to cooler elevations where moisture condenses into rain or snow. The range traps an average of 140 inches for its verdant western rain forests and 200 inches for its glaciers. It also casts a rain shadow to the northeast that produces relative dryness.

ROOSEVELT ELK PRESERVE

A PAIR OF ROOSEVELT ELK splash for the cover of the tree line. Olympic was almost named Elk National Park because it provides a home for the largest unmanaged herd of Roosevelt elk in the contiguous United States.

Larger and more skittish around humans than its Rocky Mountain cousin, the Roosevelt elk takes its name from President Theodore Roosevelt, who set aside the Olympic area as a national monument in 1909 mainly to protect these animals. Their numbers now remain stable at several thousand, the chief cause of death being the harsh winters.

Elk cows and young move in herds of 15 to 100 animals and are quite common in the rain forest valleys on the western side of the peninsula. Some groups remain in the lower forests all year, while others migrate from the high meadows in summer to the lowland forests in winter.

During the autumn rut, bulls challenge one another and lure cows into harems with a distinctive bugling sound—an eerie, soaring squeal followed by a series of hoarse grunts. They also raid competitors' harems, feigning charges and sparring with clattering antlers.

COASTAL COMMUNITIES

A CLUMP OF sea stars waits out low tide on Olympic's 57-mile strip of coastal wilderness, where sea level fluctuates at least six feet daily. Low tide exposes four horizontal life zones: a spray zone and upper, middle, and lower intertidal zones.

Hammered by the surf and baked by sunshine, the intertidal zones teem with an astounding concentration of plants and animals. Under the glassy surface of a tide pool, as many as 4,000 organisms representing 20 different species may live within a single square foot. Among these may be found crabs, tiny fish, gooseneck barnacles, limpets, sea urchins, snails, and giant green sea anemones, which can live for hundreds of years.

Sea stars comb the rocks, devouring mussels —and thereby allowing room for 25 other species of organisms that the mussels tend to crowd out.

Several kinds of whales spout offshore, including gray, blue, humpback, and sperm. Sea lions and seals cavort in the waves and sun themselves on rock ledges. River otters, mink, and raccoons raid the beaches for sea urchins, crabs, and other shellfish.

Offshore islands are sanctuaries for seabirds such as rhinoceros auklets, pigeon guillemots, and pelagic cormorants.

Olympic National Park

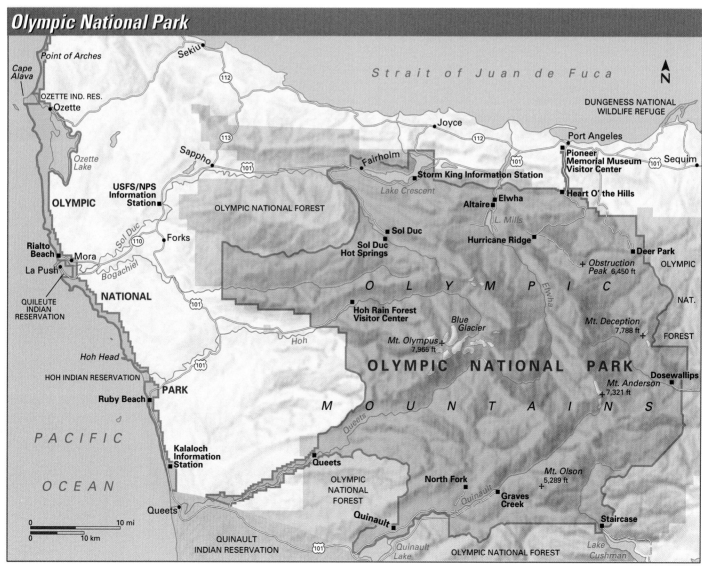

Petrified Forest

Even Jules Marcou, the first professional geologist to visit the Petrified Forest region in northern Arizona in 1853, couldn't resist collecting chunks of fossil trees. He alighted repeatedly, he reported, to "break off a piece, now of crimson, now of golden yellow, and then another, glorious in many rainbow dyes."

First noticed in 1851 by U.S. Army officers passing by, the region's colorful array of petrified wood was a tempting treasure. Collectors carted off the vivid rocks by the ton. To stop such piecemeal dismantling of this remarkable heritage, the area—then called Chalcedony Park—was declared a national monument in 1906. In 1962 it became Petrified Forest National Park.

The hourglass-shaped park set in the northern Arizona desert divides into two sections connected by a scenic drive. The northern part, largely wilderness, encompasses portions of the Painted Desert. The southern half embraces some of the world's greatest known concentrations of petrified wood. Nature paints from a vivid palette here in areas that justify their evocative names: Jasper Forest, Agate Bridge, Crystal Forest. Constantly changing clouds enhance the brilliant kaleidoscope as they cast patterns of light and shadow on the desertscape.

It is hard to picture this sere scene as a tropical floodplain of the late Triassic period 225 million years ago. In marshlike terrain thrived giant, flowerless plants and some of the earliest dinosaurs. By a fluke of nature, floods washed whole trees and foliage downstream and covered them with silt and mud, cutting off oxygen and retarding decay. Waterborne silica replaced organic matter. In some logs the actual cell structure remains. In others crystals replaced the entire organism.

Besides opening a window on ancient plant life here, these rock fossils aid in paleontological studies of early animals. For instance, scientists who discovered in 1984 the bones of a small, ancestral dinosaur could also reconstruct the world in which it lived.

Petrified logs sprawl across Blue Mesa like columns fallen from an ancient temple.

Polished slab of a petrified log reveals jewel-like hues. Yellows and reds indicate traces of iron. Early U.S. Army surveyors marveled at the "Painted Desert and its trees turned to stone." Some fossil logs measure a hundred feet in length.

STATE: Arizona
ESTABLISHED: 1962
AREA: 93,533 acres (37,851 ha)
NATURAL FEATURE: Probably the world's largest concentration of colorful petrified logs; persistent problem with visitors removing pieces of fossilized wood from the park, even though examples from outside park boundaries are available for sale
CULTURAL FEATURES: Puerco Pueblo—Indian village dating to before A.D. 1400; Agate House —8-room pueblo with walls built of petrified wood; Indian petroglyphs on sandstone block called Newspaper Rock
FLORA: Desert and grassland shrubs, cactuses, yuccas, wildflowers
FAUNA: Pronghorn, bobcats, coyotes, badgers, prairie dogs, jackrabbits

Redwood

Bathed in mist, fog, and rain, California's rugged northern coast provides an ideal climate for the lush, primeval forests of redwood trees that thrive in Redwood National Park. These ancient trees, with their massive, fluted trunks, are the tallest living things on earth. They rise 300 feet and more from a jungle-like understory of moss, ferns, berry bushes, and rhododendrons. Protected by thick bark from fire and insects, some live for as long as 2,000 years.

When logging began in 1851, roughly two million acres of redwood forest blanketed the Pacific Coast.

Today, some 95,000 acres of old-growth forest remain. Redwood, which embraces three state parks, sets aside about 40 percent of what survives.

More than a forest preserve, the park also encompasses a fascinating coastal zone where heavy surf pounds beaches, cliffs, sea stacks, and tide pools. Whales surface offshore. Seals and sea lions comb the breakers for fish and other food. Inland, prairie grasses and wildflowers grow in open areas kept free of trees by fire and grazing elk. At the park's northern end, otters hunt for fish in the Smith River, California's last major undammed river.

This giant redwood, 18 feet in diameter, was felled south of today's park in 1933. Loggers cleared 85 percent of coast redwood forests during the century prior to 1965. Then the state of California and the Save-the-Redwoods League bought up hundreds of groves and turned them into state parks, three of which now lie within the national park's borders.

PARK DATA

STATE: California

ESTABLISHED: 1968, expanded in 1978

AREA: 110,232 acres (44,609 ha), including three state parks and 36,000 acres (14,569 ha) of clear-cut terrain being reclaimed

ELEVATION: Sea level to 3,117 ft (950 m)

CLIMATE: Similar to mild, moist climate that prevailed in the Age of Dinosaurs, when redwood species grew over much of North America

NATURAL FEATURES: Coastal landscape of cliffs, bluffs, and beaches

FLORA: World's 3 tallest trees in Tall Trees Grove; tallest standing more than 367 ft (112 m) high, with trunk base 14 ft (4 m) in diameter; weight of park trees up to 500 t (454 mt), bark up to 12 in (30 cm) thick, most trees 500 to 700 years old

FAUNA: Elk, black-tailed deer, mountain lions, bobcats, coyotes, black bears; gray and killer whales; seals, porpoises, sea lions; more than 370 species of birds, mostly seabirds; sea stars, sea anemones, mussels, mole crabs

Sunshine slants through mists clinging to the canopy of a redwood forest. These trees take 400 years to mature.

Rocky Mountain

Lily pads dot the smooth surface of Nymph Lake on the park's most pop- ular hiking trail. Above the trees juts Hallet Peak's tilted summit.

*F*amous for its high, broad-backed peaks, soaring walls of bare rock, and dazzling expanse of alpine tundra, Rocky Mountain National Park straddles the Continental Divide some 60 miles northwest of Denver. Established in 1915, it encompasses a magnificent section of the glaciated Front Range, boasts 78 peaks over 12,000 feet, and cradles the headwaters of the Colorado River.

Breezy, savanna-like meadows of prairie grass and ponderosa pine sprawl over the park's eastern foothills, attracting elk, mule deer, coyotes, muskrats, hawks, and owls. Higher up, greater levels of moisture support thick evergreen forests. But starting at roughly 11,000 feet, the climate becomes so brutal—so cold, so dry, so flogged by the wind—that it resembles the Arctic winter. Trees grow as dwarfs, then not at all.

Roughly a third of the park lies in this treeless realm. It is a vast, gently rolling landscape of tiny wildflowers and heroic vistas of serried peaks. No other national park embraces a tundra zone so easily accessible. Trail Ridge Road, the nation's highest paved highway, crosses 11 miles of Rocky Mountain tundra at about 12,000 feet.

PARK DATA

STATE: Colorado
ESTABLISHED: 1915
AREA: 265,727 acres (107,536 ha)
HIGHEST POINT: Longs Peak, 14,255 ft (4,345 m)
FLORA: Ponderosa pines; Engelmann spruces and firs at elevations above 9,000 ft (2,743 m); tundra wildflowers adapted to the harsh environment
FAUNA: Bighorn sheep, moose, and other large mammals; muskrats, marmots, and many other rodents; tassel-eared Abert squirrels in ponderosa pine forests; birds including golden eagles, hawks, and hummingbirds

Saguaro

Majestic sentinels of the far Southwest, saguaros reach their northeastern limit in this newly created national park in Arizona. Largest native cactuses in the United States, these appealing giants grow only in the Sonoran Desert, which runs from northwestern Mexico into central Arizona and southeastern California.

A saguaro's shallow, widespread root system gathers water so efficiently that it can soak up some 200 gallons during a single, rare rainfall—enough to keep it going for a year. It stores water in spongy tissues beneath its tough, waxy skin, whose pleated surface expands and contracts at need like an accordion. Its life span may exceed 150 years.

The park divides into two districts. In the western one, the Tucson Mountains form a backdrop to vistas of dense saguaro forests and lowland cactus desert. In the eastern district, Cactus Forest Drive winds through an aging saguaro forest at the base of the towering Rincon Mountains. Six plant communities, ranging from lowland desert scrub to upland coniferous forest, succeed each other up the mountainside.

The park legislation of 1994 provides not only for the protection of the saguaros from encroaching development but also for the preservation of these diverse vertical life zones.

PARK DATA

STATE: Arizona
ESTABLISHED: 1994; a former national monument
AREA: 91,327 acres (36,959 ha) in two districts on either side of Tucson
HIGHEST POINT: Mica Mountain, 8,666 ft (2,641 m), in Rincon district
CLIMATE: Summer midday temperatures above 100°F (38°C); annual rainfall less than 12 in (30 cm)
FLORA: More than 600 plant species
FAUNA: Javelinas and other small mammals; Gila monsters, desert tortoises, snakes, lizards; some 200 bird species

A saguaro rears its branches above spiky brush and yellow poppies. Its first limbs sprouted as spiny balls at some 75 years of age.

Sequoia and Kings Canyon

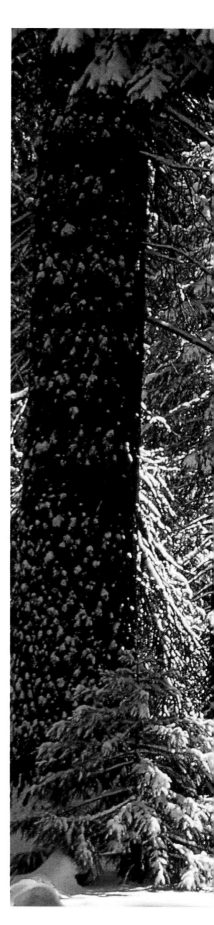

Giant sequoia trees, the world's largest living things, grow exclusively in scattered groves along the verdant western slopes of California's Sierra Nevada range. Sequoia and Kings Canyon National Parks protect the most extensive of these groves as well as the biggest individual trees —great, soaring columns of deeply furrowed bark, some the height of 30-story buildings.

Besides the trees, the adjoining parks take in the highest, most rugged portion of the Sierra Nevada, a spectacular alpine wilderness of crystalline lakes and streams, meadows, jagged peaks, plunging cascades, great domes of polished granite, glaciated canyons, dense coniferous forests, and swift, often dangerous rivers.

Sequoia contains the largest expanse of protected oak-covered foothills left in California and the highest peak in the contiguous United States, Mount Whitney, at 14,494 feet. Here, too, is a vast subterranean world of more than 100 marble caves adorned with stalactites, stalagmites, and other formations.

To the north, the awesome gash of Kings Canyon rivals the Grand Canyon for depth and Yosemite for beauty.

The Big Trees grow in groves, their cinnamon brown trunks rising from a scattered understory of seedlings and broadleaf shrubs. They share their surroundings with Jeffrey and sugar pines, white firs, and incense cedars—trees of impressive size anywhere but at the foot of a sequoia.

Giant sequoias are a bit shorter than coast redwoods, the tallest trees on earth, but they surpass the redwoods in overall size thanks to a much wider trunk. The largest sequoia, the General Sherman Tree, measures more than 36 feet across at the base—the width of a three-lane highway. Sequoias can live for thousands of years, though not as long as bristlecone pines. The oldest sequoia on record, felled at 3,200 years, was a sapling during the Trojan War.

Though sequoia wood—coarse-grained and brittle—makes poor construction lumber, one-third of the groves were cut between 1850 and 1950 to make shingles and stakes.

The colossal trunks of giant sequoias dwarf other evergreens growing among them. Sequoias depend on the 40-plus inches of water that falls as rain or snow when the Sierra trap moist air flowing inland from the Pacific. Snowmelt replenishes groundwater during the dry summer months.

PARK DATA

STATE: California

ESTABLISHED: Sequoia in 1890, the nation's second oldest national park; Kings Canyon in 1940; jointly administered since 1943

AREA: 863,700 acres (349,527 ha), most of it wilderness

ELEVATION: From 1,200 ft (366 m) to more than 14,000 ft (4,267 m)

CLIMATE: In the foothills, like the Mediterranean; above 10,000 ft (3,048 m), similar to the Arctic

FLORA: Sugar, lodgepole, ponderosa, and foxtail pines; red and white firs, incense cedars, black oaks; Pacific dogwoods, California buckeyes; yuccas, grasses, and wildflowers

FAUNA: Black bears, bighorn sheep, mule deer, mountain lions, bobcats; foxes, and many other small mammals; rattlesnakes; woodpeckers, golden eagles

UNIQUE FEATURES: World's largest living thing: General Sherman Tree, 274 ft (84 m) tall, trunk weight 1,400 t (1,270 mt), age 2,300 to 2,700 years, still growing and adding 50 cu ft (1.4 cu m) a year to its bulk; Mount Whitney, 14,494 ft (4,418 m), highest peak in the contiguous U.S.

FIRE PLAYS A CRUCIAL role in sequoia reproduction—by exposing and fertilizing mineral soils, by reducing competition from other vegetation, by opening cones, which release seeds, and by creating clearings so that sunlight can reach seedlings. Tree-ring analysis reveals that sequoia groves have a long history of small, frequent fires that clear out the underbrush and rarely damage the Big Trees, which are protected by a layer of fire-resistant bark as much as two feet thick.

After decades of fire suppression by park personnel, thickets of small trees and shrubs grew up, and leaf litter buried the forest floor to depths nature never would have allowed. Accumulated debris fueled intense fires that threatened even mature trees. Today, the Park Service sets some fires among the sequoias, to mimic the natural fires that have nurtured the Big Trees for eons.

Skiers, shown (right) in a photograph from the 1930s, enjoy a seasonal outing. The park's abundant snowfall, open forests, and meadows draw visitors keen on winter sports.

In a classic High Sierra setting (opposite), sapphire waters of Bubbs Creek glide past Center Peak and through meadows studded with slabs of granite. Hiking trails in the park ramble for hundreds of miles through such scenery.

Shenandoah

The Indians called the rolling river Shenandoah, Daughter of the Stars. East of the gentle valley where the river runs, Shenandoah National Park lies astride the adjacent rampart of the Blue Ridge Mountains.

This narrow, 75-mile-long slice of forested parkland in northwestern Virginia is a singular preserve of ever-changing beauty—rolling foothills and secluded hollows, mountain creeks and cascades, wildflowers and wild berries, sylvan trails and wide vistas—their mood dictated by the seasons.

Spring arrives here in March, creeping up the ridge and finally touching the summits by late May. Wildflowers proliferate among the deep greens of summer, followed by brilliant fall foliage. With the leaves gone, you can see forever on a clear winter's day.

Shenandoah is the mid-Atlantic region's only mountain-based national park; in fact, it is the only national park in the eastern mountains between Acadia and Great Smoky Mountains. Congress authorized its establishment in 1926. Its wild beauty today belies its past. During the 1800s, farm settlement spread from the fertile valley into the uplands. Here, scattered in isolated ridges and hollows, mountain people evolved their own rich culture. They used the mountain land for grazing, lumbering, and growing crops.

By the time Shenandoah National Park was established, more than half the population had left the mountain area, and the remaining residents sold their land or were relocated with government assistance. President Franklin D. Roosevelt dedicated the park in 1936, and recreational facilities were built by the Civilian Conservation Corps. Today, forest—boasting about a hundred different species of trees—has reclaimed more than 95 percent of the parkland, with two-fifths of it designated as wilderness. Hence, Shenandoah can claim distinction as a "recycled" park, proof of nature's ability to regenerate.

Most people experience Shenandoah along Skyline Drive, the 105-mile-long artery, completed in

Lost in a hollow below Big Meadows, Naked Creek Falls (opposite) rewards off-trail hikers.

A moisture-loving cardinal flower (below) is one of 1,100 wildflower species here.

1939, that runs the length of the park. One of the country's most popular and scenic drives, especially during the park's fall foliage spectacle, it meanders along the spine of the Blue Ridge range, affording breathtaking panoramas of the Shenandoah Valley and 40-mile-long Massanutten Mountain to the west and of the rolling Piedmont country to the east.

For those who prefer to explore Shenandoah beyond Skyline Drive, the park also offers some 500 miles of hiking trails, ranging from short leg-stretchers to a 95-mile portion of the Appalachian Trail.

On Shenandoah's Stony Man Mountain, hardy lichens, a type of sedum, and a bright pink azalea find a foothold in the cracked and weathered basalt.

Theodore Roosevelt

Rumbling tones of bison on the move; mournful crooning of coyotes—"song dogs" to the Indians; golden grasses shimmering in the never ceasing prairie wind; surreal badlandscapes sculptured by wind and water; vast open spaces of the Old West. All drew Theodore Roosevelt to Dakota Territory in the 1880s. He hunted bison, tried ranching, and always credited his strenuous outdoor life here with giving him the strength to serve as president.

To honor this 26th president, three sites in western North Dakota were dedicated as a national park in 1978. Bison, reintroduced to the area in the 1950s, flourish here, as does much other wildlife—including deer, elk, wild horses, pronghorn, prairie dogs, golden eagles, and meadowlarks, usually easily spotted from along park roads.

Besides badlands, the park contains another curious phenomenon—coal seams that, once ignited, may smolder for years.

PARK DATA

STATE: North Dakota
ESTABLISHED: 1978
AREA: 70,446 acres (28,509 ha); 3 locations along the Little Missouri River: the South Unit, the site of Roosevelt's Elkhorn Ranch, and the North Unit
NATURAL FEATURES: Colorfully striated badlands; slick bentonite clay
CULTURAL FEATURE: Maltese Cross Cabin from Roosevelt's first ranch

"The grass-land stretches…like a sea," wrote Theodore Roosevelt of the Dakota prairie. His namesake park preserves remnants of that once vast ecosystem.

Virgin Islands

*E*ast of Puerto Rico, the clear turquoise waters of the Caribbean break against a tiny volcanic island named St. John, home of Virgin Islands National Park. Roughly half the island and most of its coastal waters lie within the park, forming a remarkably diverse preserve of coral reefs, white sand beaches, coves, bays, and densely forested mountains.

Covering only 19.4 square miles, St. John is the smallest of the U.S. Virgin Islands, but its great variation in rainfall and exposure gives rise to a surprising range of vegetation. Some 800 plant species (16 of them rare or endangered) grow within the island's subtropical forests, mangrove swamps, marshes, and arid, desertlike areas. Geckos, iguana lizards, hummingbirds, fish-eating bats, insects, and other animals live among the trees, vines, shrubs, and cactus scrublands.

Nearly all of the island's native plants survive, even though the original forests were cleared in the 18th century for sugar and cotton. Ruins of plantation buildings, abandoned after slavery was abolished, still stand.

Supremely fragile coral reefs, the most complicated of marine ecosystems, fringe the island's irregular shoreline. Groupers, grunts, blueheads, yellowtail snappers, and many other wildly colorful and oddly shaped fish glide over great domes of brain coral and hide among the branches of elkhorn and staghorn corals. Eels, squids, spiny lobsters, basket sponges, and sun anemones nestle into hollows.

Along the coast lie sand flats, rocky shallows, meadows of sea grasses, and mangrove swamps. Three endangered sea turtle species—hawksbill, green, and leatherback—roam the waters and bury their eggs on the island's beaches.

PARK DATA

LOCATION: St. John, U.S. Virgin Islands

ESTABLISHED: 1956

AREA: 12,909 acres (5,224 ha); administrative headquarters on St. Thomas

CLIMATE: Average temperature about 79°F (26°C)

NATURAL FEATURE: One of the Lesser Antilles islands, exposed peaks of a submarine mountain range that forms eastern rim of Caribbean Sea

CULTURAL FEATURES: Partially restored 18th-century ruins of Annaberg Sugar Mill, Herman Farm; mysterious petroglyphs

FLORA: Includes mangoes, mangroves, soursops, palms, turpentine trees, tamarinds, organ-pipe cactuses, century plants, bay rum trees, orchids, and night-blooming cereuses —pollinated by bats

FAUNA: Breeding ground for 20 species of tropical birds, including 2 species of Caribbean hummingbirds; marine birds, including pelicans, frigate birds, boobies; August meeting place for thousands of hermit crabs, which migrate to beaches to breed and lay eggs

Five thousand acres donated by Laurance S. Rockefeller, developer of Caneel Bay resort (far left), led to creation of the park that protects half of St. John.

Voyageurs

*T*his park provides an uncrowded and welcoming place for a diverse spectrum of visitors.

Boxy houseboats bob on the lakes, the occupants casting for something fresh for the pan when they put into a sheltered cove at day's end. Motorboats crease the waters, bound for fishing grounds or for rapid transit across these big lakes—Rainy, Namakan, Sand Point, and Kabetogama.

Canoeists ply the waters for sport, more slowly than the powerboats, more carefree than the voyageurs who drove their heavily laden bark canoes to and from the fur country to the northwest. A park boundary on the Canadian border follows the path of the old Voyageurs Highway.

For backpackers, a trail across Kabetogama Peninsula leads to a favored stopping place on Rainy Lake, with fine swimming and cliffs for viewing sunset pastels.

Though winter temperatures often plunge below zero degrees Fahrenheit, the park never closes. Snowmobilers flock to the generous expanse of frozen lakes. Nordic skiers set out for the Black Bay and Ash River trails or take off cross-country.

To safeguard threatened species —bald eagles and timber wolves— park officials have closed 17 lake bays to snowmobiling, setting off a stormy protest. Park plans had envisioned the preservation of a prime recreation resource along with the recovery of a north-country wilderness—a daunting challenge.

Bur reed floats on a corner of Rainy Lake. The marsh sedge bears globular, burlike fruit.

PARK DATA

STATE: Minnesota
ESTABLISHED: 1975
AREA: 218,054 acres (88,243 ha), one-third of it water; access to interior by boat or plane in summer
CLIMATE: Summer high temperatures from 55° to 85°F (13° to 29°C); winters very cold
CULTURAL FEATURE: Historic Kettle Falls Hotel, a restored hostelry from the early 1900s
FLORA: Aspens, birches, red and white pines, black spruces; a variety of bog and marsh plants
FAUNA: Threatened timber wolves; black bears, moose, beavers, otters; loons, bald eagles, white pelicans; walleyes, northern pikes, smallmouth bass

Wind Cave

Wind Cave country lies where the rolling mixed-grass prairie of the western plains meets the rugged, ponderosa pine-clad Black Hills of South Dakota. Here, a visitor once wrote, "the lover of nature could...find his soul's delight."

The park is arguably two parks in one. While it does harbor the country's fifth longest subterranean labyrinth (ninth longest in the world and one of the oldest), named for the rushing winds at its mouth, it also encompasses some of North America's most beautiful grasslands and foothills.

What's more, the distinct ecosystems found in this transition zone between East and West—remnant prairie, hills, and forest—make this wildlife sanctuary prime mammal- and bird-watching terrain. Prairie dogs, scampering about their hummocky "towns," share this land with badgers, coyotes, cottontails, and mule deer. Free-roaming herds of pronghorn, bison, and elk have been restored to their native habitat. Prairie falcons, golden eagles, and meadowlarks live in the park, along with forest-loving nuthatches and wild turkeys. And normally separate tree species stand side by side here, such as ponderosa pines next to American elms.

PARK DATA

STATE: South Dakota
ESTABLISHED: 1903
AREA: 28,292 acres (11,449 ha)
ELEVATION: Highest point Rankin Ridge, 5,013 ft (1,528 m); lookout tower offering Black Hills panorama
CLIMATE: Summer temperatures rising to 100°F (38°C); winter very cold and dry; temperature in Wind Cave constant at 53°F (12°C)
NATURAL FEATURES: Wind Cave beginnings in a limestone bed 60 million years ago; more than 76 mi (122 km) of passageways, where significant mineral formations include calcite boxwork, and popcorn and frostwork crystals
FLORA: Mixed-grass prairie covering 75 percent of the park and ponderosa pine forest most of the remainder; a wide variety of wildflowers
FAUNA: Large mammal species—bison, pronghorn, and elk—successfully reintroduced to native ranges on Wind Cave grasslands

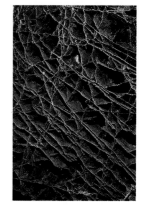

World-class boxwork, a honeycombed calcite formation, hallmarks Wind Cave.

Heads turned toward the sun, yellow sunflowers frame a distant herd of grazing bison.

Wrangell-St. Elias

*E*ven the word "enormous" fails to convey a sense of Wrangell-St. Elias, a park of truly staggering proportions. Nine of the United States' sixteen tallest mountains cut this southeastern Alaskan park into a tangle of towering white peaks. Some of the world's longest, largest, and most active glaciers flow from their flanks. The Malaspina Glacier exceeds Rhode Island in size, while the Hubbard stretches for 70 miles. The desolate wastes of the Bagley Icefield count as the continent's largest subpolar ice field. When Congress preserved this wilderness in 1980, it created a U.S. national park far larger than any other. Larger in area than New Hampshire and Vermont combined, the park's boundaries would encompass nearly six Yellowstones.

Four major mountain ranges meet within the park's more than 13 million acres: The Wrangells ripple the northern interior with volcanic peaks, including 14,163-foot Mount Wrangell, an active volcano with steaming vents that last erupted in 1930; the St. Elias Mountains rise from the Gulf of Alaska and push north; the Chugach line the southwestern coast; and the Nutzotin and Mentasta Mountains guard the park's northern border. Few but the tallest peaks have earned names, and many still remain unclimbed.

About 80 percent of the landscape consists of snow, rock, and ice—a remote and starkly beautiful high country. Hundreds of thousands of acres of forests and meadows reveal how life tenaciously reclaims land uncovered by retreating glaciers.

Wildlife flourishes here. In the interior, Dall sheep and mountain goats claim the mountain ridges, while black and grizzly bears, bison, and moose

Nature's thunderous symphony sounds in Wrangell-St. Elias as a huge column of ice sheers off Hubbard Glacier, crashing into Disenchantment Bay.

wander the lowlands, and herds of caribou roam the north and west sides of the park. The Copper River, which forms the western boundary, serves as a major flyway for migratory birds and a nesting ground for trumpeter swans.

Kayakers and rafters use the hundreds of rivers and streams flowing off the glaciers as highways into the interior. Less adventurous spirits can drive into the park on one of two roads, the legacy of mining efforts earlier this century. The promise of gold and silver still lures a hearty few, but more people come here now for a chance to sample something far more precious—a vast, raw, and little-disturbed wilderness.

MOUNTAIN-DWELLING DALL SHEEP

AGAINST A BACKDROP of dark volcanic rock, Dall sheep stand out like brilliant patches of unmelted snow. No other wild sheep bear this white coat, an adaptation to Alaska's long, severe winters.

The Dall sheep that inhabit the treeless slopes and precipitous ridges of the park's interior represent some of the world's finest herds of this species. They negotiate the impossibly steep and rocky terrain with a sure-footedness enhanced by widespread and rough-bottomed hooves. Such agility is no luxury: Good grazing spots may lie as much as 40 miles apart.

Slightly smaller cousins of the Rocky Mountain bighorns, the Dall sheep grow long, curling horns prized by hunters the world over. A fully curved horn indicates a mature ram of at least seven or eight years, a bit more than half its usual life span. A ewe's horns (above) are much smaller.

During the birth of its lamb, the ewe retreats to a rugged, protected spot, chosen for its safety. The males roam in small bands after mating, leaving ewes and young in larger herds.

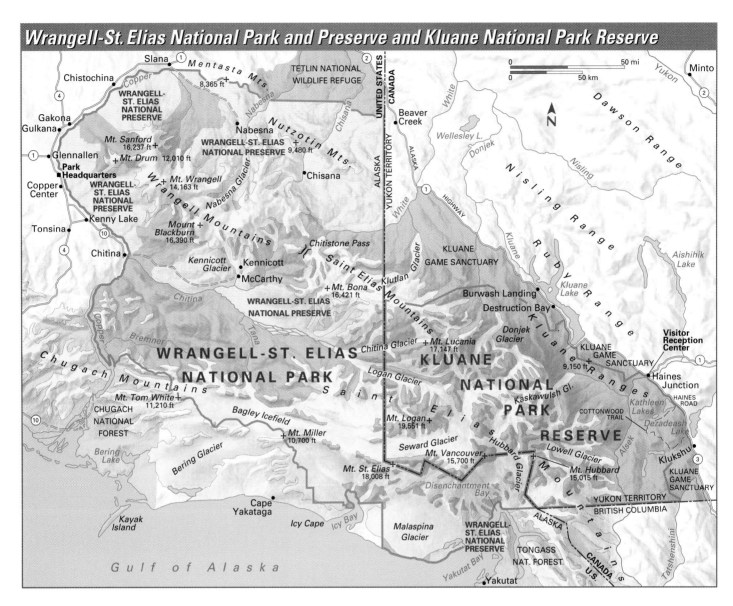

Slana
Chistochina
Mentasta Mts.
8,365 ft
TETLIN NATIONAL
WILDLIFE REFUGE
UNITED STATES
CANADA
Beaver
Creek
Copper
WRANGELL-
ST. ELIAS
NATIONAL
PRESERVE
Nabesna
Nutzotin Mts.
Chisana
50 mi
0
0   50 km
Minto
Dawson Range
Yukon
Gakona
Gulkana
Mt. Sanford
16,237 ft
Mt. Drum 12,010 ft
WRANGELL-ST. ELIAS
NATIONAL PRESERVE
9,480 ft
Nabesna
Chisana
ALASKA
YUKON TERRITORY
White
Wellesley L.
Donjek
Nisling
Nisling Range
Glennallen
Park
Headquarters
Mt. Wrangell
14,163 ft
WRANGELL-
ST. ELIAS
NATIONAL
PRESERVE
Wrangell
Mountains
Nabesna Glacier
White
HIGHWAY
Kluane
Ruby Range
Copper
Center
Kenny Lake
Aishihik
Lake
Tonsina
Mount
Blackburn
16,390 ft
Chitistone Pass
KLUANE
GAME SANCTUARY
Kluane
Chitina
Kennicott
Glacier
Kennicott
McCarthy
Saint Elias
Glacier
Klutlan
Mt. Bona
16,421 ft
WRANGELL-ST. ELIAS
NATIONAL PRESERVE
Burwash Landing
Destruction Bay
Kluane
Lake
Kluane Range
Visitor
Reception
Center
Chitina
Copper
Bremner
Tana
Chugach
Mountains
WRANGELL-ST. ELIAS
NATIONAL PARK
Chitina Glacier
Mt. Lucania
17,147 ft
Logan Glacier
Saint
KLUANE
NATIONAL
Donjek
Glacier
Kluane
Ranges
KLUANE
GAME
SANCTUARY
9,150 ft
Haines
Junction
Mt. Tom White
11,210 ft
CHUGACH
NATIONAL
FOREST
Bagley Icefield
Mt. Miller
10,700 ft
Bering Glacier
Elias
PARK
Kaskawulsh Gl.
RESERVE
COTTONWOOD
TRAIL
Kathleen
Lakes
Dezadeash
Lake
HAINES
ROAD
Bering
Lake
Mt. Logan
19,551 ft
Seward Glacier
Mt. Vancouver
15,700 ft
Hubbard Glacier
Lowell Glacier
Alsek
Mountains
Klukshu
KLUANE
GAME
SANCTUARY
Kayak
Island
Cape
Yakataga
Icy Cape
Icy Bay
Mt. St. Elias
18,008 ft
Disenchantment
Bay
Malaspina
Glacier
Mt. Hubbard
15,015 ft
WRANGELL-
ST. ELIAS
NATIONAL
PRESERVE
YUKON TERRITORY
BRITISH COLUMBIA
ALASKA
TONGASS
NAT. FOREST
CANADA
U.S.
Tatshenshini
Gulf of Alaska
Yakutat Bay
Yakutat

MINING PRECIOUS METALS

INTREPID MINERS still brave the park's freezing waters, producing perhaps an ounce of gold for a hard day's work. A portable suction dredge (left) gathers scraps of gold (right).

Mining companies pulled a billion pounds of copper from the earth here in the early 1900s. Veins of gold and silver proved less productive but still netted millions of dollars.

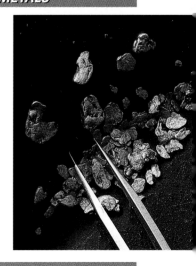

Yellowstone

Around the Grand Loop Road loom the vistas, the sights and sounds and smells that bring the world flocking to Yellowstone: Mammoth Hot Springs' amazing mineral formations; Roaring Mountain's steaming fumaroles; Fountain Paint Pot's bubbling cauldron of reddish mud; the delicate, brightly colored terraces of Grand Prismatic Spring; and the all-time favorites—the waterspouts of the Upper Geyser Basin, capped by Old Faithful. These features, together with the spectacular beauty of the Grand Canyon of the Yellowstone and the abundant wildlife, supported the area's designation in 1872 as the world's first national park. Since then, it has developed into an important wildlife haven.

Beyond the Grand Loop, off in the northeast corner of the park, the landscape mellows. Here in the Lamar Valley, long celebrated for its mountainous beauty, a new excitement stirs. In the winter of 1994-95, gray wolves howled in the valley, a milestone in the long campaign to restore a natural balance to Yellowstone's web of life.

The valley has witnessed other efforts in that campaign. Early in the century, after a historic slaughter had all but doomed the nation's bison, the park established Buffalo Ranch here to preserve a remnant herd. In the 1960s, faced with swelling elk herds, rangers corralled elk in the Lamar and trucked them off to distant ranges, or gunned them down. Part of the elk problem was that the park had achieved its goal of eliminating all wolves by the 1930s.

A half century later, Yellowstone was struggling to reverse that goal. America now cherished its imperiled species, the wolf among them. Wildlife advocates lamented this major blank spot in the assemblage of the nation's

Hills of new rock grow at Mammoth Hot Springs, at Yellowstone's northwestern gateway. Calcium carbonate, dissolved from limestone by the hot springs, rises to the surface to form these famed travertine terraces.

first national park. Mountain lions roam Yellowstone. Grizzlies, with a troubled history, total 250 or more. Bison number about 3,500. Some 38,000 elk, in nine herds, seek summer graze in Yellowstone.

"We have waited 60 years for this," said a park official, as 14 wolves in three packs, imported from Canada, settled into the wintry Lamar. If the recovery goes as planned, the wolf population may grow to 150 or 175 animals in ten or twelve packs. This could produce a significant impact on prey animals. Ranchers, concerned that Yellowstone wolves might leave the park and prey on livestock, remain opposed to the program.

As this effort progressed, Yellowstone confronted a new wildlife threat from an unexpected quarter. In 1994 a ten-year-old girl caught a 16-inch fish on Yellowstone Lake. Her guide took one look and quickly called for a lake ranger. The youngster had landed a lake trout, an exotic. Later four others turned up. Lakers dwell in park lakes just a few miles away—but across the Continental Divide from Yellowstone Lake. A natural migration seemed impossible; a mischievous transplanting seemed likely. Experts warn that an uncontrolled lake trout population could eventually eliminate 90 percent of the native cutthroat trout in Yellowstone Lake—a reverberating disaster. Grizzlies gorge on spawning cutthroats. Mink and otters eat cutthroats. Nesting eagles and ospreys and white pelicans consume tons of fish. Lake trout spawn deep, swim deep; they cannot provide a viable option. Strong measures to eliminate or suppress the invaders may give the natives a fighting chance to maintain their numbers and thus stave off a severe ecological upheaval.

Above the Grand Canyon of the Yellowstone, frozen thermal steam coats a pine.

THE GREAT FIRES of 1988, which burned across nearly half the park's 2.2 million acres, left skeleton forests and a pall of ash—with little damaging effect. "It is my lasting impression," says John Varley, director of the Yellowstone Center for Resources, "that this place took the fires in stride. Nothing ecologically skipped a beat. New forest is growing right on schedule. Eighty percent of the park is lodgepole pine

habitat. With seeds spread from serotinous cones, those that require heat to open (the rusty cones at left), a vast number of lodgepoles sprouted. The seedlings measure about 18 inches, and the total is greater by far than in pre-1988 Yellowstone."

With thick, dark forest canopies gone, a flush of green spread into the openings—grasses, forbs, forage for elk, moose, bison, and deer. The new growth, Varley reports, has increased the park's carrying capacity for those animals by 20 to 30 percent.

Wildflowers found a place in the sun; aspen seeds a perfect medium in damp ash, but no one can say how well they'll fare.

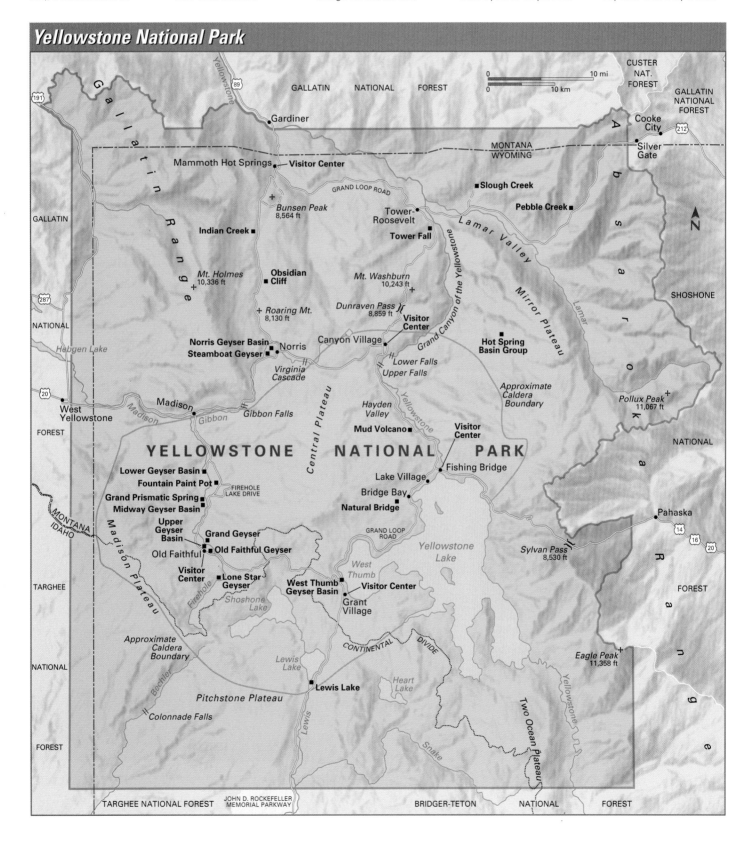

Yellowstone National Park

WHAT'S COOKING at Yellowstone? As many as 10,000 geothermal wonders, all told. The Continental Divide angles across this high Rockies plateau; waters flow eastward and westward, but also downward—and it is with these sinking waters that Yellowstone works its formidable witchery.

Great volcanic eruptions once wracked the plateau. One 600,000 years ago left a giant, elliptical caldera measuring 47 by 28 miles. The heat of molten rock, or magma, that set off the volcanic bursts keeps Yellowstone cooking.

Surface water, falling through porous rock, is superheated by a layer just above the magma and forced back upward. Where it finds a clear path, a hot spring forms. When more complex plumbing in the rock restricts the upward flow of steamy water, a geyser can spout. Fumaroles, venting steam, result from water boiling beneath the surface, with little or no moisture at ground level. Mud pots bubble where acidic gases and water decompose rock into mud and clay.

Geysers are the superstars, and Yellowstone has more of them than anywhere else on earth. Old Faithful remains true to its name but takes more time between eruptions—some 75 to 80 minutes on average, compared to the hourly average of earlier years. Change is attributed to shifts in the passageways and to vandals who throw objects into the world-famed spouter.

Faithful's neighbor, Grand, still shows the vim of the world's tallest predictable geyser, its fountain sending jets as high as 200 feet. At Norris, hottest and most changeable of the geyser basins, Echinus occasionally showers its admirers with warm water; and Steamboat, earth's tallest geyser, can shoot up nearly 400 feet, three times as high as Old Faithful—but Steamboat can remain inactive for years.

Fires aboveground have no impact on geysers and hot springs; the fires that govern their fate lie below.

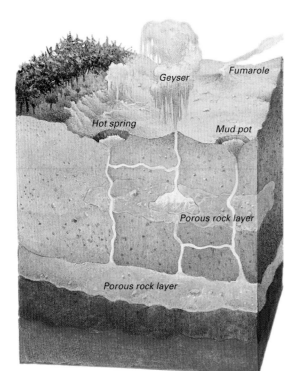

Geyser

Fumarole

Hot spring

Mud pot

Porous rock layer

Porous rock layer

Steam clouds swirl up from Norris Geyser Basin, site of earth's tallest geyser. Norris records more thermal novelties than any other site in Yellowstone.

Yosemite

olunteers of the Mariposa Battalion discovered the valley in 1851, the first non-Indians known to have seen it. An officer beheld the gossamer haze, the cloud-hung heights. His eyes watered, and he felt a "peculiar exalted sensation."

Yosemite remains a vale of awe, timeless, exalting. San Franciscans spend eight hours on the road to enjoy two hours here. The decade ending in 1994 saw visitors increase by a third, to 4.1 million; three-fourths of them surged into Yosemite Valley, a seven-mile wedge in a 1,169-square-mile park. With buses and trams, bike paths, and traffic restrictions, the park seeks to thin valley jams.

Cliffs and domes and monoliths of granite rise thousands of feet. "Every rock in its walls seems to glow with life," wrote John Muir, minstrel of Yosemite, devoted to its preservation. Near the western gateway stands the brute bulk of El Capitan, often aglow. Across the valley Bridalveil Fall bounds from a cleft, its rebounding spray wind-woven into airy veiling. When snows of the Sierra peaks are "melting into music"—Muir again—the springtime valley throbs with a crescendo of waterfalls, 13 in all, a matchless display. Three rank among the five highest on earth: Yosemite Falls, 2,425 feet; Sentinel Falls, 2,000 feet; and Ribbon Fall, 1,612 feet.

For the panoramic view, hikers—and drivers—ascend to Glacier Point, a magnificent sweep encompassing the valley and the high country. Adventurous souls set forth from the Happy Isles trailhead on a 4,900-foot ascent, past Vernal and Nevada Falls to the top of Half Dome, Yosemite's mighty emblem. This is strenuous hiking, a 17-mile round trip, but child's play

compared to the derring-do of Yosemite's climbers, famed for pioneering ascents and techniques in a world-class venue. They may take days inching up El Capitan's sheer walls, sleeping in hammocks anchored to the rock. When "free soloing," they climb without hardware, without ropes—and without companions to belay a fall. Fatal missteps are not unknown.

Spring crawls up through the park, taking as much as half the year to progress from the valley floor, at an elevation of 2,000 feet, to the Sierra heights, topping

Viewed from the Merced River, 7,569-foot El Capitan (opposite) looms over the entrance to the Yosemite Valley.

Lupines spread across a lowland meadow (below) as spring begins a slow climb to the High Sierra. Its passage awakens 1,400 kinds of flowering plants.

out more than 13,000 feet above sea level. Wildflowers celebrate the ascent of spring: baby blue eyes and poppies in the valley; paintbrushes and marsh marigolds in Tuolumne Meadows at 8,600 feet; rock primroses, mountain sorrels, and alpine saxifrages above timberline. Giant sequoias still stand tall and stolid in Yosemite; from a base that measures nearly 100 feet around, Grizzly Giant soars 209 feet—the 2,700-year-old patriarch of Mariposa Grove.

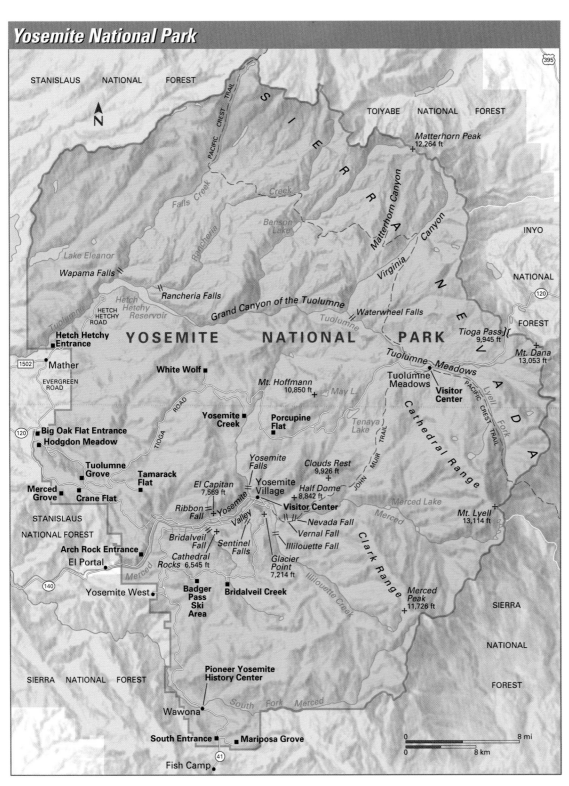

Yosemite National Park

PARK DATA

STATE: California
ESTABLISHED: 1890
AREA: 747,956 acres (302,687 ha)
CLIMATE: Summer temperatures up to 90s °F (30s °C) in the valley; winter temperatures from 26° to 54°F (−3° to 12°C), with average snowfall of 29 in (74 cm) in the valley
ELEVATION: From 2,000 ft (610 m) above sea level to more than 13,000 ft (3,962 m)
NATURAL FEATURES: Unusual number of waterfalls spilling freely over sheer cliffs (best viewed in spring before summer dries some up); wide variety of granitic formations, from domes and spires to arches and sheets
CULTURAL FEATURES: Reconstructed village of Ahwahneechee Indians, with bark houses and cultural exhibit; Wawona, site of 19th-century wayside hostel, now a hotel; pioneer history center nearby, with relocated historical buildings and horse-drawn coaches
FLORA: Three groves of giant sequoias: Mariposa (the largest), Tuolumne, and Merced; 17 conifer species; oaks, quaking aspens, cottonwoods, willows, alders; wildflowers
FAUNA: 74 mammal species, including mule deer, black bears, bighorn sheep, mountain lions; snakes, lizards; 247 bird species; rainbow trout

BEFORE THERE WAS Yellowstone, there was Yosemite. In 1864 President Abraham Lincoln signed a law granting the valley and the lordly sequoias of the Mariposa Grove to California. The nation created a park, but not yet a national park. Yellowstone was born eight years later.

John Muir pleaded that Yosemite Valley could not be saved without "its Sierran fountains"—the high country where waters gathered for the rush down valley walls. His vision prevailed; in 1890 the new Yosemite National Park embraced the high peaks and meadows and forests.

In 1903 another visionary came out to Yosemite. President Theodore Roosevelt listened to Muir's tales of "timber thieves…and other spoilers" and rode with him beneath Half Dome (above, Muir at T.R.'s right). "How happy were the days in the Yosemite I owed to you," the President wrote. Three years later, T.R. added the California grants to the national park. Muir now had his "harmonious unit" in a single preserve.

As with Yosemite, so with wildlands and wildlife across the nation. Roosevelt spent happy days in many, studied, listened, wrote, hunted big game, and set aside vast preserves. His presidential years established the first 51 national wildlife refuges, endowed the new U.S. Forest Service with more than 150 million acres of forest reserves, created 5 national parks to double the total, and designated 18 historic and scientific areas as national monuments. Among these protected areas were the Grand Canyon and the Muir Woods, the tract of California coast redwoods that honors T.R.'s companion of Yosemite.

Tuolumne Meadows Yosemite Falls Half Dome Glacier Point Vernal Fall

El Capitan

Cathedral Rocks

Bridalveil Fall

THE FORMATION OF THE

ALL AGREED that nature had created a valley of spectaculars. But how? "Glaciers," insisted John Muir, "cut and carved …until they have wrought out this royal road." Trained geologists dismissed Muir as an "ignorant sheepherder" and "ambitious amateur." Yet his long, devoted scrutiny—"constant brooding above the rocks, lying upon them for years as the ice did"—produced more truth than the expert who envisioned Yosemite as the sunken remains of a great earth catastrophe.

Science now concludes

that glaciers and wind and running waters reshaped the granite heights that emerged from the sea and were uplifted over many millions of years.

In the past two million years, glaciers flowed from the Sierra peaks three or four times. Ice sheets ground through the canyon cut by the Merced River, adding depth and width, producing a U-shaped valley about seven miles long.

The relentless ice found blocks of granite weakened at vertical joints and plucked them away. Where resistant granite stood firm, the ice scoured the walls and left such splendors as El Capitan (shown in the painting opposite and photograph below, at left). Half Dome's lofty cap was never ground by a glacier; exfoliation of rock flakes rounded the shape. As the valley deepened, tributary canyons were left hanging; their tumbling streams joined the enchantments of Yosemite.

When the last glacier departed, a lake remained. Gradually it silted up, leaving a floor where wildflower meadows spread and forests of oak and conifer grew tall.

WILDLIFE PAST AND PRESENT

FROM THE MEADOW mice in the valley to the pikas in the high country, wildlife ranges through the life zones of Yosemite: mule deer and black bears, coyotes and ground squirrels, fishers and wolverines.

So once ranged the grizzly. No more—1995 marked the centennial of the eradication of the last Yosemite grizzly.

For a time bighorn sheep and peregrine falcons also were among the missing. Now these two are back.

Bighorns, reintroduced in 1987, roam the High Sierra along the park's eastern edge. The herd has steadily increased in numbers since its reintroduction.

Peregrines course the valley skies once more, stooping swiftly to hunt gulls and swifts and swallows, skirmishing with ravens and hawks and golden eagles. The peregrine falcons raise young in five rocky aeries, and climbers are instructed to give them a wide berth.

Hunter of the night, a great gray owl bides its time amid dead tree limbs fringed with staghorn lichens.

Zion

ontradictions abound in this rumpled canyon country near Utah's border with Arizona. To the Mormon pioneer Isaac Behunin, whose people had fled persecution across the Midwest, it was a heavenly refuge— Zion. But his coreligionists who settled there during the Civil War found Zion's temperature range—from 15 below zero to 115 above—its aridity, and even its floods to be more on the infernal side, and eventually moved on.

Zion's best-known landmarks are soaring sandstone monuments some rising 3,000 feet above canyon floors. "Natural temples of God" to the early Mormons, they later inspired such names as Angels Landing, the Great White Throne, and the Altar of Sacrifice. But Zion's Paiute name, meaning "canyon like an arrow quiver," goes to the heart of this sunbaked parkland, a canyon so deep and narrow that sunlight barely pierces its base.

Through the bottom of the canyon flows the Virgin River, a watercourse that looks more like a sylvan creek. But its appearance deceives: Over the past 13 million years, the Virgin River has created this breathtaking chasm, downcutting through as much as 3,000 feet of rock. And its work continues apace. Each year the river may transport a million or more tons of rock and sediment to the Colorado River, which it joins at Lake Mead.

Most visitors view Zion Canyon from the inside out—a reversal of the usual perspective in canyon country parks. Standing streamside and peering

Rippled in ancient times by wind and stream, sandstone frames the sky's reflection in a shallow pool.

skyward, the sheer-sided walls seem, like skyscrapers, to be giant constructions. The imagination is constantly challenged to believe that all the soaring grandeur—every monolith, mesa, and cliff face—is the result, instead, of the *de*structive forces of erosion.

A vast desert before sinking beneath an inland sea, Zion's sands were cemented by calcium from decaying sea organisms and fused into stone by enormous pressures and the weight of overlying strata. Since then, water trickling through the porous sandstone has dissolved the calcium cement—at different rates, and to different effects.

In one spot, the erosion might dislodge a cliff-size slab of rock, and in another sculpture a span as improbable as the 310-foot Kolob Arch, one of the world's largest. Or, water percolating through the sandstone may burble to the surface as springs; the shower that pours from Weeping Rock first fell as rain on the plateau above 20 to 30 years earlier. There and in other hanging canyons, springwater nourishes gardens of scarlet monkey flower, golden and western columbine, and maidenhair fern. A number of small swamps are also fed by seepage through the sandstone.

Water is the greatest contradiction at Zion. Its absence parches the region to bone dryness. But its presence defines all of Zion, not just the sliver of the park that visitors to Zion Canyon see. Stretching off to the northwest boundary near Kolob Canyon, the entire plateau the park occupies is a maze of uncounted stream-cut canyons —and the towering structures that erosion has left behind.

Broom groundsel (right) blooms in profusion along a Zion trail. Manzanita, columbine, Indian paintbrush, and other wildflowers also brighten the park.

Taking to the water, a hiker wades through the Narrows (opposite), where the Virgin River flows between canyon walls sometimes only 18 feet apart.

PARK DATA

STATE: Utah
ESTABLISHED: 1919
AREA: 146,598 acres (59,326 ha)
CLIMATE: Mild winters, with little snow in canyon; pleasant spring and fall— daytime temperatures reaching 80°F (27°C); summer thunderstorms

NATURAL FEATURES: Checkerboard Mesa and other examples of cross-hatched and sculptured sandstone; arches including Great Arch of Zion, a "blind" arch (not free-standing) in a cliff wall; spectacular waterfalls during spring snowmelt

FLORA: Fremont cotton-woods, willows, ashes at riverside; piñons and junipers in lower canyons; ponderosa pines, firs, and quaking aspens on plateaus; ferns, wildflowers
FAUNA: Mule deer, bobcats, foxes, squirrels, rabbits; lizards; many birds

NATIONAL PARKS OF
Mexico

The national parks of Mexico reflect the many faces of this richly varied country. In parks such as Pico de Orizaba and Iztaccíhuatl-Popocatépetl, volcanic summits are at once sites of breathtaking scenery and windows into the fiery past of Mexico and of the earth. The panorama of the human past appears at Palenque, where the Palace tower watches over the ruined Maya city; at Tula, with its giant stone warriors defending a royal Toltec pyramid; in the preserved remains of a grand 17th-century hacienda at Molino de Flores Netzahualcóyotl. Parks such as Constitucíon de 1857 and Benito Juárez honor modern Mexican history.

A variety of settings, landscapes, and activities awaits visitors to the Mexican parks. Mountain climbers scale some of the highest peaks in North America. City dwellers find green retreats near home. Vast stretches of wilderness welcome hikers.

Cypress groves, mangrove swamps, thermal springs, turquoise lakes, pine woods, deserts, rain forests, tropical glaciers—all these and more provide habitats for a wide range of wildlife. Mexico's biodiversity ranks fourth in the world.

In the late 19th century, Mexico began to set aside areas for the conservation of its natural and historic treasures. Today, with a heightened interest in preserving its biodiversity, the country has established the National System of Protected Natural Areas. Mexico now boasts some 17 million acres of refuges and biosphere reserves in addition to the almost two million acres in its 44 national parks.

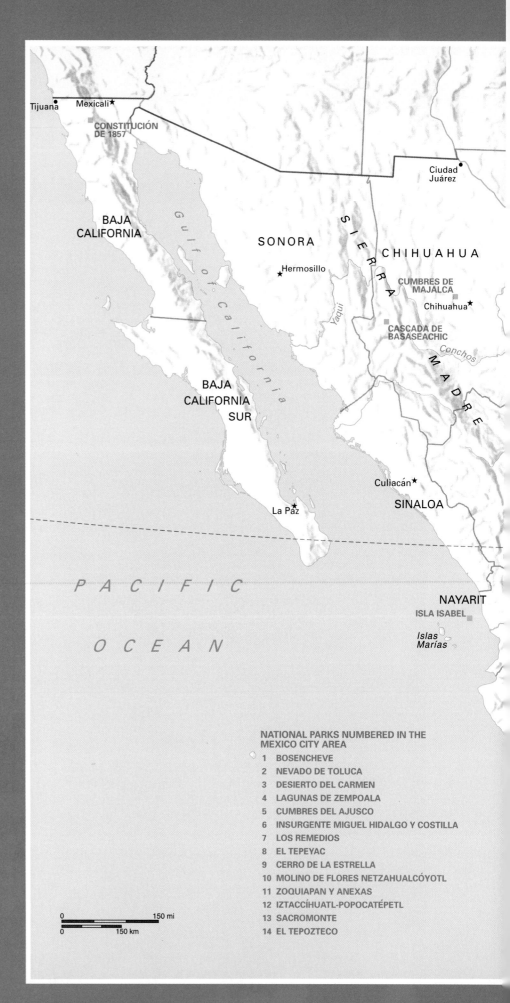

NATIONAL PARKS NUMBERED IN THE MEXICO CITY AREA

1 BOSENCHEVE
2 NEVADO DE TOLUCA
3 DESIERTO DEL CARMEN
4 LAGUNAS DE ZEMPOALA
5 CUMBRES DEL AJUSCO
6 INSURGENTE MIGUEL HIDALGO Y COSTILLA
7 LOS REMEDIOS
8 EL TEPEYAC
9 CERRO DE LA ESTRELLA
10 MOLINO DE FLORES NETZAHUALCÓYOTL
11 ZOQUIAPAN Y ANEXAS
12 IZTACCÍHUATL-POPOCATÉPETL
13 SACROMONTE
14 EL TEPOZTECO

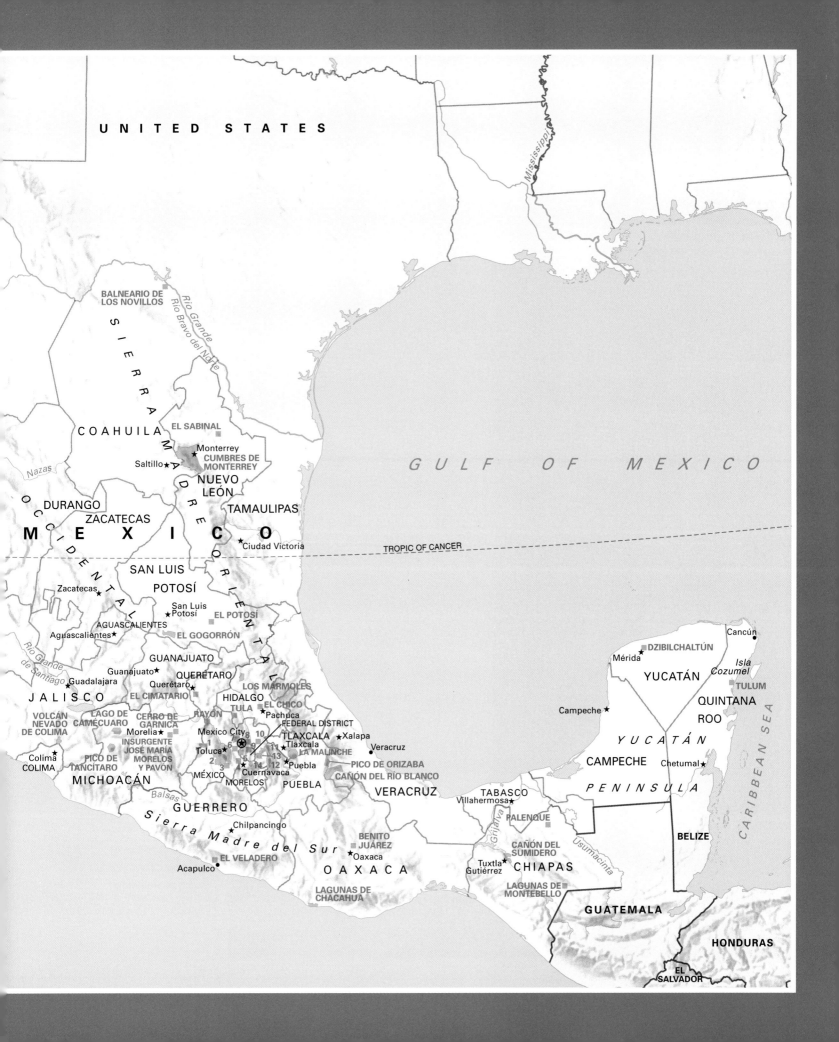

Balneario de los Novillos

*J*ust a short drive from the U.S. border at Del Rio, Texas, the park called the Baths of the Young Bulls attests to the influence of cattle ranching. Vaqueros still herd their animals near the lagoon created by the Arroyo de las Vacas—"stream of the cows." Walnut trees, oaks, willows, and poplars ring the pool, an oasis in an otherwise dry landscape of high desert plateau and hills.

PARK DATA

STATE: Coahuila
ESTABLISHED: 1940
AREA: 104 acres (42 ha)
FLORA: Walnuts, oaks, willows, poplars; Chihuahuan Desert vegetation
FAUNA: Including armadillos, black-tailed jackrabbits, ringtails (related to raccoons)

Desert bloom at Balneario: Prickly pear cactuses, wildflowers, and grasses crowd the desert floor after a surprise cloudburst.

Benito Juárez

P anoramic vistas are the hallmark of this mountainous park, named for a revered 19th-century architect of Mexican reform. From the heights of Cerro del Fortín, where the park is located, surrounding ranges reveal their beauty. Born in a local Zapotec village, Juárez rose to prominence in law and politics. He led the movement to wrest Mexico from military and ecclesiastical control and, as president, ended the French occupation of the country. Today his statue overlooks the valley-cradled city of Oaxaca.

Native son and traditional hero, Benito Juárez surveys the Oaxaca Valley from Cerro del Fortín.

Bosencheve

C alled "place of oaks" in the language of Mazahua Indians, Bosencheve features evergreen oaks but is known equally for dense stands of pine and fir overlooking mountain meadows lush with spring wildflowers.

In this wilderness park straddling the border of the states of México and Michoacán, summer rains fill the Laguna Seca and Laguna Verde, boosting fish populations and providing refuge for migrating waterbirds. Small mammals, including three species of skunk, inhabit the forests and brush.

Bosencheve's lakes teem with carp and a fish known locally as *mojarra.*

Cañón del Río Blanco

*F*rom the springs of its origin high in the peaks of Acultzingo, the Río Blanco defines the national park that bears its name. Traveling down to the lowlands, the river spills grandly over four waterfalls before reaching journey's end. Along the way it passes a varied sampling of Mexico's life zones: from conifer-studded mountains through hills green with oaks; past groves of poplar, walnut, and ash, along with avocados and grasses, to wetland gullies lush with giant ferns, bananas, and lemon trees. Few Mexican national parks embrace such diversity.

Wildlife along the river's course varies greatly as well. Common species such as white-tailed deer, weasels, and raccoons—denizens of temperate zones throughout North America—thrive in the woodlands, as do iguanas, lizards, and geckos in drier habitats. Other species lead a distinctly threatened existence in their fragile environments.

A place of great natural beauty, Río Blanco nonetheless occupies the same location in central western Veracruz state as no fewer than 16 municipalities, including the Nogales-Orizaba-Córdoba corridor with a population of some three million. As a result, the park shares its resources with industry and other human needs. Penned in reservoirs, the waters of the Río Blanco generate electricity for nearby towns and cities. Tributaries provide drinking water and carry the waste of urban populations. Less-than-pristine waters have driven away the huge flocks of migratory birds that used to alight at the river's largest reservoir, Tuxpango. Gone, too, are the wild boars that once rooted unconcernedly on the forest floors and the jaguars that roamed the jungle thickets.

PARK DATA

STATE: Veracruz
ESTABLISHED: 1938
AREA: 137,613 acres (55,690 ha)
ELEVATION: From 2,953 to 8,530 ft (900 to 2,600 m)
CLIMATE: Tropical to temperate to cold, depending on elevation
FLORA: Relict pockets of deciduous and evergreen jungle; tropical gumbo-limbos, ceibas, and lignum vitaes; temperate oaks and pines
FAUNA: White-tailed deer, raccoons, ringtails; iguanas, geckos; birds such as green parakeets, owls, falcons, partridges

Bright flame trees (opposite) punctuate the lush tropical vegetation of the Río Blanco's course in this western Veracruz parkland.

Rushing tributaries feed the Río Blanco, when they are not diverted for drinking water and other human needs.

Cañón del Sumidero

L ocal legend has it that, after a long, valiant stand against the Spanish conquistadores in the 16th century, thousands of native Chiapanecas hurled themselves off the steep cliffs of Cañón del Sumidero rather than face enslavement. Their ghosts are said to haunt still the 20-mile-long chasm that forms the backbone of this park in Mexico's southernmost state.

The name Sumidero means "sump" —a drainage pool. The joint forces of a geological fault and the erosion of the Río Grijalva carved the area's sedimentary rock into a fissure ranging from half a mile to a mile and a quarter wide and from three to four thousand feet deep. Along the way, the river cut caves into the canyon walls and exposed permeable rock, creating springs that generate spectacular waterfalls. Ancient peoples sheltered in some caves and held rituals in others; paintings and ceramics of historic value attest to their presence.

Sumidero provides an awesome backdrop to the town of Tuxtla Gutiérrez. Visitors can reach the canyon by bus, van, or car, stopping at spectacular lookouts along its rim. At the end of the canyon is the Chicoasén Dam. Completed in the early 1980s, the dam tamed the treacherous waters of the Grijalva, also known as the Río Grande de Chiapa, transforming the canyon into a narrow reservoir.

The now tranquil river has become the ideal route for exploring Sumidero. Launches embark from the nearby town of Chiapa de Corzo and wind northward—through prolific beds of waterlilies, past sunning crocodiles and cooling waterfalls—revealing on canyon walls the microenvironments engendered by differences in temperature and humidity.

PARK DATA

STATE: Chiapas
ESTABLISHED: 1980
AREA: 53,842 acres (21,789 ha)
FLORA: According to elevation and conditions; tropical mahoganies, gumbo-limbos; oaks, pines
FAUNA: 52 mammal species, including spider monkeys, peccaries, several endemics; endangered American river crocodiles; trogons, great curassows

Tour boats ply the misty waters of the Río Grijalva (opposite), showing off the awesome beauty of Sumidero Canyon.

Moss-covered rock ledges catch a cascade at Christmas Tree Falls.

Cascada de Basaseachic

T he Tarahumara Indians named it Basaseachi. In their language, this meant "place of the cascades," or, alternately, "place of the coyotes." They knew the area intimately and it contained both—the most spectacular and the highest waterfall in Mexico as well as packs of the mournful-voiced wild canines. Roaming the Chihuahuan Desert in winter, the Tarahumara, in summer, sought shelter higher up in the caves that lined canyon walls. Their isolated life centered around their rituals, including the long-distance footraces that lasted as many as 72 hours. The Spanish came and learned of the waterfall; a final "c" was added to the name to give it a Mexican sound.

At Cascada de Basaseachic in the Sierra Madre of central Chihuahua, two mountain streams have converged to produce a single channel. It flows to the edge of a jagged volcanic precipice and then leaps into space, beginning a breathtaking plunge that ends some 807 feet below in a cool, emerald pool.

The Basaseachic waterfall is only one of at least six falls that appear in the park during the summer rainy season, but none of the others approach its magnitude. Even it is changeable, depending on the season and long-term rainfall patterns, ranging from a single drop at a time in the driest years to a full-flood torrent every five to ten years. Each falls, however, alters the landscape, carving deep clefts into the varying hardness of the volcanic rock. Basaseachic itself has fashioned a natural bridge across its channel a short distance before it takes the plunge.

Even though development is pressing in around the park, the area's uneven relief of hills, mesas, and deep,

PARK DATA

STATE: Chihuahua
ESTABLISHED: 1981
AREA: 14,337 acres (5,802 ha)
ELEVATION: From 6,500 to 9,000 ft (2,000 to 2,700 m)
NATURAL FEATURES: Portions of the Sierra Madre; canyon carved by the Basaseachic River; several waterfalls
FLORA: More than 500 species of vascular plants; Douglas firs, forests of several species of pine and oak; chaparral
FAUNA: Threatened black bears, white-tailed deer; cats including pumas, jaguarundis, and bobcats; endangered river otters and beavers, ground squirrels, flying squirrels; Tarahumara frogs, salamanders, horned lizards, rattlesnakes; birds such as golden eagles, falcons, military macaws, endangered thick-billed parrots, royal eagles, and green macaws
UNIQUE FEATURE: The highest waterfall in Mexico, 807-ft-high (246-m-high) Basaseachic Falls

A rare flood-state photo of the Cascada de Basaseachic reveals its full glory as well as its rugged setting.

Tranquil green pools (opposite) await hikers who follow the Basaseachic Falls from clifftop to misty end. Autumn brings dramatic changes to the park's oaks and poplars.

Denizen of Basaseachic's forests, the thick-billed parrot faces serious threat from deforestation, grazing, and other human actions in and around the parkland.

nearly inaccessible ravines have made it a kind of natural greenhouse where endemic communities of plants and animals have flourished over eons. The park shelters more than 500 species of plants ranging from fir, pine, and oak forests to chaparral, orchids, and magnolias that hint at the region's tropical past. The coyote still figures among more than 225 vertebrate species, along with the jaguar, wolf, black bear, flying squirrel, river otter, beaver, and many species of birds and reptiles.

Reaching the Basaseachic Cascade is no longer a herculean feat. From a small parking lot near the village of the same name, it is a short hike to the top of the falls. A steep but maintained path, fortified with steps, leads to several vantage points, ultimately arriving at the plunge pool at the cascade's base—a journey of less than one hour.

Cerro de Garnica

Igh in the Oxumatlán range, a scenic but narrow road winds along the verdant hilltops to Cerro de Garnica. This small, undeveloped park is set in a rugged landscape of tall pines and steep hillsides. Once visitors find the entrance to the park, they will discover that hiking is mostly confined to the service road leading to the overlook near Garnica's microwave towers. Along the trail they may see white-tailed deer, ringtails, magpie jays, orange-fronted parakeets, and reptiles, including rattlesnakes. The overlook provides a panorama of rugged green hillsides, which gradually disappear into the distant mountain haze.

Steep hills, lush deep valleys, and winding roads characterize Cerro de Garnica.

PARK DATA

STATE: Michoacán
ESTABLISHED: 1936
AREA: 2,392 acres (968 ha)
ELEVATION: 5 prominent peaks within park; Garnica nearly 10,000 ft (3,000 m)
CLIMATE: Cool, rainy summers; cold winters
FLORA: Conifer forest of pine and fir
FAUNA: Mammals including white-tailed deer, gray foxes, ringtails, armadillos; reptiles such as rattlesnakes, horned lizards; green and magpie jays, orange-fronted parakeets

Cerro de la Estrella

*I*n the southeastern corner of one of the world's most populous cities stands an extinct volcano. Over the millennia, it has witnessed events both sacred and profane in Mexico's history. Legend records that, when the Aztec serpent god Quetzalcoatl learned of his father's murder, he gathered his parent's bones and carried them to the top of a mountain. There, Quetzalcoatl erected an altar. Every 52 years, when the secular and religious calendars coincided, people gathered at the altar to discard broken and blemished items and to accept *fuego nuevo*, "new fire," from the high priests. The arrival of the Spanish conquistadores in the early 16th century interrupted this rite, but it has since resumed its original 52-year cycle.

Today, visitors to the national park can view the site of the legendary altar and visit a museum housing artifacts from many eras. During Easter Holy Week, the number of visitors swells to the thousands as people climb the paths of the 7,812-foot mountain to observe a reenactment of Christ's Passion and death. Local people play most of the parts in this drama.

During the rest of the year, the park is an urban greensward where joggers and picnickers escape from Mexico City's noise and traffic. On clear days, Cerro de la Estrella offers broad views of the Valley of Mexico—once the mighty Aztecs' domain. At night, the valley twinkles with the lights of the modern capital of Mexico.

PARK DATA

STATE: Federal District
ESTABLISHED: 1938
AREA: 2,718 acres (1,100 ha)
CULTURAL FEATURES: Aztec archaeological site and museum
FLORA: Native vegetation largely replaced by exotic eucalyptus and pepper trees
FAUNA: Opossums; Steller's jays

Joggers take to the leafy paths of Cerro de la Estrella—"hill of the star"—a tall oasis of greenery in Mexico's capital city. Archaeological sites at the summit evoke the country's Aztec past.

Constitución de 1857

T he name of this park, evoking the document that proclaimed Mexico a representative democracy grounded in the separation of church and state, gives no hint of its topographic wonders. Centered on the western slopes of the Sierra de Juárez in northern Baja California, Constitución de 1857 park protects temperate, semihumid forests unique in the dry, desert-laden state. Many varieties of pine as well as oak and dry scrub provide critical habitat for a wide range of species from puma and bobcat to golden and bald eagle.

A high plateau reaching 5,000 feet and edged with huge mounds of ancient granite boulders provides the setting for Laguna Juárez, Baja's only interior lake. Migrating waterbirds find its warm, clear waters an ideal respite along the arduous Pacific flyway.

PARK DATA

STATE: Baja California
ESTABLISHED: 1962
AREA: 12,378 acres (5,009 ha)
NATURAL FEATURES: Laguna Juárez, also called Laguna Hanson; several canyons
FLORA: Pines, piñons, oaks, and dry scrub
FAUNA: Mule deer, bighorn sheep, pumas, bobcats, kit and gray foxes, coyotes, ringtails; reptiles such as rattlesnakes, spiny and horned lizards; birds including golden and bald eagles, acorn woodpeckers

A majestic desert bighorn sheep surveys its domain in the park. This hardy species nimbly negotiates the rocky outcroppings of Constitución de 1857.

Nature's sculptures, large granite boulders, edge Laguna Juárez. This shallow, intensely blue body of water forms the centerpiece of the national park and is an important source of water for Baja's cities and farms.

Cumbres del Ajusco

When the *capitalinos*, residents of Mexico City, want to get away from it all, they often go no farther than the volcanic range about 12 miles southwest of their city's center. At Cumbres del Ajusco National Park, spectacular 12,000-foot peaks, representing some of the earliest volcanic activity in the Valley of Mexico, poke through dense evergreen forests and subalpine meadows. In the Nahoa Indian language, the word Ajusco means "water that springs forth."

As with many landforms in this part of the country, history and legend combine to make each one a hallowed site. Among the Cumbres del Ajusco, the peak known as Cruz del Marqués bears a notable tale. Millions of years after its formation, the 12,894-foot volcano witnessed a confrontation between the forces of Nuño de Guzmán, a renegade Spanish official, and his bitter rival, the conquistador Hernán Cortés, who held the title of Marquis of the Valley of Oaxaca. The victorious Cortés raised a cross on the summit in commemoration of the battle. The cross has long since vanished, but the name remains. The peak called Santo Tomás is close to the height of Cruz del Marqués, while Pico del Águila (eagle's peak), at 12,730 feet, is known for its curved summit, shaped like the raptor's head.

The park's 2,273 acres in the Tlalpan sector of the Federal District are home to a number of small mammals as well as bird and reptile species. Visitors enjoy the striking vistas of Cumbres del Ajusco. In addition, they can climb, hike, picnic, and dine at the small, quaint restaurants that line the road up to the park.

PARK DATA

STATE: Federal District
ESTABLISHED: 1936
AREA: 2,273 acres (920 ha)
NATURAL FEATURES: Volcanic peaks, some rising nearly 13,000 ft (about 4,000 m)
CULTURAL FEATURE: Site of historic battle
FLORA: Open pine and fir forest; subalpine prairie
FAUNA: Bobcats, hognose skunks, Mexican cottontail and volcano rabbits; rattlesnakes; birds including prairie falcons, Steller's jays, blue grosbeaks, house finches

Neat, conical haystacks in a field below the volcanic peaks of Cumbres del Ajusco attest to farming within the park. Such private use and ownership continue in a number of Mexican national parks. In recent years, officials have been working toward ameliorating problems that result from such uses and threats to ecosystems.

Cumbres de Majalca

Cumbres de Majalca boasts a canyon named Salsipuedes—meaning "Climb out if you can." But the central Chihuahua park is fairly easily negotiated. It covers the southern expanse of the volcanic Sierra de Majalca, where an evenness of altitude gives the appearance of a vast tableland, forested with pine, juniper, and oak and sloping upward to the east. The rougher terrain is in the east, while the west descends gradually to a valley.

Salsipuedes Canyon is easily traveled along the stream that carved it. Although vertical walls about 200 feet high make parts of the canyon too deep for meeting the challenge of its name, fantastic scenery encourages a lingering visit. Erosion has fashioned basaltic rock into a landscape of columns and spires, many resembling puffy cushions stacked haphazardly and poised to tumble.

Early in this century, foresters worked the slopes of Cumbres de Majalca to supply a privately owned sawmill. Its overseer recognized the potential of the area as a weekend and cool summer refuge for residents of blazing hot Chihuahua city, the state capital, some 35 miles away. A road built in 1927 brought a stream of writers and other intellectuals seeking inspiration among the forests, mountains, and canyons. Cabins and vacation homes still comprise the only lodgings in the park, which continues to serve as a getaway and retirement destination for residents of Chihuahua and also of Ciudad Juárez.

PARK DATA

STATE: Chihuahua
ESTABLISHED: 1939
AREA: 11,792 acres (4,772 ha)
NATURAL FEATURES: Basaltic rock formations
FLORA: Forests of several species of pine and oak; junipers, Arizona cypresses
FAUNA: Black bears, pumas, Mexican wolves, coyotes, black-tailed and white-sided jackrabbits, red squirrels; birds such as northern goshawks, greater roadrunners, imperial woodpeckers, varied buntings, dickcissels, Montezuma quail

The rocky cliffs and knobby wooded hills of Cumbres de Majalca (left) stretch away to the southeast.

Commonly called a century plant, this agave (opposite) can take many years to mature and bloom—though not usually as long as a hundred years. For local people, the agave plant produces an array of different products. These range from food and beverages to soap and household items, such as baskets and mats, made from the plant's strong fibers.

Cumbres de Monterrey

Mountains, rivers, canyons, waterfalls, caves, scenic vistas—standard features of many national parks throughout the world. Add an industrial city of three million and nine other municipalities and you have Cumbres de Monterrey, Mexico's unique and largest national park.

Four-fifths of Peaks of Monterrey lies along the higher elevations of the Sierra Madre Oriental, the north-south extension of the Rocky Mountains and the spine of eastern Mexico. The remaining fifth is a plain supporting the city of Monterrey and other urban enclaves in Nuevo León and a long canyon, the Huasteca, that traces the western edge of Monterrey. Silver, slaves, and souls ripe for conversion brought the Spanish to the area in the 16th century.

Millions of years ago, this parkland was a seabed, with the bodies of calcareous creatures settling on the floor to create thick strata of limestone. Folding of the earth's crust tilted the strata to create some near-vertical outcrops and peaks.

With elevations ranging from 2,300 to 11,500 feet and with the influence of warm, moist winds from the Gulf of Mexico, Cumbres de Monterrey encompasses a wide assortment of climates and soils and a high degree of biodiversity. Plant communities range from the 45 species of cactus in the arid and semiarid areas to wet coniferous forests. With the world's greatest variety of pine species, Mexico—and Nuevo León in particular—is thought by many to be the birthplace of the genus *Pinus*. The park's wildlife includes black bears and bobcats among the 50 mammal species, more than 100 bird species, and 150 butterfly species.

PARK DATA

STATE: Nuevo León
ESTABLISHED: 1939
AREA: 609,115 acres (246,500 ha)
NATURAL FEATURES: Northern reaches of the Sierra Madre Oriental; several canyons; waterfalls; Grottoes of García in limestone strata
FLORA: Forests of pine and oak; cypresses; buckthorns, madronas, mesquites, agaves including lechuguillas, chollas; 8 species of orchids
FAUNA: 50 species of mammals including white-tailed deer, black bears, pumas, bobcats, jaguarundis, coyotes, collared and white-lipped peccaries, hooded skunks, armadillos, anteaters, ringtails, weasels; snakes, lizards; raptors such as golden eagles, gray, brown, and peregrine falcons; scaled and harlequin quail, sierra parakeets; 150 butterfly species
UNIQUE FEATURE: Mexico's largest national park

Agaves and ocotillos frame the sharp crests of the Sierra Madre Oriental. Here, tectonic forces thrust up limestone strata to nearly vertical angles.

Among the landforms that encourage exploration are the dozens of smaller sierras—parallel mountain ranges—that form the crests of the Sierra Madre. A cable car takes visitors to Grutas (or Grottoes) de García, a limestone cave with 16 chambers and a number of unusual stalactite and stalagmite formations, about 30 miles northwest of Monterrey.

As one might expect, balancing the needs of a burgeoning population in Mexico's third largest city with the ecological considerations of its largest park is no small task. To date, the balance seems to hang in favor of development, although measures to bolster protection of specific areas of parkland are in place. The site known as Chipinque has been designated an "ecological park" within the larger park, and plans are being formulated that would better isolate the urban from the wilderness areas.

At Cumbres de Monterrey, nature's labors produce wonders: A stream cascades over moss-covered rock to create Horsetail Falls (opposite). Deep within the Grutas de García (above), limestone deposits have fashioned a shrine to the Virgin Mary.

Desierto del Carmen

*W*aterfalls, forests, and springs drew the Carmelites to this site in the 18th century. Deep within the pine and oak woods—considered more conducive to meditation than their previous site nearer Mexico City—the monks built the Santo Desierto monastery.

Visitors must pass through a wide stone arch—Excommunication Gate—so named to remind women that if they entered the monastery they would be excommunicated. Today, both sexes come to admire the Chamber of Secrets, a barrel-vaulted room known for its excellent acoustic properties, and to view the fine artwork in the chapel.

Sunrise illuminates the stone walls of Santo Desierto monastery, considered a national monument.

Dzibilchaltún

At the spring equinox, the sun shines directly through the door of the Temple of the Seven Dolls at Dzibilchaltún. Built around the year A.D. 800, the temple was later covered by a pyramid. Sometime between 1200 and 1450 the Maya tunneled through the pyramid to build a new shrine and buried seven clay figures in the temple floor as part of the dedication ceremony. The temple is one of thousands of structures in the park. Lying in the scrub thorn forest of northern Yucatán, Dzibilchaltún, which means "place where there is writing on flat stones," once supported almost 20,000 people. A ceremonial and administrative hub, it was occupied for hundreds of years.

A museum in the park displays the seven clay dolls as well as pottery, other figurines, jewelry, and human bones recovered from a 144-foot-deep cenote in Dzibilchaltún's central plaza.

From 1956 to 1964, excavators removed tons of rubble from around the Temple of the Seven Dolls (below) before rebuilding it. Today it rises on the terrace of the ancient pyramid.

PARK DATA

STATE: Yucatán
ESTABLISHED: 1987
AREA: 1,332 acres (539 ha)
CLIMATE: Hot and dry
CULTURAL FEATURES: Maya city continuously inhabited for more than 2,500 years; the Xlacah ("old town" in Mayan) cenote, or natural well
FLORA: Original vegetation modified by human activities; secondary deciduous low forest containing gumbo-limbos, ceibas, acacias; 20 endemic flowering species
FAUNA: Small mammals, including ringtails, armadillos; birds such as great blue herons, thicket tinamous, little hermit hummingbirds; several endemic fish species

El Chico

Mexico's first national park, El Chico, began as a mining village in colonial times—the town of El Chico is now contained within the park. Established to save the forests and breathtaking landscape around the village from the ravages of overmining, the park now boasts the area's only native vegetation. Hikers and campers can enjoy sparkling clear springs; brooks that wander through rolling hills and luxurious fir, juniper, and oak groves; and waterfalls that cascade through El Chico's gorges and ravines.

An observatory on one of the park's highest peaks, La Peña del Cuervo, or "raven's rock," gives visitors a panoramic view of the park's many features. Other peaks, ranging up to 10,138 feet above sea level, include Las Ventanas and Cruz Grande.

PARK DATA

STATE: Hidalgo

ESTABLISHED: Declared a forest reserve in 1898; considered Mexico's first national park although official status not established until 1982

AREA: 6,768 acres (2,739 ha)

NATURAL FEATURES: Important natural area near Mexico City; peaks of the Pachuca Sierra

CULTURAL FEATURES: Old mining town of El Chico, as well as various villages

FLORA: 6 of 9 conifer species found in Mexico; many endemic plants; firs comprising 90 percent of the forest; rest made up of various species of oak, pine, juniper, cypress

FAUNA: Mammals including white-tailed deer, bobcats, gray foxes, ringtails, armadillos; 30 species of reptiles; 19 species of amphibians; more than 85 bird species

Unusual rock formations within El Chico, including this portion of Las Monjas—The Nuns—(left), are of volcanic origin.

Las Monjas rises beyond the grassy cemetery at El Chico.

El Cimatario

Where the northern edge of the Amealco Mountains overlaps the western edge of Querétaro state lies the broad swath of wilderness called El Cimatario. Here the solitary mountain lion, or puma, roams the semiarid hills in search of prey, perhaps a jackrabbit or squirrel. Falcons and foxes hunt for cottontails and small birds, and opossums feed on prickly pear cactuses, always keeping a watchful eye out for weasels and coyotes.

Three outstanding peaks—Santa Teresa, El Grande, and El Cimatario—tower over the park, part of a mountainous region that supplies all the water needs for nearby Querétaro city.

During colonial times an important battle called the Thirty against the Four Hundred was fought here, so named because the smaller rebel army was victorious against the Spanish viceroy's larger army of 400. The battlefield is now preserved as a historical site.

PARK DATA

STATE: Querétaro
ESTABLISHED: 1982
AREA: 6,047 acres (2,447 ha)
CULTURAL FEATURE: Battlefield from Spanish colonial era
NATURAL FEATURES: Natural area and watershed for Querétaro; peaks of Amealco Mountains
FLORA: Dry zone vegetation such as acacias, prickly pears, Mexican thistles; fire damage in recent years
FAUNA: Pumas, bobcats; other mammals including coyotes, foxes, longtail weasels, hooded skunks, hares, rabbits; birds including falcons, flycatchers, dusky and amethyst-throated hummingbirds

A cloud bank at sunrise covers all but the top of Santa Teresa Mountain, at 7,710 feet the highest peak of El Cimatario.

El Gogorrón

*T*ourists from all over Mexico come to El Gogorrón to bathe and relax in its soothing, bubbling hot springs, purported to have curative effects on a variety of arthritic conditions. The waters hover naturally at around 108°F.

Named after a hacienda that once existed just outside the park, El Gogorrón contains only a few of the dozens of thermal springs that pepper the valley just south of San Luis Potosí. Sandwiched between the Bernalejo, De la Cuesta, and San Luis Potosí mountain ranges, the park affords many scenic vistas of the great Bernalejo escarpment and prominent peaks, including Bernalejo and De la Cuesta.

Within the park a state-run resort offers hot springs, swimming pools, a restaurant, basketball and volleyball courts, horseback riding, and gardens. Visitors who want to stay overnight can sleep in comfortable cabins with their own private Roman baths.

Hikers who explore the undeveloped areas and caves outside the resort but still within the park may be fortunate enough to see coyotes, gray foxes, desert tortoises, or flying squirrels; but they need to watch where they step—the western diamondback rattlesnake also inhabits this park. The semiarid climate of the valley—hot during the day and cool at night—supports creosote bushes, mesquites, prickly pears, and organ-pipe cactuses, while pines and oaks grow high on the surrounding mountain ranges where rainfall is more abundant.

Visitors who come to take the waters at El Gogorrón usually stop off afterward in Santa María del Río, just outside the park. This town is famous for its colorful handmade shawls, called rebozos.

PARK DATA

STATE: San Luis Potosí
ESTABLISHED: 1936
AREA: 61,776 acres (25,000 ha)
NATURAL FEATURES: Natural hot springs; Bernalejo escarpment and peak; De la Cuesta peak
FLORA: Chihuahuan Desert vegetation; mesquites, creosote bushes, prickly pear and organ-pipe cactuses on the plain; piñons, oaks, and pines at higher elevations
FAUNA: Mammals such as coyotes, gray foxes, coatis, antelope jackrabbits; reptiles including desert tortoises, horned lizards, and western diamondback rattlesnakes; birds such as falcons and roadrunners

Agaves and xerophytes cling to the rocky hills of El Gogorrón. From some agave species Indians and other local people have traditionally derived food, medicine, fiber, and soap, as well as alcoholic drinks such as pulque, mescal, and tequila.

El Potosí

Millions of years ago, in the Cenozoic and Mesozoic eras, El Potosí lay at the bottom of the sea. When the sea withdrew, the marine rock that remained behind was eroded into numerous outcrops, piled on top of one another like cairns. These are only some of the many scenic attractions awaiting the intrepid hiker—the park also boasts natural overlooks, steep cliffs, and canyons. Higher up, through ravines in the hills of El Divisadero, Peña Boloña, and Joya de Ventura, rush streams that merge into the Arroyo Grande, a tributary of the Río Verde.

The climate and vegetation of El Potosí are diverse because of varied elevation and rainfall. Much of the park has a semiarid climate that supports plants such as mesquites and Mexican piñons, while the Cañada Grande, or "great gully," area is humid and overgrown with semitropical vegetation. Animals that visitors might see include coyotes, white-tailed deer, skunks, opossums, lizards, hawks, woodpeckers, phoebes, and flycatchers.

A place of great natural beauty, El Potosí is remote. Tourists who wish to visit this park to hike and camp will have trouble reaching it without a four-wheel-drive vehicle and excellent road and topographical maps. Access is from unpaved roads and rough terrain. There are no visitor facilities within the park, and all water and food must be brought in. Local residents, however, manage to farm successfully the park's rich, dark organic soil.

PARK DATA

STATE: San Luis Potosí
ESTABLISHED: 1936
AREA: 4,942 acres (2,000 ha)
FLORA: From subtropical to desert zone vegetation; piñons, pines, oaks; endemic species
FAUNA: White-tailed deer, coyotes, hognose skunks; birds including woodpeckers, trogons, phoebes

A Harris' hawk takes wing from an organ-pipe cactus.

Spanish moss drapes a nut tree in the semitropical Cañada Grande area.

El Sabinal

A tiny green jewel of a park surrounded by low hills, El Sabinal attracts visitors from nearby Monterrey and Carralvo to picnic and swim. Overhanging willows and 100-year-old Montezuma cypresses—often called "the tree of Mexico"—shade the river that wanders through the park. At a spot where the river widens lies a cool, inviting grove.

PARK DATA

STATE: Nuevo León
ESTABLISHED: 1938
AREA: 20 acres (8 ha)
FLORA: Riverine vegetation; willows, Montezuma cypresses; desert zone shrubs on low hills
FAUNA: Bobcats, ringtails, coatis, armadillos; chachalacas, quail, doves

Water-loving trees—Montezuma cypresses—thrive along the river's edge in El Sabinal.

El Tepeyac

On the slopes of the Sierra del Guadalupe lies El Tepeyac, a park of meadows and oak-forested hills that provides a respite for the people of Mexico City. The oak groves and occasional acacias and cactuses are being joined by eucalyptus and pepper trees.

On Tepeyac Hill stands the Basilica of Our Lady of Guadalupe, an 18th-century shrine honoring Mexico's patron saint. A section of the Guadalupe aqueduct, built between 1743 and 1751 to carry water to nearby villages, runs through the park.

PARK DATA

STATE: Federal District
ESTABLISHED: 1937
AREA: 746 acres (302 ha)
CULTURAL FEATURE: Colonial aqueduct arches
FLORA: Native acacias and cactuses being joined by exotic species
FAUNA: Opossums; birds including Steller's jays, house finches

Trees, wildflowers, and grasses blanket a hillside at El Tepeyac.

El Tepozteco

A top an eroded volcanic ridge stand the pre-Columbian ruins of Tepozteco, a pyramid built to the god Tepoztécatl. From the village of Tepoztlán, a long, arduous climb leads to the site. Thick stands of oak and pine shelter the cobbled gulley. From the rock shelf where the temple stands, there are views of expansive green valleys and eroded cliffs. The distant sounds from Tepoztlán form a contrast to this ancient place.

PARK DATA

STATE: Morelos and the Federal District
ESTABLISHED: 1937
AREA: 59,305 acres (24,000 ha)
NATURAL FEATURES: Eroded volcanic pinnacles
FLORA: Variation depending on elevation, tropical to temperate; endemics
FAUNA: Mammals including bobcats, foxes, and volcano rabbits; raptors such as golden eagles

The pyramidal ruins of Tepozteco (upper center) stand guard over their volcanic domain.

El Veladero

*G*ourd, gumbo-limbo, dragon's blood croton, earpod, mahogany—these are only a few of the tropical tree species growing in this mountainside park that sweeps around the beaches and bay and city of Acapulco.

When the park of El Veladero was created to preserve the scenic views from the famous resort town, the 12,500 families who lived on the mountain were relocated to a nearby town.

The park protects the wildlife around the bay and preserves the aquifers that supply Acapulco with its drinking water. Recreational areas are being created in El Veladero for those who are able to tear themselves away from the sparkling beaches that border the city.

PARK DATA

STATE: Guerrero
ESTABLISHED: 1960
AREA: 7,806 acres (3,159 ha)
CLIMATE: Tropical
FLORA: Tropical forest, including ceibas, earpod trees, mahoganies, gumbo-limbos, papayas, mangoes, coconut palms; many endemic species
FAUNA: Mammals including white-tailed deer, collared peccaries, coatis, armadillos; iguanas, snakes; birds such as doves, various species of woodcreeper

Ancient petroglyphs contrast with modern hotels, shops, and restaurants in a view from the park overlooking Acapulco Bay.

An adult and baby iguana catch the sun's rays in El Veladero.

Insurgente José María Morelos y Pavón

 Located east of the busy city of Morelia is a small national park named after a Mexican priest who, in 1811, helped lead a local insurgency against Spanish rule. The Indians and mestizos from this mountainous region joined Morelos' guerrillas. The forces maintained control of much of the country southwest of Mexico City from 1813 to 1815. Independence from Spain finally came in 1821.

Today this wooded park is mainly a weekend retreat for residents of Morelia. Near the park is El Salto— "the leap"—a waterfall reached by a short walk from the highway through a forest of oak and pine. A final, steep climb leads through sweet-smelling undergrowth to clear pools at the base of the waterfall. If the weather is warm, people may be found cooling off under the cascading water.

Water leaps over El Salto falls near the park named for the priest-hero, José María Morelos y Pavón.

Insurgente Miguel Hidalgo y Costilla

 This park, also known as La Marquesa, marks the scene of an important battle, Monte de las Cruces, fought during the start of the struggle for Mexican independence. Here, in 1810, Father Miguel Hidalgo y Costilla, a Catholic priest, led 80,000 Indians and mestizos to victory against Spanish Royalists. The park encompasses a large valley surrounded by forested mountains. Springs from the mountains pool in the valley to form a trout hatchery. Visitors from nearby Mexico City come for the day to hike and climb, as well as to ride horses and to fish in the park's artificial lake.

A statue of Miguel Hidalgo y Costilla marks the scene of his crucial battle.

Isla Isabel

*T*wo million years ago, complex geologic forces—involving both subduction and collision—raised a line of submarine mountains along Mexico's west coast. Isla Isabel was one of these, a volcano pushed up from the floor of the Pacific Ocean. Now an island park, Isla Isabel lies about 30 miles off the coast of Mexico in the Pacific Ocean and is primarily a series of small volcanic cones formed for the most part out of ash.

A seabird sanctuary, Isla Isabel hosts 42 species of birds and is one of the chief nesting grounds for 9 of them, including frigate birds, pelicans, terns, and 3 types of boobies. The park has no permanent human inhabitants and does not permit tourism, but occasional groups of scientists and researchers visit, and the island's southwestern shores are seasonally inhabited by fishermen. Introduced lemon and fig trees, along with bananas, pineapples, sugarcane, and coconut palms, compete with the native vegetation and serve as occasional food sources for the fishermen.

PARK DATA

STATE: Nayarit
ESTABLISHED: 1980; permits required
AREA: 242 acres (98 ha)
FLORA: Mangroves; dry tropical forest
FAUNA: Reptiles such as lizards, iguanas, snakes; 42 bird species, including boobies, frigate birds, pelicans, more than 145,000 pairs of sooty terns
UNIQUE FEATURE: Mexico's only island national park

Freshwater springs and rainwater feed pools and lakes (left) on Isla Isabel, including a crater lake. Small islets and cliffs act as wave breakers for nesting birds such as the brown booby (below).

Iztaccíhuatl-Popocatépetl

According to legend, an Aztec warrior named Popocatépetl fell in love with Iztaccíhuatl, the emperor's daughter. Hearing Popo had been killed in battle, Izta died of grief. When Popo returned, alive after all, he built two mountains. On one he laid Izta's body. On the other, he stood, forever holding a funeral torch.

Today the two lovers remain united in death in the forms of Popocatépetl, or Smoking Mountain, and Iztaccíhuatl, or White Lady. Steam still rises from Popo's crater, and Izta, also called "the sleeping woman," looks much like a woman lying on her back.

Visitors driving into the park enjoy spectacular views of densely forested ravines, and those who travel along the volcanoes' flanks can see their snowcapped peaks as well as oddly shaped glacier formations.

At Tlamacas, on Popo, stand both a hotel and hostel from which one can see the summit and the upper rim of Popo, as well as an occasional fumarole. It is from this vantage point that climbers begin their ascent to Popo's crater. Visitors who are not climbers may prefer a leisurely ramble through the woods near the hotel, or a hike along the many footpaths and trails around the flanks of both mountains.

The park can be divided into three levels of elevation, vegetation, and wildlife. In the first level, from 11,000 to 13,000 feet above sea level, grow Mexican fir forests, junipers, open pine groves, and grasses. Pines are found here at an elevation higher than anywhere else in the world. In the forest and grasses live skunks, coyotes,

Where the open pine forest ends (left), purple lupines and grasses begin, thriving among the cinders on the slopes of Popocatépetl.

Deep in the 2,100-foot-long, jagged crater of Popocatépetl (opposite), lies the great chimney from which the volcano vents its sulfurous eruptions.

wildcats, deer, and rattlesnakes. Among the grasses and pines live volcano rabbits, volcano mice, and moles.

At the second level—which overlaps the first—from 12,500 to 14,000 feet, are subalpine wildflower meadows and high-mountain grasses.

At the third overlapping level, from 13,000 to 16,000 feet, are mosses and lichens. Even higher lie fields of permanent snow.

The two volcanoes boast the only Neotropical glaciers in North America and are an important center for seismological and glaciological research.

The perpetual ice on both mountains feeds numerous underground springs, which are in turn the source of the many streams that supply the cities of Mexico, Puebla, and Cuautla with some of their water.

Popocatépetl has erupted some 30 times since the 14th century, and in 1993 it began to awake after a long slumber, spewing forth smoke and ash. A major eruption would threaten the two million people who live nearby.

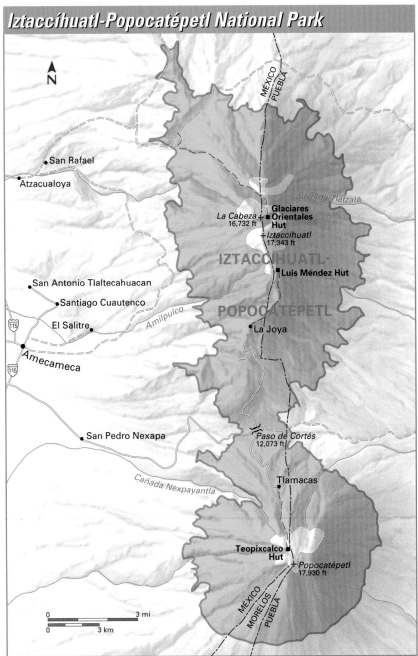

Iztaccíhuatl-Popocatépetl National Park

San Rafael
Atzacualoya
Cañada Tlatzala
Glaciares Orientales Hut
La Cabeza 16,732 ft
Iztaccíhuatl 17,343 ft
IZTACCÍHUATL-
Luis Méndez Hut
San Antonio Tlaltecahuacan
Santiago Cuautenco
POPOCATÉPETL
Amilpulco
El Salitre
La Joya
Amecameca
San Pedro Nexapa
Paso de Cortés 12,073 ft
Cañada Nexpayantla
Tlamacas
Teopixcalco Hut
Popocatépetl 17,930 ft
MÉXICO MORELOS PUEBLA
MÉXICO PUEBLA

0   3 mi
0   3 km

THE VOLCANO RABBIT

THE UNIQUE TEPORINGO, also known as the volcano rabbit, is found only in Mexico on the grassy volcanic slopes of Izta, Popo, and nearby mountains. This tiny, dark-furred creature is one of Mexico's oldest mammal species, surviving from an ancient geologic era. One of the smallest rabbits in the Americas, the teporingo is only 12 inches long, with short, round ears and a short tail and legs. Like all rabbits, it is usually nocturnal, appearing at dusk, although, during mating season or on dark days, it may emerge in the daytime. It lives in burrows or under rock piles and apparently dwells in colonies. Habitat damage and hunting have put the teporingo at risk of extinction.

WEEKEND TRIPPERS from Mexico City have a drive of only some 50 miles to reach Popo and Izta, which may explain why these are the most frequently climbed peaks in Latin America—that and the fact that they are two of the three highest volcanoes in the country. The elevation of Iztaccíhuatl is 17,343 feet. Popocatépetl is 17,930 feet high.

The volcanoes can be climbed year-round, but success, bringing an unforgettable view into Popo's crater, is more likely from October to March, when avalanches, thunderstorms, and whiteouts are at a minimum. The shelters on each mountain are often full and have no facilities, so all equipment must be packed in. Equipment can be rented at the base of Popo, and it is possible to join one of the numerous groups that climb each day.

Izta is harder to climb than Popo because its irregular shape makes finding smooth routes to the top more difficult. Izta's peaks are named after portions of the female body—the sleeping woman.

Popo can be climbed in eight hours, and Izta in two days, but reserving a week for both allows for acclimatization on the way up.

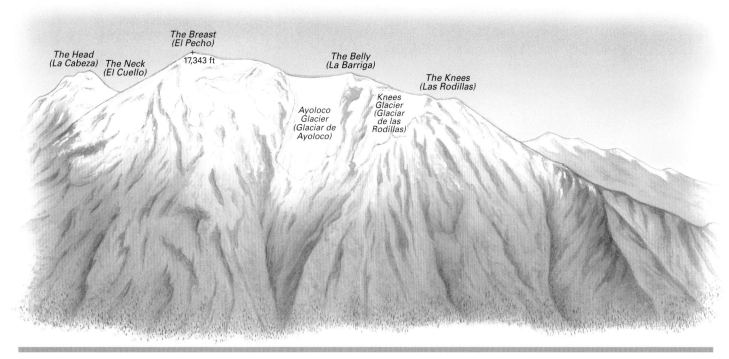

The Head (La Cabeza)

The Neck (El Cuello)

The Breast (El Pecho)

17,343 ft

The Belly (La Barriga)

The Knees (Las Rodillas)

Ayoloco Glacier (Glaciar de Ayoloco)

Knees Glacier (Glaciar de las Rodillas)

Lago de Camécuaro

According to an old legend, an Indian princess wept over the death of her king and the loss of her empire to the Spanish invaders. Her tears flowed for days and were caught by the twisted roots of ancient cypress trees surrounding a lake—which came to be called the "torrent of tears." The legend of the lake—Lago de Camécuaro—is still told, and the gnarled cypresses give a mystical atmosphere to this park.

In reality, the lake's azure waters are fed by crystalline springs. So clear is the water that boaters and swimmers can see the limestone bottom, which is marked by caves and swarming schools of small, colorful fish.

Lago de Camécuaro is small, but there is a winding path that leads around the cypress trees and the lake. The path tempts artists to set up their easels and offers pleasant picnic spots where one can watch children splashing in the cool, shaded water or listen to strolling musicians who entertain people relaxing along the lakeshore.

PARK DATA

STATE: Michoacán
ESTABLISHED: 1941
AREA: 22 acres (9 ha)
CLIMATE: Temperate, with wet summers
FLORA: Montezuma cypresses, pine and fir forests
FAUNA: Northern pintails, black-bellied tree ducks, parakeets, green jays; fish

Old stands of majestic Montezuma cypress trees (left) thrive on the shores of Lago de Camécuaro. The lake provides habitat for a variety of ducks, including the northern pintail (below).

Lagunas de Chacahua

O axaca state's image as a high, dry, cactus-covered outpost finds exception here on the lush, humid Pacific coastal plain where this remote preserve lies. Only a day trip from the coastal resort of Puerto Escondido, Chacahua is a world away, pristine and wild, an entrée to a tropical wonderland.

Mexico's only tropical national park, Chacahua covers 35,057 acres, consisting of about one-third water—lagoon, canal, and open sea—and several major ecosystems that support an array of land and sea flora and fauna.

Local Mixtec Indians called this place *minicano,* meaning "big lagoon," and Chacahua—"shrimp hollow" or "shrimp place." Set in the fertile land at the mouth of the Río Verde, where the mountains drop dramatically to the coastal plain, this low-lying park's main topographical features are its three tropical lagoons—the Pastoría, the Chacahua, and the Salinas—which are linked by navigable canals and sprinkled with islets. The park is thick with vegetation such as mahogany, ebony, orchids, and lianas. Not infrequently, heavy seasonal rains fill the lagoons, which overflow or channel their way to the sea.

Within Lagunas de Chacahua, four distinct ecozones coexist—scrubby coastal dunes, jungly mangrove, grassy savanna, and dense rain forest. In addition, cultivated plantings of coconut palms, lemon trees, bananas, maize, and sesame grow along the Río Verde.

A major wildlife refuge and bird sanctuary, the park contains a remarkable number of indigenous species, among them white-tailed deer, wildcats, wild boars, anteaters—and more than half of all the bird species found

A great egret suns on a tangle of mangrove roots in Lagunas de Chacahua National Park, where dense mangrove swamps provide a rich habitat for resident and migrating birds.

FOR CENTURIES, flotillas of female sea turtles—green, black, loggerhead, leatherback, hawksbill, and Pacific ridley—have nested along this coastline, many returning instinctively to their natal beach. The turtles drag themselves from the sea and dig their deep, sandy nests, into which they deposit as many as 200 eggs. Later the hatchlings, such as this young black turtle, vulnerable to birds and other predators, race for the safety of the water.

In 1986, to protect the six endangered species that nest here, a coastline reserve was set aside.

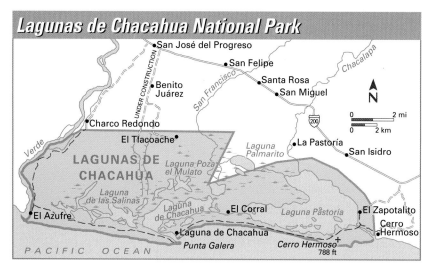

Lagunas de Chacahua National Park

San José del Progreso
San Felipe
Chacalapa
Benito Juárez
Santa Rosa
San Miguel
San Francisco
UNDER CONSTRUCTION
200
N
0   2 mi
0   2 km
Charco Redondo
Verde
El Tlacoache
Laguna Palmarito
La Pastoría
San Isidro
LAGUNAS DE CHACAHUA
Laguna Poza el Mulato
Laguna de las Salinas
Laguna de Chacahua
El Corral
Laguna Pastoría
El Zapotalito
Cerro Hermoso
El Azufre
Laguna de Chacahua
Punta Galera
Cerro Hermoso 788 ft
PACIFIC OCEAN

in Mexico. Threatened wildlife finds protection here; the list includes green and black iguanas, boa constrictors, ocelots, jaguars, ospreys, endangered spider monkeys, tapirs, and several sea turtle species.

Chacahua also operates a crocodile nursery. The park's prolific waters abound, too, with nearly 40 species of fish, along with the shrimp and other crustaceans that spawn in the brackish lagoons.

A human refuge as well, Chacahua's scattering of tiny fishing villages preserves the coast's complex cultural legacy. For centuries, the Mixtec and other Indians lived here. When the Spanish arrived, the Indians fled, soon to be replaced by runaway Africans—slaves to the conquistadores. The Africans settled here and became fishermen. Four centuries later, their descendants greet visitors to the same remote shore.

Two worlds meet: Pacific coastal dunes outline the shoreline at Lagunas de Chacahua (above, left), yielding to the mangroves that fringe lagoons, canals, and islets.

Prop roots spilling from a stand of red mangroves build up the lagoon's bank (above). Several types of mangrove thrive here, varying with the degree of wetness and salinity.

Lagunas de Montebello

No one knows how many bodies of water there are in Montebello, a spectacular, 14,881-acre preserve tucked into the forested folds of the Sierra de Chiapas on Mexico's border with Guatemala. The official estimate hovers around 60, but that's not counting the myriad small pools that appear with the rainy season.

Montebello's phenomenal lakes come in all shapes, sizes—and colors, from emerald and jade to turquoise, deep blue, red, copper, even white and black. Their names describe their hue—Esmeralda (emerald), Laguna Azul (blue lake), Agua Tinta (red water)—or character, as in Encantada (enchanted), Perol (boiling pot), Ensueño (dream), Montebello (beautiful mountain).

The geological explanation lies in the limestone, or karst, terrain, marked by underground streams, caverns, and

PARK DATA

STATE: Chiapas
ESTABLISHED: 1959
AREA: 14,881 acres (6,022 ha)
NATURAL FEATURES: Many pools; El Arco grotto
FLORA: Diverse, depending upon elevation and precipitation—coniferous and oak forests; cloud forest with sweetgums, tupelos; orchids, bromeliads; giant ferns; aquatic plants
FAUNA: Great variety, from white-tailed and brocket deer to badgers, flying squirrels to boa constrictors; endangered species including spider monkeys, golden anteaters, quetzals

A chain of Montebello's multiformed lakes sparkles blue and turquoise in its rugged forest setting. The park's 60-odd lakes are noted for their intense, varied hues.

Known locally as "the old man of the mountain," an agile, watchful tayra (right) stretches on a branch. Loss of habitat has brought this member of the weasel family close to extinction.

sinks. The reservoirs dissolve and collapse the limestone layers, creating depressions. When these clog, water accumulates. Its color is influenced by the depth, the angle of the sunlight, the composition of bottom soil, and the chemistry of the water.

A nearby historic landmark has benefited from the establishment of Montebello. The park's protection of natural areas indirectly preserves the Maya archaeological site at Chinkultic.

ARRAY OF FLORA AND FAUNA

MONTEBELLO'S FLORA and fauna, from the spotted nightingale thrush (above, left) and the nine-banded armadillo (above, right) to pine-oak woodlands, water plants, orchids, and bromeliads occupy diverse habitats teeming with life. Many rare and imperiled animals find refuge here, such as ocelots, jaguars, spider monkeys, Mexican anteaters, and yellow-faced warblers. Some species—for example, the Hercules beetle and certain butterflies—exist nowhere else on earth.

Lagunas de Montebello National Park

MAYA RUINS OF CHINKULTIC

LONG AGO, NEAR THE Lagunas de Montebello area, the Maya built a hilltop city that they called Chinkultic—"cave of the steps." Occupied from the first through the thirteenth centuries A.D., this trade and ceremonial center saw its heyday between the years 300 and 900.

Rediscovered in 1895, the 40-acre site contains some 200 earthen mounds clustered around 6 main complexes that include a large ball court and a main temple (opposite).

Standing 131 feet tall on a stepped pyramid and fronted by four platforms, the temple crowns a blufftop terrace that offers striking views of the park. Some 150 feet below lies a well, the Cenote Agua Azul, into which the Maya threw religious offerings.

Lagunas de Zempoala

Z empoala—"the place of many waters." Gloriously situated in the high, rugged, and still active volcanic country south of Mexico City, this alpine park's chief attribute is the chain of six small, turquoise lakes—two permanent, four fluctuating with seasonal rains—lying at its heart.

Millions of years ago, lava blocked off certain rivers and streams, creating Zempoala's lakes. It also cut off the drainage system between the valleys of Mexico and Cuernavaca, creating a new system that drains vital waters from the park region to the city of Cuernavaca.

Before the scenic highway was built, getting to Zempoala's isolated lakes was an adventure in itself. Today, the park, shared by the states of Morelos and México—and easily accessible from Mexico City, Cuernavaca, and Toluca—is one of the country's most popular for hiking, boating, and camping. En route, the road offers some fine views of the valley of Cuernavaca.

Zempoala's dramatic range of elevations crosses two climate zones, resulting in a great variety of flora and fauna. Pine forests predominate on the thick volcanic slopes, with stands of oak and dense upland forests of Mexican fir. Local fauna includes bobcats, white-tailed deer, armadillos, a host of rodents and other small mammals, reptiles, and birds—and the Zempoala axolotl, a unique salamander found nowhere else in the world.

PARK DATA

STATES: Morelos and México
ESTABLISHED: 1936
AREA: 11,537 acres (4,669 ha)
CLIMATE: Cool; annual average rainfall from 47 to 59 in (1.2 to 1.5 m), mostly in summer
ELEVATION: Averaging about 10,000 ft (3,000 m), with higher peaks
NATURAL FEATURES: Zempoala Peak; 6 lakes
FLORA: Variation depending on elevation—in forests of pine, oak, and fir
FAUNA: Mammals including white-tailed deer, bobcats, ringtails, coatis, spotted and hooded skunks, shrews; endemic species —a salamander, the Zempoala axolotl, and the crowned rattlesnake; birds including whippoorwills and woodpeckers

The sun burns through morning mist at Lagunas de Zempoala National Park, a sylvan preserve of sparkling lakes cupped by steep, piney volcanic slopes.

La Malinche

U pon his defeat of a Maya war
party, Spanish conquistador
Hernán Cortés took among his spoils a
beautiful young Indian woman named
Malintzin, whom the Spaniards mis-
called Malinche. She became Cortés'
mistress and interpreter—and a local
legend, inspiring the name of majestic
La Malinche volcano, centerpiece of La
Malinche National Park.

Established in 1938, the park lies
east of Mexico City in the mountainous
country on the border between the
states of Tlaxcala and Puebla, part of
the geological region known as the
Transverse Volcanic Axis. La Malinche,
now extinct, is one of the oldest volcanoes in the axis. It contains a dramatic
gorge and the ancient crater. Drainage
from the summit feeds underground
streams that water local farms.

The volcano's steep, wooded slopes
provide a habitat for a great variety of
animals and birds and a training
ground for high-caliber human
climbers. A gentle mountain road
enables other visitors to enjoy La
Malinche's cool fir and pine woods
and fabulous panoramic views.

PARK DATA

STATES: Tlaxcala and Puebla
ESTABLISHED: 1938
AREA: 112,927 acres
(45,700 ha)
NATURAL FEATURE: La
Malinche crater, 14,636 ft
(4,461 m) high
FLORA: Forests of pine, oak,
fir; subalpine meadows;
agaves, prickly pears
FAUNA: Coyotes, badgers,
ringtails, skunks, Mexican
and cottontail rabbits;
falcons, quail, long-tailed
wood partridges, dusky
hummingbirds

The volcanic crown
of La Malinche—an
extinct relic of the
Pliocene epoch—
peaks above the clouds
at 14,636 feet.

Los Mármoles

Although this spectacular preserve in the wilderness of northern Hidalgo state received national park status in 1936, it has no visitor facilities. Named for the abundance of marble found in the region's rock, the park, favored by hikers and climbers, is noted for its dramatic contrasts in elevation. The existence of two climate zones, temperate and hot, accounts for the range and bounty of vegetation and wildlife that are found here.

PARK DATA

STATE: Hidalgo
ESTABLISHED: 1936
AREA: 57,205 acres
(23,150 ha)
FLORA: Pines, madronas, alders, oaks, cypresses; dry scrubland plants— creosote bushes, agaves
FAUNA: White-tailed deer, bobcats, armadillos, bats; roadrunners, birds of prey

A medley of flora crowds the steep, marble-strewn uplands of Los Mármoles National Park.

Los Remedios

A popular green space set less than 14 miles north of Mexico City, Los Remedios sees thousands of visitors annually. The park harbors two historic landmarks: an aqueduct, and the 1574 Sanctuario de la Virgen de los Remedios—the Sanctuary of the Virgin of Help, or Remedies. The sanctuary houses a wooden image of the Virgin—brought to Mexico by the Spanish and believed to grant prayers—for which the pious leave votive offerings.

PARK DATA

STATE: México
ESTABLISHED: 1938
AREA: 988 acres (400 ha)
FLORA: Native flora damaged; introduced eucalyptus and casuarina trees taking over; some Montezuma cypresses, weeping willows; mesquites, grama grasses
FAUNA: Ringtails, variety of rodents; a number of small reptiles; lazuli buntings, American redstarts, green jays

In the national park of Los Remedios, the graceful Acueducto de los Caracoles—meaning "aqueduct of snails, or spirals"—bisects a grove of trees (above). Named for its twin towers, shown here as they appeared about 1930 (left), the aqueduct was built between 1620 and 1765.

Molino de Flores Netzahualcóyotl

In the foothills of the Sierra Nevada, on the banks of the Coxcacuaco River, stand the remains—partly restored—of a once grand hacienda, or ranch: the Molino de Flores. A mill estate, it processed grains as well as pulque, a fermented juice made from the agave. The hacienda dates from the 17th century. It was burned and looted during the Mexican Revolution of 1910.

The structures include a granary, vat house, chapels, and burial grounds. These and the main buildings and master residence—set around a central square—together with waterworks and gardens are all accessible to visitors.

Nearby stand the Baths of King Netzahualcóyotl—a pre-Hispanic ruin—thought to be the king's retreat where he meditated while composing poetry.

Sequestered on the rocky riverbank (opposite), the colorful Chapel of Our Lord of the Channel and the family burial place hold the remains of Molino de Flores' owners.

This now deserted cobbled lane (below) harbored the hacienda's guest house, at left.

Nevado de Toluca

Airy green pine woods frame the jagged peaks of the volcano Nevado de Toluca, which dominates the valley of the same name (left).

Above the trees, sub-alpine prairie prevails, then yields to a miniature world of alpine tundra mosses and lichens on the mountain's steep, rocky upland slopes.

L egend has it that the Indians called the great volcano Xinantécatl—"naked man." At once majestic and moody, Nevado de Toluca, the country's fourth highest peak at 15,387 feet, commands the wide valley south of México state's lofty capital, Toluca. This 126,024-acre national park takes in the extinct volcano and surrounding lands, as well as several small hill towns and villages. Its main attraction, though, is the mountain itself.

Part of the range composing Mexico's Transverse Volcanic Axis and forming the geological divide between North and Central America, Nevado de Toluca was built up from prolific lava flows through the Pleistocene epoch. Ice Age glaciers scraped its flanks. Then, over the course of many thousands of years, two paroxysmal explosions occurred, blowing off the volcano's top, and creating Toluca's ragged, truncated silhouette. It is marked by two main peaks: Pico del

Águila (eagle's peak) and Pico del Fraile (friar's peak) on the crater wall called Espinazo del Diablo (devil's spine). On a clear day, all afford panoramas of the surrounding scenery.

Most famous of the volcano's features, products of the glacial thaw, are its two crater lakes, Laguna del Sol and Laguna de la Luna—"lake of the sun" and "lake of the moon." Both are among the world's highest lakes. Pre-Columbian Indians, probably the Matlatzinca, regarded them as sacred places and ceremonial sites; here offerings of copal in clay vessels were made to the rain god. According to legend, anyone who dared to violate the secrets at the bottom of the Laguna del Sol would be sucked down by whirlpools. However, underwater archaeological explorations begun in the early 1960s have proceeded without incident.

Today a scenic, winding mountain road leads into the wide, often cloud-wrapped crater, right to the water's edge. Scuba enthusiasts suit up and dive for sport in the chilly waters. The lakes are stocked with rainbow trout for fishing by permit.

Nevado de Toluca's many snow-fed streams supply two of Mexico's main rivers, the Balsas and the Lerma. Climate, geology, and vegetation combine to make the mountain the main impounding area of the Río Lerma, which provides drinking water to Toluca and Mexico City. In fact, the chief incentive for establishing a park here was to protect the land and forest, the wildlife, and the water resources.

Toluca's lakes—Laguna del Sol (foreground) and Laguna de la Luna— flank a lava dome that, millennia ago, plugged the central vent.

Palenque

S equestered in the lush, green rain forest of northern Chiapas state, ever shrouded in mist, this park contains one of the most beautiful of all pre-Columbian Maya archaeological sites: the fabled lost city of Palenque. Neither the largest nor the most physically imposing of Classic Maya ruins, Palenque's spectacular setting and exceptional architectural design and detail—stucco reliefs, mansard roofs— set it apart from other Maya sites.

The road to the ruins—named Palenque, or "palisade" by the Spanish— winds upward toward the fertile ridges of the Chiapas mountains to a shelf that overlooks the valley and the wide, verdant floodplain of the Río Usumacinta. Except for the occasional scream of a howler monkey or the calls of myriad birds, steamy silence reigns here. Pressed by the encroaching jungle, the limestone ruins stand at the heart of this ancient ceremonial center.

First settled around 100 B.C., Palenque blossomed between A.D. 650 and 750, mainly under two generations of a great ruling family: Pacal, identified in hieroglyphs as Shield, and his son Chan-Bahlum, or Jaguar-Serpent. Abandoned suddenly in the ninth century, Palenque was swallowed up by

PARK DATA

STATE: Chiapas
ESTABLISHED: 1981
AREA: 4,398 acres (1,780 ha); a UNESCO world heritage site
NATURAL FEATURES: Queen's Bath; Motiepa Falls
CULTURAL FEATURES: Maya archaeological sites; Tzotzil Indian villages
FLORA: Rain forest— mahoganies, ceibas, chicle trees, breadnuts; lianas, strangler figs, bromeliads
FAUNA: White-tailed and brocket deer, howler and spider monkeys, coatis, ringtails, kinkajous; numerous kinds of reptiles and amphibians; birds including toucans, toucanets, great tinamous, great currassows, many species of parakeets, blue-headed parrots; the rare tobacco butterfly; several threatened or endangered species

Even in ruins, the labyrinthine Palace epitomizes the superlative Maya architectural achievement at Palenque. Wonders of natural design, such as this glassy-winged butterfly, fill the surrounding tropical forest.

tropical forest in an area with Mexico's highest average rainfall.

Centuries later, the Spanish began to investigate. In the 1780s, an artillery captain, Antonio del Río, explored and excavated there. Palenque was probably the first pre-Columbian site known to Europeans. In 1841, American explorer-archaeologist John Lloyd Stephens brought Palenque to public attention. His books led the way for scientific archaeology in the region. Still, only a fraction of the site's nearly 500 buildings (which cover several square miles) has been excavated.

One of Palenque's unusual aspects is its naturalistic plan. A creek meanders between and beneath the buildings, thanks to a one-of-a-kind, underground aqueduct. During Palenque's heyday, the entire city was painted in bright colors. The builders created a plan at once free and enclosed, and adapted to the hilly site—as in the case of the pyramid-based Temple of the Inscriptions, which was built right into the hillside. The majestic temple's name refers to its three stone tablets covered with hieroglyphs, which apparently chronicle 200 years of Palenque's ruling family.

The enormous Palace complex and site, Palenque's centerpiece, contains twelve buildings flanking four grassy courts, dozens of small rooms and corridors, underground galleries, a drainage system, and a unique four-story tower, as well as exquisite stucco bas-reliefs. Beyond here are clusters of smaller temples perched on grassy knolls—the Temple of the Cross, for example, and the lovely Temple of the Sun, with its lacy stone roof comb.

THE DISCOVERY OF PACAL'S SARCOPHAGUS

IN 1952, THE TEMPLE of the Inscriptions gave up a major secret. Three years earlier, while exploring the edifice, archaeologist Alberto Ruz Lhuillier had noticed a curious flagstone in the temple floor. He also observed that the temple walls seemed to extend below floor level.

Deciding to investigate, he pulled up the stone and found a rubble-filled stairway leading down into

the temple's interior.

Excavators worked for three seasons to clear the stairs. They found a cache of votive offerings outside a masonry wall and behind this, a huge, triangular, standing stone slab and the remains of six sacrificial youths. Beyond the slab was a great funerary crypt, perfectly preserved after nearly 1,300 years. Along with stately figures in stucco relief and various grave goods, the chamber held a sarcophagus with a stone lid (opposite), measuring about 7 by 12 feet and weighing 5 tons. The bas-relief portrays the death and rebirth of the great ruler Pacal, who is seated on the sun god, with a cruciform and a heavenly bird above him. Symbols of death flank the figure, and glyphs frame the surface of the slab. The sarcophagus held Pacal's jade-covered remains.

The Temple of the Inscriptions is the only known Maya pyramid base to have served as a tomb.

Palenque National Park

PALENQUE

North Group
Temple of the Count
Temple 10
Museum
Ball Court
Temple 11
East Court of the Palace
Palace
Otulum
Entrance
Tower
Temple 12
Temple 13
Temple of the Inscriptions
Temple of the Sun
Temple 14
Temple of the Cross
Temple of the Foliated Cross
Temple of the Lion
Temple 18
Lookout
Temple 18A

N

Aqueduct

0   400 feet
0   100 meters

THE TEMPLE OF the Foliated Cross, dedicated in A.D. 692, lost its front facade and stairway when its stepped pyramid base shifted, exposing the central wall (above). The earlier photograph (top), taken about 1900, hints at the scale of the clearing effort. Inside, a carved panel features a cross symbolizing the god of maize—the staff of life—emerging from the earth. The tablet also shows an image of a ceiba, or silk-cotton tree, the Maya sacred World Tree, thought by them to unite the Universe.

Pico de Orizaba

*A*ztecs called it Citlaltépetl— "mountain of the star"— because its snowy peak reflects the full moon's light like a giant star. Better known as Pico de Orizaba, Mexico's highest mountain soars to 18,855 feet. It is the uncontested draw of this park, which straddles the boundary between the states of Puebla and Veracruz. The border runs across the mountaintop.

Snow permanently caps the cone of this dormant volcano, which last erupted in 1687. A conspicuous land-mark even for ships at sea, Orizaba served as a beacon for Spanish vessels navigating the Gulf of Mexico. Today, only experienced climbers should attempt to scale it; other visitors with four-wheel-drive vehicles can usually reach the base camp.

However, Orizaba's beauty can be enjoyed from below. The park encom-passes several towns and Indian villages in the warm, lush valley of Acultzingo. Both temperate and cold, Orizaba's main ecosystems are pine, fir, oak, and cypress forests, subalpine meadows, and alpine tundra.

PARK DATA

STATES: Veracruz and Puebla
ESTABLISHED: 1937
AREA: 48,803 acres (19,750 ha)
FLORA: Oaks, pines, firs
FAUNA: White-tailed deer, various small mammals; blue grosbeaks, tropical mockingbirds, raptors such as hawks, falcons,
UNIQUE FEATURE: Pico de Orizaba, at 18,855 ft (5,747m), Mexico's highest peak

African tulip trees frame the distant, snow-capped summit of Pico de Orizaba.

In Orizaba's temperate zone, an *Abronia* lizard blends with its verdant habitat.

Pico de Tancítaro

*T*owering above the lush but rugged western region of Michoacán is the extinct volcano, Tancítaro. Reaching nearly 13,000 feet above sea level, Tancítaro is the highest peak in this area. It looms over an immense volcanic field dotted with hundreds of smaller and younger cones. Now the steep slopes and pine-covered hillsides are interlaced with valleys where orchards thrive.

PARK DATA

STATE: Michoacán
ESTABLISHED: 1940
AREA: 72,441 acres (29,316 ha)
NATURAL FEATURES: Pico de Tancítaro, extinct volcano, some 13,000 ft (about 4,000 m) high; numerous other volcanoes
FLORA: Temperate forests of fir, pine, and oak
FAUNA: White-tailed deer, gray foxes, armadillos, ringtails; various birds

Volcano El Paracutín, in the foreground, vents sulfurous steam. Extinct Pico de Tancítaro looms in the left distance.

Rayón

*R*ayón is a small park that provides a picnic spot overlooking surrounding farms and the village of Tlalpujahua. The park's site is a historic one. From this hill, the Rayón brothers fought off a long siege by the Spanish during Mexico's War of Independence.

The hillside of Rayón looks down on the village of Tlalpujahua.

PARK DATA

STATE: Michoacán
ESTABLISHED: 1952
AREA: 84 acres (34 ha)
CULTURAL FEATURE: Cerro de Gallo—"hill of the rooster"—where besieged Rayón brothers held off government forces
FLORA: Pine and fir forests
FAUNA: White-tailed deer, ringtails, armadillos; birds such as hawks and brown-barred woodpeckers

Sacromonte

*T*he pride of the quiet market town of Amecameca, in the state of México, this small park harbors some big sights. Its centerpiece is a steep, conical hill, a fine vantage point for viewing the volcanoes, Iztaccíhuatl and Popocatépetl in neighboring Izta-Popo National Park. Landmarks include a hilltop parish church dedicated to the Virgin of Guadalupe. Once a beloved missionary's retreat, the church is now a pilgrimage site.

PARK DATA

STATE: México
ESTABLISHED: 1939
AREA: 111 acres (45 ha)
CULTURAL FEATURE:
Baroque church and monastery
FLORA: Native oak species replaced by exotic eucalyptus
FAUNA: Mammals such as ringtails, hognose skunks, armadillos; birds including falcons, blue grosbeaks, dusky hummingbirds

Popocatépetl commands the view beyond the church that crowns Sacromonte hill.

Tula

*T*horny cactuses and scrub brush cover the high, lonely plateau of the southern Chihuahuan Desert, where this park protects the archaeological ruins of Tula. Long ago called Tollan—"place of the reeds"—Tula was the revered capital of the legendary Toltecs, who dominated central Mexico from about 900 to 1200. Their influence spread throughout Mesoamerica, even to the Maya of distant Yucatán, and the Aztecs later claimed that legacy. The Toltecs were ultimately overcome by invaders, and Toltec power split into dozens of small city-states.

The site of Tula consists of several sections. The main ceremonial area, with its large plazas and carved walls, holds the ball court, the Burnt Palace complex, and the Pyramid of Quetzalcoatl, hero-god of ancient Mexico, with four giant warriors carved in stone.

PARK DATA

STATE: Hidalgo
ESTABLISHED: 1981
AREA: 245 acres (99 ha)
CULTURAL FEATURES: Archaeological site of Toltec ruins; museum; 16th-century Franciscan chapel with fine facade
FLORA: Chihuahuan Desert scrubland vegetation such as creosote bushes, mesquites, acacias, piñons, prickly pears, organ-pipe cactuses, yuccas, various agaves including lechuguillas
FAUNA: Small mammals such as wood rats, cottontails, shrews; reptiles including horned lizards, rattlesnakes; birds including mourning and white-winged doves, sparrows

Panorama of past glory, the pyramid and colonnades of Tula rise from the desert plateau.

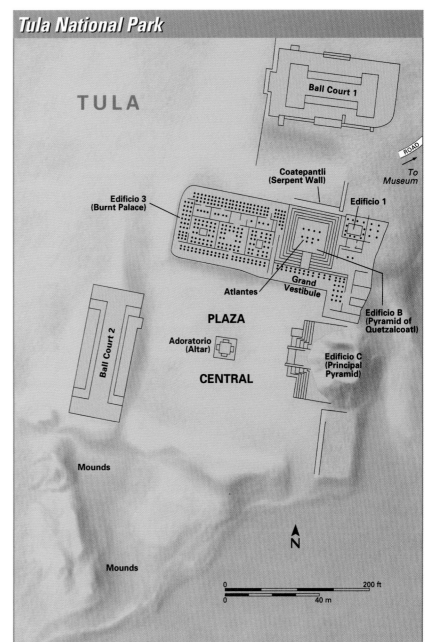

TULA

Ball Court 1

ROAD
To Museum

Coatepantli
(Serpent Wall)

Edificio 3
(Burnt Palace)

Edificio 1

Atlantes

Grand
Vestibule

Edificio B
(Pyramid of
Quetzalcoatl)

PLAZA

Ball Court 2

Adoratorio
(Altar)

Edificio C
(Principal
Pyramid)

CENTRAL

Mounds

N

Mounds

0   200 ft
0   40 m

TOLTEC HISTORY entwines thoroughly with myth and legend. According to the Aztecs, who glorified these claimed ancestors, the Toltecs were master artists and craftsmen, endowed with all knowledge by Quetzalcoatl. This priest-king founded the city of Tula and took the name Feathered Serpent. The 15-foot-tall warriors (opposite), each a massive basalt column carved in four pieces and tenoned together, once supported the roof of Quetzalcoatl's pyramid.

The figures are armed with spear throwers and wear the insignias of Quetzalcoatl.

A counterpart to the giant sculptures, this 32-inch warrior in quilted armor (above) held up an altar. The figure reflects the mingling of militarism and religion that was characteristic in Tula and all over Mesoamerica.

A detail from the Serpent Wall (right) on the pyramid's main frieze shows a skull in the fangs of a snake—an aspect of the god Quetzalcoatl.

Tulum

*T*here are actually three Tulums—the Maya ruins, the beach, and the highway-side village. The first two compose the heart of Tulum National Park, which lies on the eastern coast of the Yucatán Peninsula in Quintana Roo state.

Tulum's dramatic setting gives this place its rich appeal. The fortified ruins themselves command a limestone bluff, part of the surface of the vast, flat peninsula. The bluff overlooks the dazzling, turquoise expanse of the Caribbean, whose clear waters lap at a beautiful, white sandy beach below the 40-foot escarpment. The narrow cove once served as a landing area for canoes that traded along the coast.

Surrounded on three sides by a stone wall (originally from 10 to 15 feet tall, and 20 feet thick) and open to the sea, with a jungly plain outside the walls, the 16-acre religious and trading center claims fame for its superb stucco mural paintings, best represented in the Temple of the Frescoes.

The park's natural features complement its man-made sights. Vegetation ranges from dune shrubs to mangrove swamps to a jungle-like growth, where breadnut, gumbo-limbo, and chicle trees grow. These varied habitats support ocelots, anteaters, armadillos, manatees, and spider monkeys, as well as motmots, pelicans, Aztec parakeets, ospreys, and herons.

Tulum sprawls at cliff's edge above the blue Caribbean. The only known sizable walled town built on the coast, it shelters a palm-fringed beach below the grand Castillo, or Castle.

STATE: Quintana Roo
ESTABLISHED: 1981
AREA: 1,707 acres (691 ha)
NATURAL FEATURES:
Spectacular location of Maya ruins on limestone bluff; white-sand Caribbean beach and clear, tropical waters; cenotes, or natural freshwater wells; springs
CULTURAL FEATURES:
Extensive, picturesque ruins of Maya coastal trading complex of the Postclassic Period—from A.D. 900 to 1521
FLORA: Coastal zone— mangroves, dune vegetation; inland—tropical jungle including breadnuts, gumbo-limbos, chicle trees
FAUNA: Manatees, ocelots, foxes, spider monkeys, anteaters, armadillos; lizards; birds including ospreys, herons, pelicans, parakeets; colorful reef fishes, lobsters, shrimps

A CITY-FORT

CUSTODIANS OF the past, modern-day Maya preserve the legacy of their ancestors. A master mason (right), using methods passed down over the centuries, sets guide strings for repositioning fallen stones on a Tulum structure.

Founded before the year 1200, Tulum—Mayan for "fortress" or "wall"— became a busy port of call on the Yucatán sea-trade route before the arrival of the Spanish. In 1518, Spanish explorers thought the city as grand as Seville. Specializing in the export of honey, as well as jade, feathers, cotton, wax, and salt, Tulum may have been governed by rich merchants like this coddled trader (below).

THE CARIBBEAN FLANK of the Yucatán Peninsula boasts outstanding beaches—blinding white sand with crystal blue water and coconut palms. Here stretches part of the largest barrier reef in the Americas. It traces the length of the peninsula and is habitat for a colorful array of reef life (such as this spiny squirrelfish), making Tulum and its neighboring towns and resorts prime snorkeling and scuba diving destinations. Scattered cenotes provide a freshwater alternative to the salty sea. The coast also offers year-round fishing, both deep-sea and inshore, as well as other water sports.

Tulum National Park

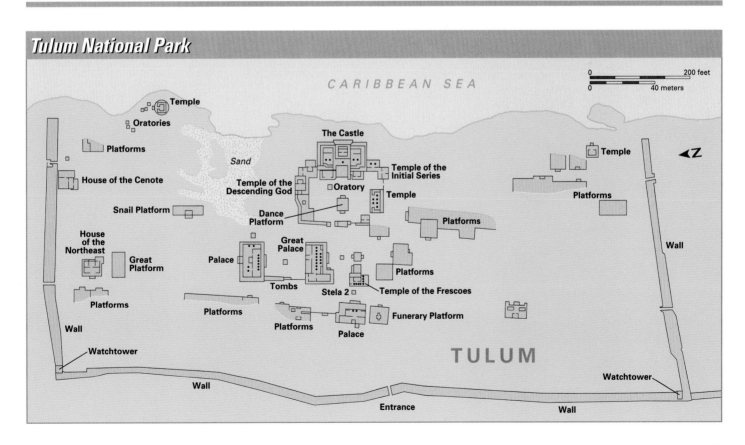

Volcán Nevado de Colima

*R*ising from the fertile plains that surround the cities of Colima and Guzmán are two of Mexico's highest volcanic peaks. Volcán de Fuego last erupted in 1994 and is still active, with steam drifting from its cone. Its extinct neighbor, Nevado de Colima, with a jagged top that reaches nearly 14,000 feet, is ringed with thick forests of sapodilla, an evergreen that grows throughout Mexico. Outside El Fresnito, a steep dirt road takes you to just below Nevado de Colima's summit where a ridge provides a superb overlook.

In western Mexico, the two highest peaks in a volcanic chain are Volcán Nevado de Colima (left, in the background) and Volcán de Fuego.

A foggy sunset (below) highlights a flank of Volcán Nevado de Colima.

PARK DATA

STATES: Jalisco and Colima
ESTABLISHED: 1936
AREA: 55,599 acres (22,500 ha)
NATURAL FEATURES: Two very high volcanoes, one active, one extinct
FLORA: Forests of pine, fir, and oak; basswoods, hornbeams, madronas; subalpine meadows
FAUNA: Pumas, whitetailed deer, gray foxes, armadillos, coatis, hognose and hooded skunks, cottontails; reptiles such as lizards, rattlesnakes; birds including falcons, hawks, magpie jays, northern mockingbirds, common bobwhites, tinamous, quail, and Mexican woodnymph hummingbirds

Zoquiapan

A high-country park lying in the volcanic district east of Mexico City, Zoquiapan contains lofty peaks—Tláloc, Telapón, and Papayo—that reach nearly 13,000 feet. Dense pine forests predominate on the park's rugged slopes, which are marked by spectacular canyons and scenic streams that water valleys far to the east and west of the park and supply more than 22 million people. Rich sub-alpine meadows and alpine tundra grow at higher elevations in Zoquiapan. Wildlife abounds in the park.

Of archaeological interest, on the summit of Tláloc, are the remains of an ancient Anáhuac ceremonial site dedicated to the worship of the god Tláloc. A more recent chapter in Zoquiapan's history—the 19th-century influx of bandits around the town of Río Frío—was popularized in Manuel Payno's novel, *The Bandits of Río Frío*.

PARK DATA

STATES: México and Puebla

ESTABLISHED: 1937; full name is Zoquiapan y Anexas

AREA: 47,983 acres (19,418 ha)

NATURAL FEATURES: Volcanic peaks rising 13,000 ft (4,000 m)

FLORA: Forests of pine, fir, and alder

FAUNA: White-tailed deer, bobcats, coyotes, armadillos, longtail weasels, cottontail and volcano rabbits; reptiles including mesquite lizards, rattlesnakes; tree frogs, salamanders; birds such as kestrels, Montezuma quail; broad-tailed, blue-throated, and fork-tailed emerald hummingbirds

Haystacks stud a high meadow and echo the summit of Iztaccíhuatl volcano, peering above Zoquiapan's slopes.

Illustrations Credits

Dust Jacket: front, Carr Clifton. back (t) Raymond Gehman; (c) Susan G. Drinker, Drinker/Durrance Graphics; (b) Patricio Robles Gil/Sierra Madre.

Front Matter: 2-3, Sam Abell, NGP. 4-5, Galen Rowell/Mountain Light. 6-7, David Alan Harvey. 8-9, Dick Durrance II, Drinker/Durrance Graphics. 10-11, James Balog. 12-13, Jonathan Blair.

Canada: 16-17, *Canadian Heritage*/Parks Canada. 18-19, Barbara Brundege/Eugene Fisher. 19, Bob Firth/Firth Photobank. 20-21, George F. Mobley. 23 (t), George F. Mobley; (b), courtesy Canadian Pacific Railway Company. 24 (t), Lisa Biganzoli; (b), H. Armstrong Roberts. 25 (both), courtesy Canadian Pacific Railway Company. 26-27 (both), Raymond Olsenius. 28-29, Raymond Gehman. 30 (t), Anne King; (b), John Eastcott and Yva Momatiuk. 31, Michael Melford. 32-33, Darwin Wiggett/First Light. 34-35 (all), Jim Brandenburg. 36-37, Michael Melford. 38 George F. Mobley. 39, Parks Canada/Brian Atkinson. 40-41 (both), Richard Olsenius. 42, Byron Harmon. 42-43, George F. Mobley. 44-45 (both), Raymond Gehman. 46-47, Sam Abell, NGP. 48-49, Raymond Gehman. 49, Smithsonian Institution. 51-52 (both), Raymond Gehman. 52-53 (t), Robert S. Semeniuk; (bl), Royal British Columbia Museum, Victoria, B.C., cat. # 9498. 53 (bc), Royal British Columbia Museum, Victoria, B.C., cat. # 9787; (br), University of British Columbia, Museum of Anthropology, cat. # A7059. 54-55, Raymond Gehman. 56, George W. Calef. 57-59, Raymond Gehman. 61 (t), Dean Conger; (bl), Robert Hynes; (br), Georg Gerster,

Zumikon, Switzerland. 62 (t), James Balog; (b), Whyte Museum of the Canadian Rockies, cat. # NA66-1197. 63, J.A. Kraulis/Masterfile. 64, Stephen J. Krasemann. 64-65, Sam Abell, NGP. 67, Frank Oberle. 68-69, Michael Melford. 69 (both), Robert Hynes. 70, James Balog. 71 (both), James P. Blair. 72-73 (both), Richard Olsenius. 74, Michael Melford. 75, J.A. Kraulis/Masterfile. 76, Matt Bradley. 76-77, Michael Odesse. 78-79, Sherman Hines/Masterfile. 80-82 (all), Sam Abell, NGP. 83 (l), James N. Flynn; (r), Stephen J. Krasemann. 84-85, Hans Blohm/Masterfile. 86, Brian Sytnyk/Masterfile. 87, Tim Fitzharris/Masterfile. 88-89, J.A. Kraulis/ Masterfile. 90-91 (both), Medford Taylor. 92, Des & Jen Bartlett. 93, Parks Canada. 94, Sam Abell, NGP. 95, Yukon Gov't. 96-97, Sarah Leen. 99 (t), Erwin and Peggy Bauer; (b), Lowell Georgia. 100-102 (both), Raymond Gehman. 103 (t), Jennifer C. Urquhart; (b), Raymond Gehman. 104, Thomas D. Mangelsen/Images of Nature. 105, James L. Stanfield.

United States: 108-109, Susan G. Drinker, Drinker/Durrance Graphics. 110, Raymond Gehman. 111, Larry Ulrich. 112-113, Dewitt Jones. 115 (t), Lyle Rosbotham; (b), David Muench. 116-117, Jim Brandenburg. 118-119, Bill Wright. 120 (t), Bill Wright; (b), Tom Algire. 121 (t), Medford Taylor; (b), Stephen Frink. 122-123, Jack Dykinga. 124, Robert F. Sisson. 124-127 (both), David Muench. 128, Stephen J. Krasemann. 129-131 (both), Michael Nichols. 132, Tibor Toth. 133 (t), James P. Blair; (b), Norbert Wu. 134-135, Galen Rowell/Mountain Light.

135, Ray Atkeson Photo Library. 136-137, Lyle Rosbotham. 138-139, Danny Lehman. 141, Libby Mills. 142, Brian Okonek. 143, Emory Kristof. 144-145, Dick Durrance II, Drinker/Durrance Graphics. 146 (t) Kevin Fleming; (b), Comstock Inc./P. Greenburg. 147, Michael Freeman. 148, Connie Toops. 150-153 (both), Galen Rowell/Mountain Light. 154, Great Northern Railway by Haynes. 155-156 (both), Galen Rowell/Mountain Light. 157, Jeff Gnass. 158-159, Lyle Rosbotham. 160-161 (t), Susan G. Drinker, Drinker/Durrance Graphics; (b), Tibor Toth. 162 (l), Smithsonian Institution; (r), Bruce Dale. 163, Jeff Foott/DRK Photo. 164-165, Tom Algire. 166-167, José Azel. 168, Richard Olsenius. 168-169, Jim Brandenburg. 170, John Netherton. 171, Connie Toops. 172 (t), Connie Toops; (b), Randy Olson. 173 (bl), Jay Dickman; (br), Tom Nebbia. 174-177 (all), David Muench. 178-179, Susan G. Drinker, Drinker/Durrance Graphics. 180, Robert W. Madden, NGS. 181, Alex Tait/Equator Graphics. 182, Connie Toops. 183, Mitch Kezar. 184-185, Phil Schermeister. 186-187 (both), Tom Bean. 188-189, David Muench. 190 (t), John Milton; (b), Jim Brandenburg. 191, Connie Toops. 192-194 (all), Chip Clark. 195 (t), Chip Clark; (b), Caufield and Shook, Inc. 196-197, James L. Amos. 198 (tl), Art Institute of Chicago; (tr), David Brill; (b), Jerry Jacka. 199 (t), David Muench; (b) Richard Alexander Cooke III. 200, from H.B. Cunningham. 201, Pat O'Hara. 202, Danny Lehman. 203, Bob & Ira Spring. 204-205, Susan G. Drinker, Drinker/Durrance Graphics. 206 (l), Cartographic Division,

NGS; (r), Sam Abell, NGP. 207, Pat O'Hara. 208, Stock Boston. 208-209, David Muench. 210, courtesy of Redwood Empire Association. 211, James A. Sugar/Black Star. 212, Tom Algire. 213-215 (both), Jim Brandenburg. 216 (t), Paul Chesley; (b), George L. Maugher. 217, Galen Rowell/Mountain Light. 218-219 (both), Pat Toops. 220, David Muench. 221, Michael Melford. 222-223, Cary Wolinsky. 224, Richard Olsenius. 225 (t), Tom Bean/DRK Photo; (b), Jim Brandenburg. 226-227, Chris Johns. 228, Fred Hirschmann. 229 (both), George F. Mobley. 230-231, Raymond Gehman. 232 (t), Jeff Vanuga; (b), Steven Fuller. 234, courtesy National Park Service, Robert Hynes. 234-235, Lyle Rosbotham. 236, Galen Rowell/ Mountain Light. 237, William Neill. 239, Theodore Roosevelt Collection, Harvard College Library. 240, adapted from a map by Pali Arts Communications/American Park Network. 240-241, Dick Durrance II, Drinker/Durrance Graphics. 241, Michael Frye. 242-244, Sam Abell, NGP. 245, Lyle Rosbotham.

Mexico: 248, Richard D. Fisher. 249 (t), Jonathan Blair; (b), Danny Lehman. 250, Adalberto Rios Szalay/Sexto Sol. 251-252 (both), María de Lourdes Alonso/Sexto Sol. 253, Adalberto Rios Szalay/Sexto Sol. 254-256 (both), Richard D. Fisher. 257 (t), Fulvio Eccardi; (b), Richard Olsenius. 258-259, Danny Lehman. 260-261, Jonathan Blair. 261, Patricio Robles Gil/Sierra Madre. 262-263, Danny Lehman. 264, Jonathan Blair. 265, Richard D. Fisher. 266-268 (both), Jonathan Blair. 269 (t), Jonathan Blair; (b), Danny Lehman. 270-271, David Alan Harvey. 271, Bates Littlehales. 272, Agustín Ortega Esquinca. 272-273, Jonathan Blair. 274-279

(all), Danny Lehman. 280 (t), Richard D. Fisher; (b), José Luis Mallard/Sexto Sol. 281, María de Lourdes Alonso/Sexto Sol. 282 (t), Richard Olsenius; (b), Patricio Robles Gil/Sierra Madre. 283 (t), Richard Olsenius; (b), Danny Lehman. 284-285 (both), Claudio Contreras/Sierra Madre. 286-287 (both), Antonio Vizcaíno/Sierra Madre. 288, Patricio Robles Gil/Sierra Madre. 289 (t), Banco de Mexico by Hugo Brehme; (b), Al Kettler. 290-291, Richard Olsenius. 291, Patricio Robles Gil/Sierra Madre. 292-293, Jonathan Blair. 294, Patricio Robles Gil/Sierra Madre. 294-295, Jonathan Blair. 295, Antonio Vizcaíno/Sierra Madre. 296-297, Bob Schalkwijk/Sierra Madre. 297, Fulvio Eccardi. 298 (both), Patricio Robles Gil/Sierra Madre. 299, Bob Schalkwijk/Sierra Madre. 300-301, Richard Olsenius. 302-303, Patricio Robles Gil/Sierra Madre. 304, Jonathan Blair. 305 (t), Danny Lehman; (b), Banco de Mexico by Hugo Brehme. 306, Danny Lehman. 307, Agustín Ortega Esquinca. 308-309, Danny Lehman. 309-311 (both), Antonio Vizcaíno/Sierra Madre. 312, Claudio Contreras/Sierra Madre. 312-313, Lyle Rosbotham. 314, Merle Greene Robertson. 315 (tr), Peabody Museum of Harvard University by T. Maler; (br), Lyle Rosbotham. 316-317, Bob Schalkwijk/Sierra Madre. 317, Antonio Ramirez/Sierra Madre. 318-319 (both), Richard Olsenius. 319, Danny Lehman. 320-321, Mark Godfrey. 322, Jonathan Blair. 323 (t), Mark Godfrey; (b), Jorge Contreras Chacel. 324-325, María de Lourdes Alonso/Sexto Sol. 326 (t), David Alan Harvey; (b), NGS Labs. 327, Pablo Cervantes. 328-329, Bob Schalkwijk/Sierra Madre. 329, Richard Olsenius. 330-331, Danny Lehman.

Park Directory

Aulavik
General Delivery
Sachs Harbor, NT
X0E 0Z0
(403) 690-3904

Auyuittuq
Box 353
Pangnirtung, NT
X0A 0R0
(819) 473-8612

Banff
Box 900
Banff, AB T0L 0C0
(403) 762-1500

Bruce Peninsula
Box 189
Tobermory, ON N0H 2R0
(519) 596-2233

Cape Breton Highlands
Ingonish Beach
Cape Breton, NS B0C 1L0
(902) 285-2691 or
(800) 565-9464

Elk Island
R.R. 1, Site 4
Fort Saskatchewan, AB
T8L 2N7
(403) 992-6380

Ellesmere Island
Box 353
Pangnirtung, NT
X0A 0R0
(819) 473-8828

Forillon
Box 1220
Gaspé, QC G0C 1R0
(418) 892-5553

Fundy
Box 40
Alma, NB E0A 1B0
(506) 887-6000

Georgian Bay Islands
Box 28
Honey Harbor, ON P0E 1E0
(705) 756-2415

Glacier
Box 350
Revelstoke, BC V0E 2S0
(604) 837-5155

Grasslands
Box 150
Val Marie, SK S0N 2T0
(306) 298-2257

Gros Morne
Box 130
Rocky Harbor, NF
A0K 4N0
(709) 458-2417

Gwaii Haanas
Box 37
Queen Charlotte City, BC
V0T 1S0
(604) 559-6319

Ivvavik
Box 1840
Inuvik, NT X0E 0T0
(403) 979-3248

Jasper
Box 10
Jasper, AB T0E 1E0
(403) 852-6161

Kejimkujik
Box 236
Maitland Bridge
Annapolis City, NS
B0T 1B0
(902) 682-2772

Kluane
Box 5495
Haines Junction, YT
Y0B 1L0
(403) 634-2251

Kootenay
Box 220
Radium Hot Springs, BC
V0A 1M0
(604) 347-9615

Kouchibouguac
Kouchibouguac, NB
E0A 2A0
(506) 876-2443

La Mauricie
794 5th St., Box 758
Shawinigan, QC G9N 6V9
(819) 536-2638

Mingan Archipelago
1303 de la Digue St.
Box 1180
Havre-Saint-Pierre, QC
G0G 1P0
(418) 538-3331

Mount Revelstoke
Box 350
Revelstoke, BC V0E 2S0
(604) 837-5155

Nahanni
Box 348
Fort Simpson, NT
X0E 0N0
(403) 695-3151

North Baffin
Box 353
Pangnirtung, NT
X0A 0R0
(819) 473-8828

Pacific Rim
Box 280
Ucluelet, BC V0R 3A0
(604) 726-7721

Point Pelee
R.R. 1
Leamington, ON N8H 3V4
(519) 322-2365

Prince Albert
Box 100
Waskesiu Lake, SK
S0J 2Y0
(306) 663-5322

Prince Edward Island
2 Palmers Ln.
Charlottetown, PE
C1A 5V6
(902) 566-7050

Pukaskwa
Highway 627
Hattie Cove, Box 39
Heron Bay, ON P0T 1R0
(807) 229-0801

Riding Mountain
General Delivery
Wasagaming, MB R0J 2H0
(204) 848-2811

St. Lawrence Islands
2 County Road 5, R.R. 3
Mallorytown Landing,
ON K0E 1R0
(613) 923-5261

Terra Nova
General Delivery
Glovertown, NF A0G 2L0
(709) 533-2801

Vuntut
105-300 Main St.
Whitehorse, YT Y1A 2B5
(403) 667-3970

Waterton Lakes
Waterton Park, AB
T0K 2M0
(403) 859-2224

Wood Buffalo
Box 750
Fort Smith, NT X0E 0P0
(403) 872-2349

Yoho
Box 99
Field, BC V0A 1G0
(604) 343-6324

Acadia
P.O. Box 177
Bar Harbor, ME 04609
(207) 288-3338

Arches
P.O. Box 907
Moab, UT 84532
(801) 259-8161

Badlands
P.O. Box 6
Interior, SD 57750
(605) 433-5361

Big Bend
P.O. Box 129
Panther Junction
Big Bend National Park
TX 79834
(915) 477-2251

Biscayne
P.O. Box 1369
Homestead, FL 33090
(305) 230-7275

Bryce Canyon
Bryce Canyon, UT 84717
(801) 834-5322

Canyonlands
2282 S. West Resource Blvd.
Moab, UT 84532
(801) 259-7164

Capitol Reef
HC70, Box 15
Torrey, UT 84775
(801) 425-3791

Carlsbad Caverns
3225 National Parks Hwy.
Carlsbad, NM 88220
(505) 785-2232

Channel Islands
1901 Spinnaker Dr.
Ventura, CA 93001
(805) 658-5730

Crater Lake
P.O. Box 7
Crater Lake, OR 97604
(503) 594-2211

Death Valley
P.O. Box 579
Death Valley, CA 92328
(619) 786-2331

Denali
P.O. Box 9
Denali Park, AK 99755
(907) 683-2294

Dry Tortugas
P.O. Box 6208
Key West, FL 33041
(305) 293-0152

Everglades
40001 State Road 9336
Homestead, FL 33034
(305) 242-7700

Gates of the Arctic
P.O. Box 74680
Fairbanks, AK 99707
(907) 456-0281

Glacier
P.O. Box 128
West Glacier, MT 59936
(406) 888-5441

Glacier Bay
P.O. Box 140
Gustavus, AK 99826
(907) 697-2232

Grand Canyon
P.O. Box 129
Grand Canyon, AZ 86023
(520) 638-7888

Grand Teton
P. O. Drawer 170
Moose, WY 83012
(307) 739-3300

Great Basin
Baker, NV 89311
(702) 234-7331

Great Smoky Mountains
107 Park Headquarters Rd.
Gatlinburg, TN 37738
(615) 436-1200

Guadalupe Mountains
HC 60, Box 400
Salt Flat, TX 79847
(915) 828-3251

Haleakala
P.O. Box 369
Makawao, HI 96768
(808) 572-9306

Hawaii Volcanoes
P.O. Box 52
Hawaii National Park
HI 96718
(808) 967-7184

Hot Springs
P.O. Box 1860
Hot Springs, AR 71902
(501) 624-3383

Isle Royale
800 East Lakeshore Dr.
Houghton, MI 49931
(906) 482-0984

Joshua Tree
74485 National Park Dr.
Twentynine Palms, CA
92277
(619) 367-7511

Katmai
P.O. Box 7,
King Salmon, AK 99613
(907) 246-3305

Kenai Fjords
P.O. Box 1727
Seward, AK 99664
(907) 224-3175 or -3176

Kobuk Valley
P.O. Box 1029
Kotzebue, AK 99752
(907) 442-3890

Lake Clark
4230 University Dr. # 311
Anchorage, AK 99508
(907) 271-3751

Lassen Volcanic
P.O. Box 100
Mineral, CA 96063
(916) 595-4444

Mammoth Cave
Mammoth Cave, KY 42259
(502) 758-2328

Mesa Verde
P.O. Box 8
Mesa Verde, CO 81330
(303) 529-4465

Mount Rainier
Tahoma Woods
Star Route
Ashford, WA 98304
(360) 569-2211

North Cascades
2105 State Route 20
Sedro Woolley, WA 98284
(206) 856-5700

Olympic
600 E. Park Ave.
Port Angeles, WA 98362
(360) 452-4501

Petrified Forest
P.O. Box 2217
Petrified Forest, AZ 86028
(520) 524-6228

Redwood
1111 Second St.
Crescent City, CA 95531
(707) 464-6101

Rocky Mountain
Estes Park, CO 80517
(970) 586-1206

Saguaro
3693 S. Old Spanish Trail
Tucson, AZ 85730
(520) 733-5100

Sequoia and Kings Canyon
Three Rivers, CA 93271
(209) 565-3134

Shenandoah
Route 4, Box 348
Luray, VA 22835
(703) 999-3500

Theodore Roosevelt
P.O. Box 7
Medora, ND 58645
(701) 623-4466

Virgin Islands
6310 Estate Nazareth 10
St. Thomas, VI 00802
(809) 775-6238

Voyageurs
3131 Highway 53
International Falls, MN
56649
(218) 283-9821

Wind Cave
Route 1, Box 190 WCNP
Hot Springs, SD 57747
(605) 745-4600

Wrangell-St. Elias
P.O. Box 29
Glennallen, AK 99588
(907) 822-5234

Yellowstone
P.O. Box 168
Yellowstone National
Park, WY 82190
(307) 344-7381

Yosemite
P.O. Box 577
Yosemite, CA 95389
(209) 372-0200

Zion
Springdale, UT 84767
(801) 772-3256

MEXICO

The government agency
with responsibility for
the national parks:
Secretaría de Medio
Ambiente, Recursos
Naturales y Pesca
Instituto Nacional de
Ecología
Dirección General de
Aprovechamiento
Ecológico de los
Recursos Naturales
Río Elba #20, 10 Piso
Col. Cuauhtémoc
Mexico City, Mexico

A conservation agency
that works with the parks:
Pronatura
Camino al Ajusco No. 124
Fracc. Jardines en la
Montaña
C.P. 14210 Mexico City,
Mexico

Index

Boldface entries indicate
illustrations or broad
treatment of a topic,
including illustrations.
(NP=National Park;
R=Reserve; M=Marine)

335

Map Key

	National park
	Other Nat. park system lands
	State or provincial lands
	Indian reservation or reserve
	National forest
	Wildlife refuge or sanctuary
	Glacier
	Swamp or marsh

●	Populated place
■	Point of interest
⋇	Falls
+	Elevation in feet
⤳	Pass
∴	Ruin
⌒	Dam
⇥⊨	Tunnel

ROADS
Paved
Unpaved
Trans-Canada / U.S. Interstate / Mexican Federal
U.S. Federal
Provincial / State
Forest or local

International border
State or provincial border
Continental Divide
Railroad — — — — — Ferry
Trail ⊣⊢⊣⊢ Canal

Acknowledgments

The Book Division wishes to thank particularly the personnel of the U.S. National Park Service and of Parks Canada for their assistance. In addition to individuals, groups, or organizations mentioned in the text, we are also grateful to the following: In Canada, the Porcupine Caribou Management Board, the Department of Indian Affairs and Northern Development; in the U.S., George H. Billingsley, Bill Loftus, John Quinley; in Mexico, the editorial staff at Editorial Jilguero *México Desconocido,* Mexico City.

This book was printed and bound by R. R. Donnelly & Sons, Willard, Ohio. Color separations by Digital Color Image, Pennsauken, N.J.; Graphic Art Service, Inc., Nashville, Tenn.; Lanman Progressive Co., Washington, D.C.; North American Color, Inc., Portage, Minn. Dust jacket printed by Inland Press, Milwaukee, Wis.

Library of Congress CIP Data

National parks of North America : Canada, United States, Mexico / prepared by the Book Division, National Geographic Society, Washington, D.C.
   p.   cm.
   Includes index.
   ISBN 0-7922-2954-1. — ISBN 0-7922-2955-X (deluxe)
   1. National parks and reserves—North America.   I. National Geographic Society (U.S.).   Book Division.
E43.5.N38 1995
917.0—dc20   95-10989
                                                                                    CIP